‖‖‖ ‖‖‖‖‖‖‖ ‖ ‖‖‖‖ ‖ ‖‖‖‖‖‖‖‖‖‖ ‖‖ ‖‖

W9-BRD-177

WILEY

GAAP
for Governments
Field Guide

2002

including the new Financial Reporting Model

Warren Ruppel

JOHN WILEY & SONS, INC.

This text is printed on acid-free paper. ∞

Copyright © 2002 by John Wiley & Sons, Inc., New York.
All rights reserved. Published simultaneously in Canada.

No part of this publication may be reproduced, stored in a re-
trieval system or transmitted in any form or by any means,
electronic, mechanical, photocopying, recording, scanning or
otherwise, except as permitted under Section 107 or 108 of
the 1976 United States Copyright Act, without either the prior
written permission of the Publisher, or authorization through
payment of the appropriate per-copy fee to the Copyright
Clearance Center, 222 Rosewood Drive, Danvers, MA 01923,
(978) 750-8400, fax (978)750-4744. Requests to the Publisher for permission should be addressed to the Permissions
Department, John Wiley & Sons, Inc., 605 Third Avenue,
New York, NY 10158-0012, (212)850-6011, fax (212)850-
6008, E-Mail: PERMREQ@WILEY.COM

This publication is designed to provide accurate and authoritative information in regard to the subject matter covered. It
is sold with the understanding that the publisher is not engaged in rendering legal, accounting, or other professional
service. If legal advice or other expert assistance is required,
the services of a competent professional person should be
sought.

To order books or for customer service, call
(800) CALL WILEY (225-5945)

ISBN 0-471-13852-5

Printed in the United States of America
10 9 8 7 6 5 4 3 2 1

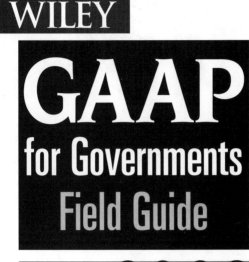

WILEY

GAAP
for Governments
Field Guide

2002

including the new
Financial
Reporting Model

CONTENTS

PREFACE

Governmental accounting is a specialized area that has undergone significant changes over the past few decades. As governmental accounting standards have developed, the complexities of preparing financial statements for governmental entities have greatly increased. Providing meaningful financial information to a wide range of users is not an easy task. Adding to these challenges, the Governmental Accounting Standards Board (GASB) has brought sweeping changes to governmental financial statements with its new financial reporting model, as promulgated by GASBS 34.

Given this rapidly changing environment, the financial statement users and readers need a technical resource that provides more than accurate, competent technical information in a succinct and readable format. While covering all of the major governmental accounting areas and concepts, this Field Guide eliminates many of the lessor important details, providing a usable, convenient reference tool. This Field Guide provides the latest implementation material available on GASBS 34, which almost completely rewrites government financial statement accounting and presentation. This Field Guide has been updated to reflect all of the new requirements.

This book would not have come to fruition without the hard work and perseverance of a number of individuals. John DeRemigis of John Wiley & Sons had the confidence in me to work with me in developing the original concept for the book and bringing it to completion. Pam Miller's efforts in producing the book are greatly appreciated.

Of course, none of the technical skills or publishing resources work well without a supportive family, for which I am grateful to my wife Marie, and my sons Christopher and Gregory.

Warren Ruppel
New York
February 2002

ABOUT THE AUTHOR

Warren Ruppel, CPA, is the assistant comptroller for accounting of the City of New York, where he is responsible for all aspects of the City's accounting and financial reporting. He has over twenty years of experience in governmental and not-for-profit accounting and financial reporting. He began his career at KPMG after graduating from St. John's University, New York, in 1979. His involvement with governmental accounting and auditing began with his first audit assignment—the second audit ever performed of the financial statements of the City of New York. From that time he served many governmental and commercial clients until he joined Deloitte & Touche in 1989 to specialize in audits of governments and not-for-profit organizations. Mr. Ruppel has also served as the chief financial officer of an international not-for-profit organization.

Mr. Ruppel has served as instructor for many training courses, including specialized governmental and not-for-profit programs and seminars. He has also been an adjunct lecturer of accounting at the Bernard M. Baruch College of the City University of New York. He is the author of three other books, *OMB Circular A-133 Audits*, *Not-for-Profit Organization Audits*, and *Not-for-Profit Accounting Made Easy*.

Mr. Ruppel is a member of the American Institute of Certified Public Accounts as well as the New York State Society of Certified Public Accountants, where he serves on the Governmental Accounting and Auditing and Not-for-Profit Organizations Committees. He is also a member of the Institute of Management Accountants and is a past president of the New York Chapter. Mr. Ruppel is a member of the Government Finance Officers Association and serves on its Special Review Committee.

1 NEW DEVELOPMENTS

INTRODUCTION

The 2002 Governmental GAAP Field Guide incorporates all of the pronouncements issued by the Governmental Accounting Standards Board (GASB) through December 2001. This chapter is designed to bring the reader up to date on all Pronouncements recently issued by the GASB, as well as to report on all of the Exposure Drafts for proposed new Statements or Interpretations that are currently outstanding. Other relevant publications from other organizations such as the American Institute of Certified Public Accountants (AICPA) are also included. The GASB has issued its long-awaited new financial reporting model standard, which is discussed extensively in this chapter. This chapter also includes relevant information on the GASB's Technical Agenda for the upcoming year.

Specifically, this chapter addresses the following documents:

- GASB Statement 34, *Basic Financial Statements—and Management's Discussion and Analysis—for State and Local Governments* (GASBS 34)
- GASB Statement 35, *Basic Financial Statements—and Management's Discussion and Analysis—for Public Colleges and Universities, an Amendment of GASB Statement 34.*
- GASB Statement 37, *Basic Financial Statements— and Management's Discussion and Analysis—for State and Local Governments: Omnibus*
- GASB Statement 38, *Certain Financial; Statement Note Disclosures*
- Exposure Draft, *The Financial Reporting Entity— Affiliated Organizations, an Amendment of GASB Statement 14*

NOTE: This guide is updated annually. The "new developments" chapter analyzes all recent documents (whether Exposure Drafts or final Pronouncements) that have been issued by the GASB, or if applicable to governmental accounting, the AICPA.

GASB STATEMENT 34, *BASIC FINANCIAL STATEMENTS—AND MANAGEMENT'S DISCUSSION AND ANALYSIS—FOR STATE AND LOCAL GOVERNMENTS*

Since the issuance of GASB Statement 11 (GASBS 11), *Measurement Focus and Basis of Accounting—Governmental Fund Operating Statements*, the GASB has been attempting to provide a financial reporting framework for the basis of accounting (full accrual basis) and measurement focus (financial resources) that were prescribed by GASBS 11. While the effective date of GASBS 11 has been deferred indefinitely, the resulting debate over a financial reporting model has gone on for almost ten years. Over this time, various reporting models and modifications of the original requirements of GASBS 11 have been developed. The reporting model that will be required by GASBS 34 is very different from that originally contemplated when GASBS 11 was first issued. GASBS 34 will have a profound impact on financial reporting by governmental entities.

NOTE: Implementing GASBS 34 will be a significant challenge for governments. As discussed later in this section, one of the most difficult aspects will be capitalizing infrastructure assets and recording depreciation on these, as well as all other, capitalized fixed assets. Requirements vary depending on the size of the government and alternatives that exist, requiring careful analysis and planning.

GASBS 34 results in a financial reporting model for governmental entities that would include states, cities, towns, villages, and special-purpose governments such as school districts and public utilities. GASBS 35 amends GASBS 34 to include the accounting and financial reporting by public colleges and universities within its scope.

The provisions of GASB Statement 34 and 35 have been incorporated throughout this guide.

Effective Dates

GASBS 34 has a phased implementation schedule. Early implementation is allowed. If a primary government implements GASBS 34 early, all of its component units should also implement early in order to provide the required information for the government-wide financial statements.

GASBS 34 is effective in three phases based on a government's total annual revenues in the first fiscal year ending after June 13, 1999.

- Phase 1 governments, with total annual revenues of $100 million or more, should apply the requirements in financial statements for periods beginning after June 15, 2001.
- Phase 2 governments, with total annual revenues of $10 million or more but less than $100 million, should apply the requirements in financial statements for periods beginning after June 15, 2002.
- Phase 3 governments, with total annual revenues of less than $10 million, should apply the requirements in financial statements for periods beginning after June 15, 2003.

Exhibit 1 provides a sample note to the financial statements that governments may consider using prior to implementation of GASBS 34. While it may present more information than required, it is designed to respond to financial statement readers' and users' strong interest in the impact of the new financial reporting model.

Exhibit 1: Sample note disclosure for GASBS 34 for pronouncements used but not effective (assumes a government with a June 30th fiscal year-end with over $100 million of total annual revenues)

In June 1999, GASB issued Statement 34, *Basic Financial Statements—and Management's Discussion and Analysis—for State and Local Governments.* The Statement significantly changes the financial reporting model for state and local governments and will result in significant changes to the financial statements of the City of Anywhere. The City has not completed the complex analysis of the impact of Statement 34 on its financial statements. Statement 34 requires government-wide financial statements to be prepared using the accrual basis of accounting and the economic resources measurement focus. Government-wide financial statements will not provide information by fund or account group, but will distinguish between the City's governmental and business-type activities and the activities of its discretely presented component units on the City's statement of net assets and statement of activities. Significantly, the City's statement of net assets will include both noncurrent assets and noncurrent liabilities of the City, which are currently recorded in the General Fixed Assets Account Group and the General Long-term Obligations Account Group. In addition to the fixed assets now recorded in the General Fixed Assets Account Group, the City will be required to retroactively capitalize infrastructure assets that were acquired beginning with the City's fiscal year ended

June 30, 1981. The City's government-wide statement of activities will reflect depreciation expense on the City's fixed assets, including infrastructure. If certain conditions are met, the City may use an alternative method to recording depreciation on infrastructure assets.

In addition to the government-wide financial statements, the City will be required to prepare fund financial statements. Governmental fund financial statements will continue to use the modified accrual basis of accounting and current financial resources measurement focus. Proprietary funds will continue to use the accrual basis of accounting and the economic resources measurement focus. Accordingly, the accounting and financial reporting for the City's General Fund Capital Projects Funds, Debt Service Funds, and Internal Service Funds will be similar to that currently presented in the City's financial statements, although the format of the financial statements will be modified by Statement 34.

Statement 34 also requires two components of required supplementary information: Management's discussion and analysis will include an analytical overview of the City's financial activities. Budgetary comparison schedules will compare the adopted and modified general fund budget with actual results on the same accounting basis used to prepare the budget.

The City will be required to implement Statement 34 in the fiscal year ending June 30, 2002, except that the City can delay the retroactive recording of infrastructure assets until the fiscal year ending June 30, 2006. The component units currently included in the City's financial reporting entity will also be required to implement Statement 34 at the same time the City implements this Statement. The City is continuing the complex analysis of determining the financial statement impact of implementing Statement 34.

Implementation Issues

Required implementation of GASBS 34 for medium-sized and smaller governments seems far off. Retroactive reporting of infrastructure assets is even further in the future. Few governments have ventured to implement GASBS 34 earlier than required. The above discussion is meant to highlight the key changes that will result from GASBS 34. Governments of all sizes, however, need to begin now to plan for the major changes that result from this statement.

NOTE: Financial statement preparers may have a tough time in getting the resources necessary to undertake this implementation effort, particularly in the area of retroactive recording of infra-

structure assets. Required implementation dates extend beyond the terms of office for current office holders with four-year terms. Waiting to address implementation issues could have serious effect on the probability of successful implementation.

The following are some suggestions for governments to begin doing now so that implementation will be as smooth as possible.

- Establish an implementation plan that contains the major activities and the time they are required to be completed. Planning should include determining whether the government is a Phase 1, 2, or 3 government, whether early implementation will be considered, and when retroactive reporting of infrastructure assets will be adopted.
- Make sure all components will implement at the same time as the reporting entity government.
- Determine whether the government's own staff will undertake the major implementation or whether outside consultants or independent auditors will be engaged. If both resources will be used, a determination of who is responsible for which portion is important.
- Review systems capabilities to determine how financial data will be accumulated under different bases of accounting and measurement focuses. While the GASB has been extremely careful to remove all references to "dual-perspective" reporting discussed in earlier documents, the fact remains that much of a government's financial activity will be reported under two bases of accounting and two measurement focuses. For governments that do not budget on a GAAP basis, an additional basis (budget basis) will be required. A likely approach is to maintain the general ledger on a cash basis and make separate adjustments as required for financial reporting purposes.
- Assess whether financial systems are capable of calculating and recording depreciation.
- Determine which infrastructure assets are considered major for purposes of retroactive recording of these assets.
- Assess the availability of records that would allow retroactive capitalization of infrastructure assets. Determine whether cost estimation techniques will be used. Be aware that different cost estimation techniques may be used for different types of assets. For example, actual cost records may be available for major

bridge construction or reconstruction projects. Deflated replacement cost information may be used for smaller bridges, such as highway overpasses.
- Perform preliminary analyses to determine whether it appears that depreciation on infrastructure assets will be reported in a traditional manner or whether the modified approach will be used.

GASB STATEMENT 35, *BASIC FINANCIAL STATEMENTS—AND MANAGEMENT'S DISCUSSION AND ANALYSIS—FOR PUBLIC COLLEGES AND UNIVERSITIES, AN AMENDMENT OF GASB STATEMENT 34*

GASBS 35 is effective using the same dates in the phased approach as GASBS 34, including the delayed effective dates for retroactive reporting of infrastructure assets. Definition of the different phases is the same as for GASBS 34. For purposes of determining which phase a public college or university belongs in, "revenues" includes all of the revenues of the primary institution, excluding additions to investment in plant or other financing sources and extraordinary items. In addition, if the public college or university is a component unit, GASBS 35 should be implemented in the same year that the primary government implements GASBS 34, regardless of revenues.

GASB STATEMENT 37, *BASIC FINANCIAL STATEMENTS—AND MANAGEMENT'S DISCUSSION AND ANALYSIS—FOR STATE AND LOCAL GOVERNMENTS: OMNIBUS*

In June 2001, the GASB issued GASBS 37 to fine-tune some of the requirements of GASBS 34. In some cases, the fine-tuning is simply a clarification of requirements that were originally included in GASBS 34. In other cases, the requirements of GASBS 34 are modified to reflect some implementation difficulties that had come to light relating to some of the requirements of GASBS 34.

The following are some of the key provisions of GASBS 37:

- Escheat property. Escheat property should generally be reported as an asset in the governmental or proprietary fund to which the property ultimately escheats. Escheat property held for individuals, private organizations, or another government should be reported in a private-purpose trust or an agency fund, as appropriate (or the governmental or proprietary fund in which escheat property is otherwise reported, with a corresponding liability).

When escheat property is reported in governmental or proprietary funds, escheat revenue should be reduced and a governmental or proprietary liability reported to the extent that it is probable that escheat property will be reclaimed and paid to claimants.

Escheat-related transactions reported in the government-wide financial statements should be measured using the economic resources measurement focus and the accrual basis of accounting. Escheat transactions reported in private-purpose trust funds or in agency funds should be excluded from the government-wide financial statements.

- Management's Discussion and Analysis (MD&A). The topics covered by MD&A should be limited to those contained in GASBS 34. Information that does not relate to the required topics should not be included in MD&A.
- Capitalized interest. Capitalization of construction period interest is no longer required to be considered part of the cost of capital assets used in governmental activities.
- Changing to the modified approach for reporting infrastructure. A government that changes from depreciating infrastructure assets to using the modified approach should report this change as a change in accounting estimate, which would not require restatement of prior periods.
- Levels of detail for activities accounted for in enterprise funds. The minimum level of detail reported presented in an enterprise fund's statement of activities is by different identifiable activities. An activity within an enterprise fund is identifiable if it has a specific revenue stream and related expenses and gains and losses that are accounted for separately.
- Identification of program revenues. For identifying the function to which a program revenues pertains, the determining factors for services is which function generates the revenue. For grants and contributions, the determining factor is the function to which the revenues are restricted. If the source of program revenue is not clear, governments should adopt a classification policy for assigning those revenues and apply it consistently.

Charges for services include fines and forfeitures because they result from direct charges to those who are otherwise directly affected by a program or service, even though they receive no benefit.

- Definition of a segment. A segment is now defined as an identifiable activity (or group of activities) reported as or within an enterprise fund or another stand-alone entity that has one or more bonds or other debt instruments outstanding. In addition, the activity would be considered a segment if the activity's revenues, expenses, gains and losses, and assets and liabilities are required (by an external party) to be accounted for separately. Disclosure requirements for each segment should be met by identifying the types of goods and services provided and by presenting condensed financial information in the notes.
- Budgetary information. The notes to the required supplementary information should disclose excesses of expenditures over appropriations to individual funds presented in the budgetary comparison.

Effective Date

GASBS 37 should be implemented simultaneously with GASBS 34.

GASB STATEMENT 38, *CERTAIN FINANCIAL STATEMENT NOTE DISCLOSURES*

In June 2001, the GASB issued GASBS 38 as a result of its project to review financial statement note disclosures. A need to reevaluate note disclosures in the context of the new financial reporting model established by GASBS 34 provided the impetus for the GASB to issue this Statement before most governments begin implementing the new financial reporting model.

The GASB reevaluated note disclosures that have been in existence since 1994 and not under reevaluation under some other project. Readers expecting a wholesale change in the note disclosures as a result of GASBS 38 will be disappointed. Several new note disclosures have been added, while relief from previous disclosure requirements is rare. While the effect of the potential changes will vary from government to government, it appears that disclosures relating to interfund balances and transfers appear to be the most significant. The following describes the significant changes proposed by this new Statement:

1. Summary of significant accounting policies

    a. Descriptions of the activities accounted for in each of the following columns (major funds, internal service funds and fiduciary fund types) presented in the basic financial statements

    b. The period of availability used for revenue recognition in governmental fund financial statements should be disclosed

    c. The requirement to disclose the accounting policy for encumbrances has been eliminated.

2. Significant violations of finance-related legal or contractual requirements and actions to address these violations should be disclosed.

3. The following details of debt service requirements to maturity should be disclosed:

    a. Principal and interest requirements to maturity, presented separately for each of the five succeeding fiscal years and in five-year increments thereafter. Interest requirements for variable-rate debt should be made using the interest rate in effect at the financial statement date.

    b. The terms by which interest rates change for variable-rate debt.

    c. For capital and noncancelable operating leases, the future minimum payments for each of the five succeeding fiscal years and in five-year increments thereafter should be disclosed.

    d. Details of short-term debt should be disclosed, even if no short-term debt exists at the financial statement date. Short-term debt results from borrowings characterized by anticipation notes, uses of lines of credit, and similar loans. A schedule of changes in short-term debt, disclosing beginning- and end-of-year balances, increases, decreases, and the purpose for which short-term debt was issued.

    e. Balances of receivables and payables reported on the statement of net assets and balance sheet may be aggregations of different components, such as balances due to or from taxpayers, other governments, vendors, beneficiaries, employees, etc. When the aggregation of balances on the statement of net assets obscures the nature of significant individual accounts, the governments should provide details in the notes to the financial statements. Significant receivable balances not expected to be collected within one year of the date of the financial statements should be disclosed.

f. For interfund balances reported in the fund financial statements, the following disclosures would be required:

 (1) Identification of amounts due from other funds by individual major fund, nonmajor funds in the aggregate, internal service funds in the aggregate, and fiduciary fund type

 (2) A description of the purpose for interfund balances

 (3) Interfund balances that are not expected to be repaid within one year from the date of the financial statements

g. For interfund transfers reported in the fund financial statements, the following disclosures would be required:

 (1) Identification of the amounts transfered from other funds by individual major fund, nonmajor funds in the aggregate, internal service funds in the aggregate and fiduciary fund type

 (2) A general description of the principal purposes for interfund transfers

 (3) A general description and the amount of significant transfers that

  (a) Are not expected to occur on a routine basis and/or

  (b) Are inconsistent with the activities of the fund making the transfer—for example, a transfer from a capital projects fund to the general fund.

Effective Date

GASBS 38 is effective over the same time frame as GASBS 34, with the exception that Phase 1 governments are given an additional year to include the short-term debt, disaggregation of balances, and interfund transfers and balances disclosures.

EXPOSURE DRAFT—*THE FINANCIAL REPORTING ENTITY—AFFILIATED ORGANIZATIONS*

In July 2001, the GASB issued an Exposure Draft that "revives" a project that has long been on hold regarding affiliated organizations. While the project originally was to address whether fundraising foundations were part of a governmental college or university's financial reporting entity, the project expanded to include all types of affiliated organizations and related organizations.

The Exposure Draft states that certain affiliated organizations for which a primary government is not financially accountable nevertheless warrant inclusion as part of the financial reporting entity because of the nature and significance of their relationship with the primary government, including their financial support of the primary government and its other component units.

A legally separate, tax-exempt affiliated organization should be reported as a component unit (discretely presented) of a reporting entity if all of the following criteria are met:

- The economic resources of the separate affiliated organization entirely or almost entirely directly benefit the primary government, its component units, or its constituents.
- The primary government or its component units are entitled to, or can otherwise access, the majority of the economic resources of the separate affiliated organization.
- The economic resources that the specific primary government is entitled to, or can otherwise access, are significant to that primary government.

In addition, the Exposure Draft states that other organizations should be evaluated as potential component units if they are closely related to, or financially integrated with, the primary government. It is a matter of professional judgment as to whether the nature and the significance of a potential component unit's relationship with the primary government warrant inclusion in the reporting entity.

Effective Date

The Exposure Draft indicates that the provisions of the resulting Statement would be effective for periods beginning after June 15, 2003, with earlier application encouraged.

GASB TECHNICAL AGENDA

The current GASB Technical Agenda focuses on some major new projects including the following:

- The GASB has two areas that it is working on relating to its conceptual framework—communications (Exposure Draft expected in the first quarter of 2003) and elements of financial statements (Exposure Draft expected in the second quarter of 2004).
- The GASB is addressing the area of other postemployment benefits and expects to issue an Exposure Draft in the first quarter of 2002. Should this project follow the accounting currently used in the private sector, this project could result in significant implementation efforts by governments. An approach similar to GASBS 27 for defined benefit pension plans is expected.
- The GASB has undertaken a new project to examine disclosures about deposit and investment risks. An Exposure Draft is planned for the second quarter of 2002.
- The GASB has undertaken a project to develop criteria for when as asset's impairment should be recognized and to determine if reported changes in asset condition levels (associated with the modified approach of accounting for infrastructure assets) can be measured in monetary terms. An Exposure Draft is planned for the fourth quarter of 2002.
- The GASB has undertaken a project to determine if additional guidance is needed to account for liabilities associated with environmental laws. Timing for any resulting Exposure Draft is not yet known.

SUMMARY

This chapter describes some of the important actions recently taken by the GASB as well as certain Pronouncements that are being readied for finalization. Governmental entities should take this information into consideration in planning the changes that they may need to make in their financial reporting systems and processes to implement new standards in an effective and efficient manner.

2 OVERVIEW OF ACCOUNTING AND FINANCIAL REPORTING BY GOVERNMENTS

INTRODUCTION

The field of governmental accounting and auditing has undergone tremendous growth and development over the last twenty years. Generally accepted accounting principles for governments were once a loosely defined set of guidelines followed by some governments and governmental entities, but now have developed into highly specialized standards used in financial reporting by an increasing number of these entities. Because of this standardization, users are able to place additional reliance on these entities' financial statements.

The Governmental Accounting Standards Board (GASB) has completed its work on a new model for financial reporting by governments that results in a radically different look to governmental financial statements as well as substantive changes in the accounting principles used by governments. Governmental financial statement preparers, auditors, and users must have a complete understanding of both current and new requirements to fulfill their financial reporting obligations.

ENTITIES COVERED BY GOVERNMENTAL ACCOUNTING PRINCIPLES

This field guide addresses this topic in much more detail throughout its later chapters as specific types of entities are discussed. However, in general, the following entities are covered by governmental generally accepted accounting principles

- State governments
- Local governments such as cities, towns, counties, and villages
- Public authorities such as housing finance, water, and airport authorities
- Governmental colleges and universities
- School districts
- Public employee retirement systems
- Public hospitals and other health care providers

Throughout this field guide, when "governmental entities" or "governments" are mentioned, the reference is to these types of entities. This field guide applies to both "general-purpose" governments, such as states, cities, and towns, as well as special-purpose governments that only have one function, such as a governmental hospital.

Not-for-profit organizations are not included within the scope of governmental accounting standards unless they are considered governmental not-for-profit organizations, nor are the federal government and its various agencies and departments. Governmental not-for-profit organizations must follow the financial reporting model for governments as promulgated by GASBS 34. Not-for-profit organizations and the federal government are sometimes confused with the governments that this book is addressing when they are homogenized into something commonly referred to as the "public sector." Not all public-sector entities (as described above) are subject to governmental accounting principles and standards.

OBJECTIVES OF GOVERNMENTAL ACCOUNTING AND FINANCIAL REPORTING

In describing the history of the governmental accounting standards development process, one could logically ask the question "Why were separate accounting and financial reporting standards needed for governments?" The answer to this depends on the identities of the groups of readers and users of the financial statements of state and local governments, the objectives of these readers and users, and the overall objectives of governmental financial reporting.

GASB Concepts Statement 1

The GASB addressed this basic question relatively soon after it was created to serve as an underpinning for all of its future standards-setting work. In 1987, the GASB issued Concepts Statement 1, *Objectives of Financial Reporting* (GASBCS 1), which identifies the primary users of the financial statements of state and local governments and their main objectives.

GASBCS 1 describes what the GASB set forth as the financial reporting objectives for governments. All of the financial reporting objectives listed and described below flow from what the GASB believes to be the most important objective of financial reporting for governments: accountability. The GASB concluded that the same objectives apply to governmental-type activities as to business-type activities, since the business-type activities are really part of the government and are publicly accountable.

The following are the financial reporting objectives contained in GASBCS 1:

- Financial reporting should assist in fulfilling government's duty to be publicly accountable and should enable users to assess that accountability.
- Financial reporting should assist users in evaluating the operating results of the governmental entity for the year.
- Financial reporting should assist users in assessing the level of services that can be provided by the governmental entity and its ability to meet its obligations as they become due.

NOTE: These financial reporting objectives are meant to provide the user of the financial statements with information as to how financially capable the government is to continue to provide services to its constituents. For example, can the government continue to collect sufficient tax revenues to support its current level of service? Has the government made significant investments in capital resources that are available to benefit future generations of citizens and taxpayers?

HIERARCHY OF GOVERNMENTAL ACCOUNTING STANDARDS

The GASB is responsible for promulgating accounting principles for governments. As described earlier in this chapter, the GASB and the Financial Accounting Standards Board are both under the jurisdiction of the Financial Accounting Foundation.

The levels of authority of the various types of established accounting principles and other accounting literature for governments was clarified by the American Institute of Certified Public Accountants (AICPA). The AICPA issued Statement on Auditing Standards 69, *The Meaning of "Present Fairly in Conformity with Generally Accepted Accounting Principles" in the Independent Auditor's Report* (SAS 69). The purpose of SAS 69 was to define the framework of generally accepted accounting principles that an auditor should use to judge whether financial statements are presented fairly within that framework. SAS 69 provides that the auditor's opinion on the fair presentation of the financial statements in conformity with generally accepted accounting principles is based on the auditor's judgment as to whether

- The accounting principles selected and applied are generally accepted
- The accounting principles are appropriate for the circumstances
- The financial statements, including the related notes, are informative on matters that may affect their use, understanding, and interpretation
- The information presented in the financial statements is classified and summarized in a reasonable manner; for instance, it is neither too detailed nor too condensed
- The financial statements reflect the underlying transactions and events in a manner that presents the financial position, results of operations, and (if applicable) the cash flows stated within a range of acceptable limits; for instance, limits that are reasonable and practical to attain in the financial statements

These considerations are required for auditors. Financial statement preparers should find these considerations helpful when preparing the financial statements for a governmental entity.

SAS 69 divides established accounting principles and other accounting literature into two main categories: other-than-governmental entities and governmental entities. Within each category, established accounting principles are divided into four categories (or levels), A through D, with Category A being the highest level of authority.

Following is the hierarchy of generally accepted accounting principles for governmental entities:

Level A   Officially established accounting principles consist of GASB Statements and Interpretations, as well as AICPA and FASB Pronouncements specifically made applicable to state and local governmental entities by GASB Statements or Interpretations.

Level B   GASB Technical Bulletins and, if specifically made applicable to state and local governmental entities by the AICPA and cleared by the GASB, AICPA Industry Audit and Accounting Guides and AICPA Statements of Position.

Level C   AICPA AcSEC Practice Bulletins, if specifically made applicable to state and local governmental entities and cleared by the

GASB, as well as consensus positions of a group of accountants organized by the GASB that attempts to reach consensus positions on accounting issues applicable to state and local governmental entities. (This group, which would function as an Emerging Issues Task Force, has not been organized by the GASB.)

Level D   Level D includes Implementation Guides (Q&As) published by the GASB staff and practices that are widely recognized and prevalent in state and local governments.

Other accounting literature.   In the absence of a pronouncement or another source of established accounting literature, the financial statement preparer or auditor may consider "other accounting literature," depending on its relevance to state and local governmental entities. Other accounting literature includes

- GASB Concepts Statements
- The accounting pronouncements in levels A through D applicable to nongovernmental entities when not specifically made applicable to state and local governmental entities by the GASB or by the organization issuing them
- FASB Concepts Statements
- AICPA Issues Papers
- International Accounting Standards of the International Accounting Standards Committee
- Pronouncements of other professional associations or regulatory agencies
- Technical Information Service Inquiries and Replies included in AICPA Technical Practice Aids
- Accounting textbooks, handbooks, and articles

Levels A through D for nongovernmental entities (included in "other accounting literature" for consideration by state and local governmental entities) consist of the following:

- Level A—FASB Statements and Interpretations, APB Opinions, and AICPA Accounting Research Bulletins
- Level B—FASB Technical Bulletins, AICPA Industry Audit and Accounting Guides, and AICPA Statements of Position
- Level C—Consensus positions of the FASB Emerging Issues Task Force and AICPA Practice Bulletins

- Level D—AICPA Accounting Interpretations, "Q&As" published by the FASB staff, as well as widely recognized and prevalent industry practices

SAS 69 reminds the auditor (and by default, the financial statement preparer) that the appropriateness of other accounting literature depends on its relevance to particular circumstances, the specificity of the guidance, and the general recognition of the issuer or author as an authority. It also states that GASB Concepts Statements would normally be more influential than any other sources in the category.

SUMMARY

This chapter provides a basic foundation for the governmental accounting and financial reporting environment. Understanding this environment will help the reader understand and apply the details of the accounting and financial reporting principles discussed throughout the rest of this book.

3 ACCOUNTING FUNDAMENTALS— FUND ACCOUNTING FUNDAMENTALS AND BASIS OF ACCOUNTING/ MEASUREMENT FOCUS

INTRODUCTION

To understand the accounting and financial reporting principles of state and local governments, financial statement preparers and auditors must be familiar with two key concepts: fund accounting and the basis of accounting and measurement focus used by funds. This chapter discusses the following information:

- A definition of *fund* and the purposes of fund accounting
- A synopsis of the various types of funds used by governments for accounting and financial reporting
- A definition of *basis of accounting* and *measurement focus*
- A description of which basis of accounting and measurement focus are used by each type of fund

These concepts are key components of the fundamental differences between the accounting and financial reporting for governments and private enterprises. Under the GASBS 34 financial reporting model, financial statement preparers and their auditors will need to understand these concepts in understanding the differences between government-wide and fund financial statements. This chapter includes some summarized information to give the reader an overview of the governmental accounting and financial reporting structure. More detailed information is contained in later chapters, which examine the accounting and the uses of the various types of funds and how typical transactions of these funds are reflected in the accounting records.

DEFINITION OF *FUND* AND THE PURPOSE OF FUND ACCOUNTING

Fund was defined by Statement 1 of the National Council on Governmental Accounting (NCGAS 1), entitled *Governmental Accounting and Financial Reporting Principles*, as follows:

> *A fund is defined as a fiscal and accounting entity with a self-balancing set of accounts recording cash and other financial resources, together with all related liabilities and residual equities or balances, and changes therein, which are segregated for the purpose of carrying on specific activities or attaining certain objectives in accordance with special regulations, restrictions, or limitations.*

This definition requires some explanation and clarification to be useful.

First, a fund is a separate entity for accounting and financial reporting purposes. A fund in itself is not a separate legal entity, although it may be established to comply with laws that require that certain transactions be segregated and accounted for as a separate "fund."

Second, a fund has a self-balancing set of accounts that record assets, liabilities, fund balance, and the operating activities of the fund. In other words, a balance sheet and operating statement can be prepared for individual funds. A fund's financial statements would not necessarily include all of the accounts for assets and liabilities that one would expect to find in a commercial enterprise's financial statements. As will be discussed later in this chapter, capital assets or certain long-term obligations are not recorded in the financial statements of funds classified as "governmental." Rather, these assets and liabilities would be displayed only on the government-wide statement of net assets. Thus, *self-balancing* shouldn't be taken to mean a complete picture. It should indicate that the transactions that are supposed to be recorded in a fund are self-balancing; for instance, the debits equal the credits (its trial balance balances), and that assets less liabilities equals the fund's residual (or, stated differently, its equity or fund balance).

Why Do Governments Use Fund Accounting?

Fund accounting for governments was developed in response to the need for state and local governments to be fully accountable for their collection and use of public resources. Funds help governments demonstrate their compliance with how they are required to allocate and spend their resources.

How Is the Number of Funds to Be Established Determined?

The number of separate funds to be established should be based on either legal requirements or management judgment for sound financial administration. In other words, where statute or law requires the establishment of particular funds, certainly these funds must be established by the government. Similarly, establishment of separate funds may be required by contracts into which the government enters, such as bond indentures. As will be discussed later, funds are also categorized as major and nonmajor for financial reporting purposes.

Beyond these legal and contractual requirements, management should determine how many funds should be established to segregate the activities related to carrying on specific activities or attaining certain objectives in accordance with special regulations, restrictions, or limitations. As discussed below, there are different fund types, and most governments will find that they have at least one fund in each fund type.

However, other governments have multiple funds in each fund type. The financial management of these governments should consider, however, that the establishment of too many funds is likely to result in cumbersome accounting and financial reporting procedures. The development of more sophisticated accounting software, with increasingly greater capability to segregate transactions within expanding account code structures, is likely to encourage governments to use fewer funds. Accountability may be achieved with better account coding, rather than with the establishment of many funds.

VARIOUS TYPES OF FUNDS USED BY GOVERNMENTS FOR ACCOUNTING AND FINANCIAL REPORTING

The following introduces the various types of funds that a government may have. Each fund type is more fully discussed in later chapters.

The fund types are categorized into three different activities: governmental, proprietary (i.e., business-type), and fiduciary.

1. Governmental

    a. General fund
    b. Special revenue funds
    c. Capital projects funds
    d. Debt service funds
    e. Permanent funds

2.   Proprietary (business-type)

    a.   Enterprise funds

    b.   Internal service funds

3.   Fiduciary

    a.   Pension and other employee benefit trust funds

    b.   Private-purpose trust funds

    c.   Investment trust funds

    d.   Agency funds

Each of these fund types is described in later chapters of this Field Guide.

A DEFINITION OF BASIS OF ACCOUNTING AND MEASUREMENT FOCUS

Two of the most important distinguishing features of governmental accounting and financial reporting are the basis of accounting and measurement focus used. Additionally, as discussed in the next section, not all of the funds of a government use the same basis of accounting and measurement focus, further distinguishing and complicating governmental accounting and financial reporting. Furthermore, for governmental funds, the basis of accounting and measurement focus used in the fund financial statements is different than that used for the same governmental activities presented in the government-wide financial statements. A simple rule of thumb to help clarify the difference between the two concepts is that the basis of accounting determines *when* transactions will be recorded and the measurement focus determines *what* transactions will be recorded.

Basis of Accounting

Basis of accounting refers to when revenues, expenditures, expenses, and transfers (and the related assets and liabilities) are recognized and reported in the financial statements. Most accountants are familiar with the cash and accrual bases of accounting. Commercial enterprises generally use the accrual basis of accounting. There are exceptions to this general rule, however. Small businesses may use the cash basis of accounting. Other businesses, such as real estate tax-shelter partnerships, may prepare financial statements on an income-tax basis, and still other commercial enterprises, such as utilities, may prepare special reports on a regulatory basis of accounting.

For governmental accounting, an additional basis of accounting, the modified accrual basis, is used by certain funds of a government. To understand the modified accrual basis of accounting, the accountant first needs to understand the cash and accrual bases of accounting.

Cash basis of accounting. Under the cash basis of accounting, revenues and expenditures are recorded when cash is received or paid. For example, an entity purchases goods that are received and used by the entity. However, the bill for the goods is not paid until two months after the goods were received. Under the cash basis of accounting, the expense for the purchased goods is not recognized in the financial statements until the bill is actually paid, regardless of when the goods were received or consumed by the entity. Using a strict interpretation of the cash basis of accounting, an entity's balance sheet would have two accounts: cash and equity. The statement of activities under the pure cash basis consists solely of a listing of cash receipts and cash disbursements for the period. As a practical matter, entities using the cash basis of accounting often record some transactions not strictly in accordance with the cash basis, such as inventory and accounts payable.

Accrual basis of accounting. The accrual basis of accounting is generally recognized as a better method than the cash basis for accounting for the economic resources of an organization, both commercial and governmental. The accrual basis of accounting presents a better presentation of the financial condition and results of operations of organizations, including governments. The accrual basis accounts for transactions when they occur. Revenues are recorded when *earned* or when the organization has a right to receive the revenues. Expenses are recorded when incurred. Unlike the cash basis, revenues and expenses are recorded when they occur, regardless of when the related cash is received or disbursed.

Modified accrual basis of accounting. As will be discussed throughout this book, governmental funds use the modified accrual basis of accounting. The modified accrual basis of accounting can be categorized as falling somewhere between the cash basis of accounting and the full accrual basis of accounting. This accounting basis was promulgated in NCGAS 1, which stated that while the accrual basis of accounting was recommended for use to the *fullest extent possible* in the governmental environment, there were differences in the environment and in the accounting measurement objectives for governmental funds that justified a divergence from the full accrual to the modified accrual basis. NCGAS 1 noted that these modifications to the accrual basis were both practical and appropriate for governmental funds to use.

The most important feature of the modified accrual basis of accounting involves the recognition of revenue in the financial statements. NCGAS 1 specifies that revenues (and other governmental fund financial resource increments) are recognized in the accounting period in which they become *susceptible to accrual*; that is, when they become both *measurable* and *available* to finance expenditures of the current period. In determining whether revenues are measurable, the government does not have to know the precise amount of the revenue in order for it to be subject to accrual. Reasonable calculations of revenues based on cash collections subsequent to the end of the fiscal year are the most likely way in which revenues become measurable. Governments are not precluded, however, from using other means to measure revenues, including historical collection patterns. In addition, a government may be able to measure revenues under cost-reimbursable grants and programs based on the amount of the expenditures claimed as revenue under each grant or program.

Determining whether revenues are available to finance expenditures of the current period is a unique consideration for governments in deciding whether revenues are subject to accrual. *Available* means that the revenue is collectible within the current period or soon enough thereafter to pay liabilities of the current period. Since governmental funds generally only record current liabilities, the availability criteria result in governmental funds only recording revenues related to the current fiscal year and received after year-end to be received within a relatively short period after the end of the fiscal year to meet the availability criteria. Assessing the criteria for the various types of revenues typically found in governments is described in later chapters.

Recording expenditures and liabilities under the modified accrual basis of accounting more closely approximates the accrual basis of accounting for other than long-term liabilities than does the recording of revenues. Expenditures in governmental funds recorded using the modified accrual basis of accounting are recorded when the related liability is incurred. Expenditures for goods and services received prior to a governmental fund's fiscal year-end are recorded in the year received, just as under the accrual basis of accounting. However, in applying this general principle, there are several important distinctions to keep in mind, as follows:

- The basis of accounting describes when transactions are recorded, not what transactions are recorded. Accordingly, as described below concerning measurement focus, allocations such as depreciation and amortization are not recorded as expenditures of governmental funds, nor are long-term liabilities.
- The most significant exception to the liability-incurred criterion for expenditure recognition involves payments of debt service on general long-term obligations. Debt service is recognized as an expenditure in the accounting period in which it is paid. There is no expenditure accrual; for example, for accrued interest on debt service up to the date of the fiscal year-end. Rather, both principal and interest are recognized as expenditures at the time that they are paid. (Chapter 9 describes an exception to the general rule when resources for debt service are accumulated in the current year and paid early in the subsequent year. It also describes the impact of GASBI 6 on this exception.)
- A second exception for expenditure recognition on the modified accrual basis of accounting involves inventory items, such as materials and supplies. Inventory may either be considered to be an expenditure when purchased (known as the *purchase method*) or may be recorded as an asset and recognized as an expenditure when consumed (known as the *consumption method*).
- Finally, the expenditures for insurance and similar services extending over more than one fiscal year do not have to be allocated between or among the fiscal years to which they relate. Rather, insurance and similar services may be recognized as expenditures in the period during which they were acquired.

More detailed information on the modified accrual basis of accounting and its application to various types of revenues and expenditures is contained in the following chapters, which cover the different types of governmental funds.

Interpretation 6—*Recognition and Measurement of Certain Fund Liabilities and Expenditures in Governmental Fund Financial Statements*

In the course of deliberations on GASBS 34, the GASB discussed areas where there were divergences in practice in the application of the modified accrual basis of accounting and current financial resources measurement focus. Because this basis of accounting and measurement focus will continue to be used by governmental funds in the fund financial statements under GASBS 34, GASBI 6 clarifies the recording of certain fund liabilities and expenditures.

GASBI 6 applies to governments that use the modified accrual basis of accounting and the current financial resources measurement focus. As discussed later in this section, it is meant to be implemented at the same time as GASBS 34 and, accordingly, will apply to the fund financial statements of governmental funds. It addresses when certain liabilities should be recorded as fund liabilities of governmental funds. Specifically, it includes within its scope liabilities that fall within the following categories:

- Those that are generally required to be recognized when due (debt service on formal debt issues, such as bonds and capital leases)
- Those that are required to be recognized to the extent that they are normally expected to be liquidated with expendable available financial resources (such as compensated absences, judgments and claims, landfill closure and postclosure care costs, and special termination benefits)
- Those for which no specific accrual modification has been established

GASBI 6 does not address whether, when, or the amount that a government should recognize as a liability, but rather clarifies the standards for distinguishing the parts of certain liabilities that should be reported as governmental fund liabilities. It also does not address the financial reporting for liabilities associated with capital leases with scheduled rent increases, employer contributions to pension plans, or postemployment health care plans administered in accordance with GASB Statement 27, *Accounting for Pensions by State and Local Government Employers*.

Governmental funds should report matured liabilities as fund liabilities. Matured liabilities include

- Liabilities that normally are due and payable in full when incurred
- The matured portion of general long-term debt, (i.e., the portion that has come due for payment)

In the absence of an explicit requirement (i.e., the absence of an applicable modification, discussed below) a government should accrue a governmental fund liability and expenditure in the period in which the government incurs the liability. Examples of these types of expenditures include salaries, supplies, utilities, professional services, etc. These types of liabilities generally represent claims against current financial resources to the extent that they are not paid.

As described in GASBI 6, there is a series of specific accrual modifications that have been established in generally accepted accounting principles for reporting certain forms of long-term indebtedness, such as

- Debt service on formal debt issues (bonds and capital leases) should be reported as a governmental fund liability and expenditure when due (i.e., matured). An optional additional accrual method (described below) may be used in certain limited circumstances.
- Liabilities for compensated absences, claims and judgments, special termination benefits, and landfill closure and postclosure care costs should be recognized as governmental fund liabilities and expenditures to the extent that they are normally expected to be liquidated with expendable available resources. Governments are normally expected to liquidate liabilities with expendable available resources to the extent that they mature (i.e., come due for payment). In other words, if the liability hasn't come due, the governmental fund should not record a liability and expenditure.

  — For example, consider an employee that terminates employment with a government and is owed accrued vacation time. A liability for the employee's unused vacation leave does not become due until the employee terminates employment. A fund liability and expenditure is not recorded until the employee actually terminates employment and the amounts are due him or her. Accordingly, if a government's fiscal year ends on June 30, and the employee terminates employment on July 1 and is paid for unused vacation time on July 20, no liability or expenditure would be recorded for the June 30 financial statements of the governmental fund. On the other hand, if the employee terminates employment on June 29 and is paid on July 20, a fund liability and expenditure would be recognized in the June 30 fund financial statements because the amount is due the employee as of June 30.

— GASBI 6 specifies that the accumulation of net assets in a governmental fund for the eventual payment of unmatured long-term indebtedness does not constitute an outflow of current financial resources and should not result in the recognition of an additional fund liability or expenditure. Accumulated net assets should be reported as part of fund balance.

Effective Date

The effective date of GASBI 6 coincides with the effective date of GASBS 34 and should be implemented simultaneously with GASBS 34.

As mentioned above, an additional accrual of a liability and expenditure for debt service is permitted under generally accepted accounting principles if a government has provided financial resources to a debt service fund for payment of liabilities that will mature early in the following period. GASBI 6 specifies that a government has provided financial resources to a debt service fund if it has deposited in or transferred to that fund financial resources that are dedicated for the payment of debt service. In addition "early in the following year" is defined as a short period of time, usually one or several days, but not more than one month. In addition, accrual of an additional liability and expenditure is not permitted for financial resources that are held in another government or that are nondedicated financial resources transferred to a debt service fund at the discretion of management.

Measurement Focus

In addition to the basis of accounting used, the other term that is key to having a full understanding of governmental accounting is *measurement focus*. As mentioned earlier, measurement focus determines what transactions will be reported in the various funds' operating statements.

Governmental funds use a measurement focus known as the *flow of current financial resources*. The operating statement of a governmental fund reflects changes in the amount of financial resources available in the near future as a result of transactions and events of the fiscal period reported. Increases in spendable resources are reported as *revenues* or *other financing sources* and decreases in spendable resources are reported as *expenditures* or *other financing uses*. Since the focus is on the financial resources available in the near future, the operating statements and balance sheets of governmental funds reflect transactions and events that involved current financial resources; for instance, those assets that will be turned into cash and spent and those liabilities that will be satisfied with those current financial resource assets. In other words, long-term assets and those assets that will not be turned into cash to satisfy current liabilities will not be reflected on the balance sheets of governmental funds. At the same time, long-term liabilities (those that will not require the use of current financial resources to pay them) will not be recorded on the balance sheets of governmental funds.

Proprietary funds use the flow of economic resources measurement focus. This measurement focus, which is generally the same as that used by commercial enterprises, focuses on whether the proprietary fund is economically better off as a result of the events and transactions that have occurred during the fiscal period reported. Transactions and events that improve the economic position of proprietary funds are reported as *revenues* or *gains*, and transactions and events that diminish the economic position of proprietary funds are reported as *expenses* or *losses*. In other words, proprietary funds reflect transactions and events regardless of whether there are current financial resources. This results in reporting both long-term assets and liabilities on the balance sheets of proprietary funds.

A SYNOPSIS OF BASIS OF ACCOUNTING AND MEASUREMENT FOCUS USED BY EACH TYPE OF FUND

Exhibit 1 serves as a reference for determining the basis of accounting and measurement focus used by the different fund types used in governmental accounting and financial reporting. For specific information on how the common transactions found in each particular fund type are treated under the particular fund's measurement focus, government financial statement preparers and auditors should refer to the specific chapters covering each of the fund types.

Exhibit 1

Fund	*Measurement focus*	*Basis of accounting*
General	Flow of current financial resources	Modified accrual
Special revenue	Flow of current financial resources	Modified accrual
Capital projects	Flow of current financial resources	Modified accrual
Debt service	Flow of current financial resources	Modified accrual
Enterprise	Flow of economic resources	Accrual
Internal service	Flow of economic resources	Accrual
Private-purpose trust	Flow of economic resources	Accrual
Permanent	Flow of current financial resources	Modified accrual
Pension (and other employee benefit) trust	Flow of economic resources	Accrual
Investment trust	Flow of economic resources	Accrual
Agency	Not applicable	Modified accrual

SUMMARY

Understanding the concepts of basis of accounting and measurement focus is important to understanding the nuances of governmental accounting. The differences in basis of accounting and measurement focus found in governmental accounting represent attempts by standard setters to better attain the financial reporting objectives discussed in Chapter 2.

4 THE IMPORTANCE OF BUDGETS TO GOVERNMENTS

INTRODUCTION

Almost all organizations—governmental, commercial, or not-for-profit—operate using some form of budgeting to ensure that resources are used in accordance with management's intentions and to facilitate obtaining results of operations consistent with management's plans. In the governmental environment, budgets take on greater importance, because they provide the framework in which public resources are spent. From an accounting and financial reporting viewpoint, budgets in government are a key component in achieving the accountability objective described in Chapter 2. Budgets in government generally represent adopted law, which is far more significant than simply a financial planning tool. Because many governments do not follow GAAP to prepare their budgets, achieving the accountability objective by comparing a non-GAAP-based budget with GAAP-based results presents some unique challenges.

This chapter provides an overview of the budgeting process in governments and highlights the important areas in which budget information is incorporated into the financial statements of governments.

BUDGET BACKGROUND

NCGAS 1, *Governmental Accounting and Financial Reporting Principles,* and NCGA Interpretation 10 (NCGAI 10), *State and Local Government Budgetary Reporting,* provide useful background information on the budgeting process typically found in state and local governments. One of the difficulties in understanding the budgeting process is the definition of a *typical* budgetary process, because it is the result of legislative actions, and accordingly, many governmental units are far from typical. However, the following discussion provides sufficient general information on the subject to enable governmental accountants and auditors to handle any budgeting situation encountered in any particular state or local governmental unit.

There are various components of a governmental budget.

- Executive budget
- Appropriated budget
- Nonappropriated budget

Executive Budget

The budgetary process typically begins with the preparation of an executive budget by the executive branch of the government (for example, the governor, mayor, or county executive) for submission to the legislature. NCGAI 10 defines the *executive budget* as "the aggregate of information, proposals, and estimates prepared and submitted to the legislative body by the chief executive and the budget office." This budget represents the efforts of the chief executive to accumulate and filter all of the budget requests for spending authority submitted by the various agencies and departments of the government. It also includes estimates of the expected revenues and other financing sources that will be used to pay for that spending authority. In addition to specific agency requests, the executive budget should also reflect the executive branch's calculations of expenditures for required payments. For example, expenditures for debt service are seldom at the discretion of the government in terms of amounts to be paid or whether the payments will be made. Pension contributions are another example of expenditures that are usually determined centrally by the executive branch.

Appropriated Budget

The executive branch usually submits the executive budget to the legislative branch of the government. After discussion and negotiation between the executive branch and the legislature, the legislature will pass the budget for signature by the executive branch. At this point, the budget is known as an *appropriated budget*. NCGAI 10 defines an appropriated budget as "the expenditure authority created by the appropriation bills or ordinances which are signed into law and related estimated revenues. The appropriated budget would include all reserves, transfers, allocations, supplemental appropriations, and other legally authorized legislative and executive changes." The importance of the appropriated budget is that it contains the legally authorized level of expenditures (the appropriations) that the government cannot legally exceed.

Nonappropriated Budget

Certain aspects of the government may operate under a financial plan that does not need to go through the formal appropriations process described above. This type of budget is referred to as a *nonappropriated budget*. A nonappropriated budget is defined by NCGAI 10 as "a financial plan for an organization, program, activity, or function approved in a manner authorized by constitution, charter, statute, or ordinance but not subject to appropriation and therefore outside the boundaries of the definition of the appropriated budget." The extent to which governments use nonappropriated budgets depends on the extent to which these types of expenditures are specifically authorized (as described in the definition).

Budgetary Execution and Management

NCGAI 10 defines budgetary execution and management as "all other suballocation, contingency reserves, recision, deferrals, transfers, conversions of language appropriations, encumbrance controls, and allotments established by the executive branch, without formal legislative enactment.   These transactions may be relevant for various accounting control and internal reporting purposes, but are not part of the appropriated budget."   Budget execution and management are the link between the higher-level appropriated budget described above and the more detailed budget that enables management of the government and its various agencies and departments to use the budget as a management and resource allocation tool.

NOTE: The importance of effective budgeting is highlighted by the existence of the Government Finance Officers' Association's Distinguished Budget Presentation Awards Program. Interested governments can submit budgetary documents to the GFOA under this program for consideration of the award, similar to the way that Comprehensive Annual Financial Statements (discussed in Chapter 5) can be submitted to the GFOA for consideration for its Certificate of Achievement for Excellence in Financial Reporting Award.

Budget Amendments

After adoption of a budget for a government's fiscal year, it often become necessary to make changes in the budget during the fiscal year. There are any number of reasons why budgets of governments might need to be amended. For example

- Tax revenues may fall short of expectations, requiring the approved level of expenditures to be decreased.
- Unusual weather circumstances (above normal snowfalls, hurricanes, floods, etc.) may result in the unforeseen use of significant amounts of a government's resources

- Policy issues developing during the year may result in a government desiring to shift spending authority to new or different programs
- Overtime and employee benefit costs may be more or less than expected

When budgets are legally adopted, the budget modification process will be dictated by the local laws of the government. Frequently, government agencies are given the ability to shift budgetary funds for relatively small amounts among their various budget categories. In addition, there may be limits as to shifting funds between budget amounts for personal service expenditures and other than personal service expenditures. When budgetary changes are for other than insignificant amounts, the legislative body will usually be required to adopt a budget amendment to formally amend the budget.

As part of the local requirements mentioned above, the period of time during which the budget may be modified will vary among governments. For example, a budget amendment adopted on the last day of the government's fiscal year provides no control over the use of governmental resources, but may be used by a government to disguise large variances from an originally budgeted amount. Local laws may prevent this type of manipulation, although some governments actually have the ability to modify their budgets months after the end of their fiscal year.

GASBS 34 requires governments to include in the Required Supplementary Information (RSI) a budgetary comparison schedule containing original budget amounts, final budget amounts, and actual amounts for the general fund and for each major special revenue fund for which a budget is legally adopted. Instead of presenting this information as RSI, a government may elect to report the budgetary comparison information in a budgetary comparison statement as part of the basic financial statements. The actual amounts presented should be on the same basis of accounting on which the budget is prepared. In addition, Management's Discussion and Analysis is required to include an analysis of significant variations between original and final budget amounts and between final budget amounts and actual budget results for the general fund, or its equivalent. The analysis should contain any currently known reasons for those variations that are expected to have a significant effect on future services or liquidity.

DIFFERENCES BETWEEN THE
BUDGET AND GAAP

As previously mentioned, there may be differences between budgetary accounting and reporting and GAAP-based accounting and reporting. As will be described in Chapter 5, a government's financial statements will include a financial statement that is actually prepared on the budgetary basis of accounting. NCGAI 10 describes the most significant categories that might give rise to these differences. These categories follow.

Basis of Accounting Differences

A government may choose to prepare its budget on a different basis of accounting than that required by GAAP. For example, while GAAP requires that the general fund use the modified accrual basis of accounting, a government may prepare its general fund budget on a different basis, such as the cash basis. Alternatively, a government may prepare its general fund budget on the modified accrual basis, with the exception of certain items that it elects to budget on a different basis, such as the cash basis.

Timing Differences

Budgets may be prepared using different time frames than the funds to which they relate use for financial reporting purposes. In addition, certain items (such as carryovers of appropriations) may be treated differently for budget purposes than for GAAP accounting and reporting. In some infrequent cases, governments adopt biennial budgets. One of the more common instances occurs when there are long-term projects that are budgeted for several years, while the fund that accounts for the construction activities (such as the capital projects fund) prepares an annual budget.

Perspective Differences

Differences sometimes arise because the fund structure that governs the way in which transactions are reported under GAAP may differ from an organizational or program structure used for budgeting purposes. NCGAI 10 defines the *organizational structure* as ". . . The perspective of a government that follows from the formal, usually statutory, patterns of authority and responsibility granted to actually carry out the functions of the government." In other words, it reflects the organizational chart and the superior/subordinate relationships that exist in actually running the government. These relationships may be different than those that would be reported for GAAP purposes within the fund structure. The program structure is defined by NCGAI 10 as ". . . The grouping of the activities, assignments of personnel, uses of expenditure authority, facilities, and equipment all intended to achieve a common purpose." In other words, budgeting may be performed on a project basis, while there may be various funds that pay for (a) the personnel assigned to the project (such as the general fund), (b) construction of the assets that the project personnel are using (such as the capital projects fund), and (c) the debt service on the money borrowed to construct the assets that the project personnel are using (such as the debt service fund).

Entity Differences

A government's appropriated budget may not include all of the entities included in its reporting entity. This is particularly important when component units are "blended" with the funds that make up the primary government. (More information is provided on the reporting entity in Chapter 6.) Governments may also legally adopt budgets for some funds within a fund type, but not for all funds within the fund type. These other funds would fall within the "nonappropriation budget" described earlier in this chapter.

The question naturally arises of what to do when budgetary reporting differs from reporting under GAAP. NCGAI 10 affirms that differences between the government's budget practices and GAAP not otherwise reconciled in the general-purpose financial statements that are attributable to basis, timing, perspective, and entity differences should be reconciled in the footnotes.

SUMMARY

As mentioned at the beginning of this chapter, budgets are an important part of maintaining control of a government's finances and are a means of achieving the financial reporting objective of accountability. Careful attention and reporting of budget-related matters is an important consideration in governmental accounting and financial reporting.

5 FINANCIAL STATEMENTS PREPARED BY GOVERNMENTS

INTRODUCTION

This chapter describes some of the unique aspects of the financial statements prepared by governments. While the basic financial statement elements of a balance sheet, operating statement, and in some cases cash flow statement exist in a significantly modified way for governments, there are some concepts unique to financial reporting for governments. One of these unique concepts is the distinction between basic financial statements and a comprehensive annual financial report. Another difference in governmental financial statements concerns the reporting of information on a government-wide as well as a fund-based basis. In addition, when budgets are legally adopted for some funds, additional operating statements are presented on the basis of accounting used for budgetary purposes, and budget to actual comparisons are displayed on that operating statement. In addition, the rules for preparation and presentation of the cash flow statement are different for governments than for commercial entities. A cash flow statement is required only for certain fund types, and is not required to be presented as one of the government-wide financial statements. The presentation categories and certain other requirements are also different for governments than for commercial entities.

This chapter provides information and discussion on the following topics:

- Basic financial statements
- Comprehensive annual financial report
- Cash flow statement preparation and reporting

This chapter focuses on the overall financial reporting for governments. There are a number of specific reporting and presentation issues that relate to specific fund types. These issues are discussed in later chapters. The financial statement discussion in this chapter assumes that the GASBS 34 reporting model is being used. The new financial reporting model for governments prescribed by GASBS 34 will significantly impact governments' financial statements.

GASBS 34 results in a financial reporting model for governmental entities that would include states, cities, towns, villages, and special-purpose governments such as school districts and public utilities. GASBS 35 amends GASBS 34 to include the accounting and financial reporting by public colleges and universities within its scope.

The components of the general-purpose financial reporting for the governmental entities included in the scope of GASBS 34 are as follows:

- Management's discussion and analysis
- Basic financial statements

    — Government-wide financial statements
    — Fund financial statements

- Notes to the financial statements
- Required supplementary information (RSI)

Each of the elements is described more fully below.

Management's Discussion and Analysis

Management's discussion and analysis (MD&A) is an introduction to the financial statements that provides readers with a brief, objective, and easily readable analysis of the government's financial performance for the year and its financial position at year-end. The analysis included in MD&A should be based on currently known facts, decisions, or conditions. For a fact to be currently known, it should be based on events or decisions that have already occurred, or have been enacted, adopted, agreed upon, or contracted. This means that governments should not include discussions about the possible effects of events that might happen. (Discussion of possible events that might happen in the future may be discussed in the letter of transmittal that is prepared as part of a Comprehensive Annual Financial Report.) MD&A should contain a comparison of current year results with those of the prior year.

GASBS 34 provides some very specific topics to be included in MD&A, although governments are encouraged to be creative in presenting the information using graphs, charts, and tables. The GASB intends MD&A to be a useful analysis that is prepared with thought and insight, rather than boilerplate material prepared by rote every year.

Current year information is to be addressed in comparison with the prior year, although the current year information should be the focus of the discussion. If the government is presenting comparative financial data with the prior year in the current year financial statements, the requirements for MD&A apply to only the current year. However, if the government is presenting comparative financial statements, that is, a complete set of financial statements for each year of a two-year period, then the requirements of MD&A must be met for each of the years presented. The requirements may be met by including all of the required information in the same presentation, meaning that two completely separate MD&As for comparative financial statements are not required, provided that all of the requirements relating to each of the years are met in the one discussion.

In addition, MD&A should focus on the primary government. Governments must use judgment in determining whether discussion and analysis of discretely presented component unit information is included in MD&A. The judgment should be based upon the significance of an individual component unit's significance to the total of all discretely presented component units, as well as its significance to the primary government.

The minimum requirements for MD&A contained in GASBS 34 are as follows:

1. Brief discussion of the basic financial statements, including the relationships of the statements to each other and the significant differences in the information that they provide. (This is where governments should explain the differences in results and measurements in the government-wide financial statements and the fund financial statements.)

2. Condensed financial information derived from the government-wide financial statements, comparing the current year to the prior year. GASBS 34 specifies that the following elements are included:

    a. Total assets, distinguishing between capital assets and other assets

    b. Total liabilities, distinguishing between long-term liabilities and other liabilities

    c. Total net assets, distinguishing among amounts invested in capital assets, net of related debt; restricted amounts; and unrestricted amounts

    d. Program revenues, by major source

    e. General revenues, by major source

    f. Total revenues

    g. Program expenses, at a minimum by function

    h. Total expenses

    i. The excess or deficiency before contributions to term and permanent endowments or permanent fund principal, special and extraordinary items

    j. Contributions

    k. Special and extraordinary items

       l.   Transfers

       m. Change in net assets

       n. Ending net assets

3.   Analysis of the government's overall financial position and results of operations. This information should assist users in determining whether financial position has improved or deteriorated as a result of the current year's operations. Both governmental and business-type activities should be discussed. GASBS 34 requires that reasons for significant changes from the prior year be described, not simply the computation of percentage changes.

4.   Analysis of the balances and transactions of individual funds

5.   Analysis of significant variations between original and final budgeted amounts and between financial budget amounts and actual budget results for the general fund (or its equivalent)

6.   Description of significant capital asset and long-term debt activity during the year

7.   For governments that use the modified approach to report some or all of their infrastructure assets, the following should be discussed:

       a.   Significant changes in the assessed condition of eligible infrastructure assets

       b   How the current assessed condition compares with the condition level the government has established

       c.   Significant differences from the estimated annual amount to maintain/preserve eligible infrastructure assets compared with the actual amounts spent during the year

8.   Description of currently known facts, decisions or conditions that are expected to have a significant effect on financial position or results of operations.

NOTE: In implementing the MD&A requirements of GASBS 34, two matters should be considered.

- *First, the relationship between MD&A and the letter of transmittal presented as part of a CAFR must be addressed. Including any information required in MD&A in a letter of transmittal does **not** fulfill any of the requirements for MD&A since MD&A is a required part of the general-purpose financial statements of a government and the letter of transmittal of a CAFR is not. On the other hand, certain information that is required in MD&A may formerly have been included in the letter of* *transmittal. This information may be moved from the transmittal letter to MD&A. However, the Government Finance Officers Association (GFOA) will soon be issuing guidance for the requirements of the letter of transmittal for its Certificate of Achievement for Excellence in Financial Reporting program. Governments that intend to apply for the GFOA Certificate of Achievement should make sure that they do not remove information from the letter of transmittal that will be required by the Certificate Program.*

- *MD&A is a required supplementary part of the basic financial statements of a government. These statements are frequently included in Official Statements prepared by governments when the governments are selling debt to the public. Official Statements generally include a significant amount of analytical information about the financial condition and financial performance of the government. Care must be taken that analytical information included in MD&A about currently known facts, decisions, and conditions are consistent with statements made in the Official Statement, after taking into consideration the passage of time between the issuance of financial statements and the issuance of an Official Statement.*

Government-Wide Financial Statements

Government-wide financial statements include two basic financial statements—a statement of net assets and a statement of activities. These statements should include the primary government and its discretely presented component units (presented separately), although they would not include the fiduciary activities, or component units that are fiduciary in nature. The statements would distinguish between governmental activities (which are those financed through taxes, intergovernmental revenues, and other nonexchange revenues) and business-type activities (which are those primarily financed through specified user fees or similar charges). Presentation of prior year data on the government-wide financial statements is optional. Presenting full prior year financial statements on the same pages as the current year financial statements may be cumbersome because of the number of columns that might need to be presented. Accordingly, a government may wish to present summarized prior year data. On the other hand, if full prior year statements are desired (for presentation in an Official Statement for a bond offering, for example) the prior year statements may be reproduced and included with the current year statements. In this case, footnote disclosure should also be reviewed to make sure that both years are addressed.

Basis of accounting and measurement focus. The government-wide financial statements are prepared using the economic resources measurement focus and the accrual basis of accounting for all activities.

The government-wide financial statements should present information about the primary government's governmental activities and business-type activities in separate columns, with a total column that represents the total primary government. Governmental activities generally include those activities financed through taxes, intergovernmental revenues, and other nonexchange revenues. Business-type activities are those activities financed in whole or part by fees charged to external parties for goods or services (i.e., enterprise fund activities). Discretely presented component units are presented in a separate column. A column which totals the primary government and the discretely presented component units to represent the entire reporting entity is optional, as is prior year data.

Reporting for governmental and business-type activities should be based on all applicable GASB pronouncements as well as the following pronouncements issued on or before November 30, 1989:

- Financial Accounting Standards Board (FASB) Statements and Interpretations
- Accounting Principles Board Opinions
- Accounting Research Bulletins of the Committee on Accounting Procedures

Consistent with GASB Statement 20, *Accounting and Financial Reporting for Proprietary Funds and Other Governmental Entities*, (GASBS 20) business-type activities may elect to also apply FASB pronouncements issued after November 30, 1989, except for those that conflict with or contradict GASB pronouncements. Consistent with GASBS 20, this option does not extend to internal service funds.

Statement of Net Assets

GASBS 34 provides several examples of how the statement of net assets may be presented. There are several key presentation issues that must be considered in implementing this Statement. These are summarized as follows:

- The difference between assets and liabilities is labeled "net assets." GASBS 34 encourages the use of the format that presents assets, less liabilities, to arrive at net assets. This difference should not be labeled as equity or fund balance.

- Governments are encouraged to present assets and liabilities in order of their relative liquidity but may instead use a classified format which distinguishes between current and long-term assets and liabilities.
- Net assets are comprised of three components.
    — Invested in capital assets, net of related debt
    — Restricted net assets (distinguishing among major categories of restrictions)
    — Unrestricted net assets

The net asset components listed above require some additional explanation and analysis.

- Invested in capital assets, net of related debt—This amount represents capital assets (including any restricted capital assets), net of accumulated depreciation, and reduced by the outstanding bonds, mortgages, notes or other borrowings that are attributable to the acquisition, construction or improvement of those assets. If there are significant unspent debt proceeds that are restricted for use for capital projects, the portion of the debt attributable to the unspent proceeds should not be included in the calculation of net assets invested in capital assets, net of related debt. Instead, that portion of the debt would be included in the same net asset component as the unspent proceeds, which would likely be net assets restricted for capital purposes. This net asset category would then have both the asset (proceeds) and the liability (the portion of the debt) recorded in the same net asset component.
- Restricted net assets—This amount represents those net assets that should be reported as restricted because constraints are placed on the net asset use that are either
    — Externally imposed by creditors (such as those imposed through debt covenants), grantors, contributors, or laws or regulations of other governments
    — Imposed by law through constitutional provisions or enabling legislation

Basically, restrictions are not unilaterally established by the reporting government itself and cannot be removed without the consent of those imposing the restrictions or through formal due process. Restrictions can be broad or narrow, provided that the purpose is narrower than that of the reporting unit in which it is reported. In addition, the GASBS 34 Implementation Guide clarifies that legislation that "earmarks" that a portion of a tax be used for a specific purpose does not constitute "enabling legislation" that would result in those assets being reported as restricted.

When permanent endowments or permanent fund principal amounts are included in restricted net assets, restricted net assets should be displayed in two additional components—expendable and nonexpendable. Nonexpendable net assets are those that are required to be retained in perpetuity.

- Unrestricted net assets—This amount consists of net assets that do not meet the definition of restricted net assets or net assets invested in capital assets, net of related debt.

Exhibit 1 presents a sample classified statement of net assets, based on the examples provided in GASBS 34.

Statement of Activities

GASBS 34 adopts the net (expense) revenue format, which is easier to view than describe. See Exhibit 2 for an example of a statement of activities based on the examples provided in GASBS 34.

The objective of this format is to report the relative financial burden of each of the reporting government's functions on its taxpayers. The format identifies the extent to which each function of the government draws from the general revenues of the government or is self-financing through fees or intergovernmental aid.

The statement of activities presents governmental activities by function (similar to the current requirements) and business-type activities at least by segment. Segments are identifiable activities reported as or within an enterprise fund or another stand-alone entity for which one or more revenue bonds or other revenue-backed debt instrument are outstanding.

Expense Presentation

GASBS 34 requires that the statement of activities present expenses of governmental activities by function in at least the level of detail required in the governmental fund statement of revenues, expenditures and changes in fund balances.

Categorization and level of detail are basically the same for governmental activities by function in pre-GASBS 34 financial statements. Expenses for business-type activities are reported in at least the level of detail as by segment, which GASBS 34 defines as an identifiable activity reported as or

Exhibit 1: Sample classified statement of net assets

City of Anywhere
Statement of Net Assets
June 30, 20XX

	Primary Government			Component units
	Governmental activities	Business-type activities	Total	
Assets				
Current assets:				
Cash and cash equivalents	$ xx,xxx	$ xx,xxx	$ xx,xxx	$ xx,xxx
Investments	xx,xxx	xx,xxx	xx,xxx	xx,xxx
Receivables (net)	xx,xxx	xx,xxx	xx,xxx	xx,xxx
Internal balances	xx,xxx	(xx,xxx)	--	--
Inventories	xx,xxx	xx,xxx	xx,xxx	xx,xxx
Total current assets	xxx,xxx	xxx,xxx	xxx,xxx	xxx,xxx
Noncurrent assets:				
Restricted cash and cash equivalents	xx,xxx	xx,xxx	xx,xxx	--
Capital assets				
Land and infrastructure	xx,xxx	xx,xxx	xx,xxx	xx,xxx
Depreciable buildings, property, and equipment, net	xx,xxx	xx,xxx	xx,xxx	xx,xxx
Total noncurrent assets	xxx,xxx	xxx,xxx	xxx,xxx	xxx,xxx
Total assets	$xxx,xxx	$xxx,xxx	$xxx,xxx	$xxx,xxx

Exhibit 1: Sample classified statement of net assets (continued)

| | Primary Government | | | Component units |
	Governmental activities	Business-type activities	Total	
Liabilities				
Current liablities:				
Accounts payable	$ xx,xxx	$ xx,xxx	$ xx,xxx	$ xx,xxx
Deferred revenue	xx,xxx	xx,xxx	xx,xxx	xx,xxx
Current portion of long-term obligations	xx,xxx	xx,xxx	xx,xxx	xx,xxx
Total current liabilities	xxx,xxx	xxx,xxx	xxx,xxx	xxx,xxx
Noncurrent liabilities:				
Noncurrent portion of long-term obligations	xx,xxx	xx,xxx	xx,xxx	xx,xxx
Total liabilities	xxx,xxx	xxx,xxx	xxx,xxx	xxx,xxx
Net assets				
Invested in capital assets, net of related debt	xx,xxx	xx,xxx	xx,xxx	xx,xxx
Restricted for:				
Capital projects	xx,xxx	--	xx,xxx	xx,xxx
Debt service	xx,xxx	xx,xxx	xx,xxx	--
Community development projects	xx,xxx	--	xx,xxx	--
Other purposes	xx,xxx	--	xx,xxx	--
Unrestricted	xx,xxx	xx,xxx	xx,xxx	xx,xxx
Total net assets	xxx,xxx	xxx,xxx	xxx,xxx	xxx,xxx
Total liabilities and net assets	$xxx,xxx	$xxx,xxx	$xxx,xxx	$xxx,xxx

Exhibit 2: Sample statement of activities

City of Anywhere
Statement of Activities
For the Fiscal Year Ended June 30, 2002

Functions/Programs	Expenses	Charges for services	Operating grants and contributions	Capital grants and contributions	Governmental activities	Business-type activities	Total	Component units
						Net (expense) revenue and changes in net assets		
						Primary government		
Primary government:								
Governmental activities								
General government	$ xx,xxx	$ xx,xxx	$ xx,xxx	$ --	$ (xx,xxx)	$ --	$(xx,xxx)	$ --
Public safety	xx,xxx	xx,xxx	xx,xxx	xx,xxx	(xx,xxx)	--	(xx,xxx)	--
Public works	xx,xxx	xx,xxx	--	xx,xxx	(xx,xxx)	--	(xx,xxx)	--
Health and sanitation	xx,xxx	xx,xxx	xx,xxx	--	(xx,xxx)	--	(xx,xxx)	--
Community development	xx,xxx	--	--	xx,xxx	(xx,xxx)	--	(xx,xxx)	--
Education	xx,xxx	--	--	--	(xx,xxx)	--	(xx,xxx)	--
Interest on long-term debt	xx,xxx	--	--	--	(xx,xxx)	--	(xx,xxx)	--
Total governmental activities	xxx,xxx	xxx,xxx	xxx,xxx	xxx,xxx	(xxx,xxx)	--	(xxx,xxx)	--
Business-type activities:								
Water and sewer	xx,xxx	xx,xxx	--	xx,xxx	--	xx,xxx	xx,xxx	--
Parking facilities	xx,xxx	xx,xxx	--	--	--	(xx,xxx)	(xx,xxx)	--
Total business-type activities	xxx,xxx	xxx,xxx	--	xxx,xxx	--	xxx,xxx	xxx,xxx	--
Total primary government	$xxx,xxx	$xxx,xxx	$xxx,xxx	$xxx,xxx	xxx,xxx	xxx,xxx	(xxx,xxx)	--
Component units:								
Landfill	$xx,xxx	$xx,xxx	--	$xx,xxx	--	--	--	$ xx,xxx
Public school system	xx,xxx	xx,xxx	$ xx,xxx	--	--	--	--	(xx,xxx)
Total component units	$xxx,xxx	$xxx,xxx	$xxx,xxx	$xxx,xxx	--	--	--	$(xxx,xxx)

Exhibit 2: Sample statement of activities (continued)

| | Net (expense) revenue and changes in net assets | | | |
| | Primary government | | | |
	Governmental activities	Business-type activities	Total	Component units
General revenues:				
Taxes:				
Property taxes	xx,xxx	--	xx,xxx	--
Franchise taxes	xx,xxx	--	xx,xxx	--
Payment from City of Anywhere	--	--	--	xx,xxx
Grants and contributions not restricted to specific programs	xx,xxx	--	xx,xxx	xx,xxx
Investment earnings	xx,xxx	xx,xxx	xx,xxx	xx,xxx
Miscellaneous	xx,xxx	xx,xxx	xx,xxx	xx,xxx
Special item—Gain on sale of baseball stadium	xx,xxx	--	xx,xxx	--
Transfers	xx,xxx	(xx,xxx)	--	--
Total general revenues, special items, and transfers	xxx,xxx	xxx,xxx	xxx,xxx	xxx,xxx
Change in net assets	(xxx,xxx)	xxx,xxx	xxx,xxx	xxx,xxx
Net assets—beginning	xxx,xxx	xxx,xxx	xxx,xxx	xxx,xxx
Net assets—ending	$xxx,xxx	$xxx,xxx	$xxx,xxx	$xxx,xxx

within an enterprise fund or another stand-alone entity for which one or more revenue bonds or other revenue-backed debt instruments are outstanding. A segment has a specific identifiable revenue stream pledged in support of revenue bonds or other revenue-backed debt and has related expenses, gains and losses, assets, and liabilities that can be identified.

Governments should report all expenses by function except for those expenses that meet the definitions of special items or extraordinary items, discussed later in this chapter. Governments are required, at a minimum, to report the direct expenses for each function. Direct expenses are those that are specifically associated with a service, program, or department and, accordingly, can be clearly identified with a particular function.

There are numerous government functions—such as the general government, support services, and administration—that are actually indirect expenses of the other functions. For example, the police department of a city reports to the mayor. The direct expenses of the police department would likely be reported under the function "public safety" in the statement of activities. However the mayor's office (along with payroll, personnel, and other departments) supports the activities of the police department although they are not direct expenses of the police department. GASBS 34 permits, but does not require, governments to allocate these indirect expenses to other functions. Governments may allocate some but not all indirect expenses, or they may use a full-cost allocation approach and allocate all indirect expenses to other functions. If indirect expenses are allocated, they must be displayed in a column separate from the direct expenses of the functions to which they are allocated. Governments that allocate central expenses to funds or programs, such as through the use of internal service funds, are not required to eliminate these administrative charges when preparing the statement of activities, but should disclose in the summary of significant accounting policies that these charges are included in direct expenses.

The reporting of depreciation expense in the statement of activities requires some careful analysis. Depreciation expense for the following types of capital assets is required to be included in the direct expenses of functions or programs:

- Capital assets that can be specifically identified with a function or program
- Capital assets that are shared by more than one function or program, such as a building in which several functions or programs share office space

Some capital assets of a government may essentially serve all of the functions of a government, such as a city hall or county administrative office building. There are several options for presenting depreciation expense on these capital assets, as enumerated in the GASBS 34 Implementation Guide. These options are

- Include the depreciation expense in an indirect expense allocation to the various functions or programs
- Report the depreciation expense as a separate line item in the statement of activities (labeled in such a way as to make clear to the reader of the financial statements that not all of the government's depreciation expense is included on this line)
- Reported as part of the general government (or its equivalent) function

Depreciation expense for infrastructure assets associated with governmental activities should be reported in one of the following ways:

- Report the depreciation expenses as a direct expense of the function that is normally used for capital outlays for and maintenance of infrastructure assets
- Report the depreciation expense as a separate line item in the statement of activities (labeled in such a way as to make clear to the reader of the financial statements that not all of the government's depreciation expense is included on this line)

Interest expense on general long-term liabilities should be reported as an indirect expenses. In certain limited circumstances where the borrowing is essential to the creation or continuing existence of a program or function and it would be misleading to exclude interest from that program or function's direct expenses, GASBS 34 would permit that interest expense to be reported as a direct expense. The GASBS 34 Implementation Guide also prescribes that interest on capital leases or interest expense from vendor financing arrangements should not be reported as direct expenses of specific programs.

Revenue Presentation

Revenues on the statement of activities are distinguished between program revenues and general revenues.

- Program revenues are those derived directly from the program itself or from parties outside the government's taxpayers or citizens, as a whole. Program revenues reduce the net cost of the program that is to be financed from the government's general revenues. On the statement of activities, these revenues are deducted from the expenses of the functions and programs discussed in the previous section. There are three categories into which program revenues should be distinguished.

— Charges for services. These are revenues based on exchange or exchange-like transactions. This type of program revenues arises from charges to customers or applicants who purchase, use, or directly benefit from the goods, services, or privileges provided. Examples include water use charges, garbage collection fees, licenses and permits such as dog licenses or building permits, and operating assessments, such as for street cleaning or street lighting.

— Program-specific operating grants and contributions. (See the following discussion on program-specific capital grants and contributions.)

— Program-specific capital grants and contributions. Both program-specific operating and capital grants and contributions include revenues arising from mandatory and voluntary nonexchange transactions with other governments, organizations, or individuals, that are restricted for use in a particular program. Some grants and contributions consist of capital assets or resources that are restricted for capital purposes, such as purchasing, constructing, or renovating capital assets associated with a particular program. These revenues should be reported separately from grants and contributions that may be used for either operating expenses or capital expenditures from a program, at the discretion of the government receiving the grant or contribution.

• General revenues are all those revenues that are not required to be reported as program revenues. GASBS 34 specifies that all taxes, regardless of whether they are levied for a specific purpose, should be reported as general revenues. Taxes should be reported by type of tax, such as real estate taxes, sales tax, income tax, franchise tax, etc. (Although operating special assessments are derived from property owners, they are not considered taxes and are properly reported as program revenues.) General revenues are reported after total net expense of the government's functions on the statement of activities.

Extraordinary and special items. GASBS 34 provides that a government's statement of activities may have extraordinary and special items. Extraordinary items are those that are unusual in nature and infrequent in occurrence. This tracks the private sector accounting definition of this term.

Special items are a new concept under GASBS 34. They are defined as "significant transactions or other events within the control of management that are either unusual in nature or infrequent in occurrence." Special items are reported separately in the statement of activities before any extraordinary items.

The GASBS 34 Implementation Guide cites the following events or transactions that may qualify as extraordinary or special items:

Extraordinary items

- Costs related to an environmental disaster caused by a large chemical spill in a train derailment in a small city
- Significant damage to the community or destruction of government facilities by natural disaster or terrorist act. However, geographic location of the government may determine if a weather-related natural disaster is infrequent.
- A large bequest to a small government by a private citizen

Special items

- Sales of certain general government capital assets
- Special termination benefits resulting from workforce reductions due to sale of the government's utility operations
- Early-retirement program offered to all employees
- Significant forgiveness of debt

Eliminations and reclassifications. GASBS 34 requires that eliminations of transactions within the governmental business-type activities be made so that these amounts are not "grossed-up" on the statement of net assets and statement of activities. Where internal service funds are used, their activities are eliminated where their transactions would cause a double recording of revenues and expenses.

Fund Financial Statements

There are many similarities between the way in which fund financial statements under GASBS 34 are prepared and the way in which they are currently prepared. One of the most notable similarities is that governmental funds will continue to use the modified accrual basis of accounting and the current financial resources measurement focus in the fund financial statements. However, there are also many important differences in the way these statements are prepared. The following discussion highlights these differences.

Fund financial statements are prepared only for the primary government. They are designed to provide focus on the major funds within each fund type. The following are the types of funds included in fund-type financial statements:

- Governmental funds
    - — General fund
    - — Special revenue funds
    - — Capital projects funds
    - — Debt service funds
    - — Permanent funds
- Proprietary funds
    - — Enterprise funds
    - — Internal service funds
- Fiduciary funds and similar component units
    - — Pension (and other employee benefit) trust funds
    - — Investment trust funds
    - — Private-purpose trust funds
    - — Agency funds

Major Funds

As mentioned above, fund financial statements focus on major funds. For governmental and proprietary funds (fiduciary fund requirements are discussed later in this chapter), fund financial statements should present each major fund in a separate column. Nonmajor funds are aggregated and displayed in a single column. GASBS 34 provides the following guidance for determining what is a major fund.

- The main operating fund (the general fund or its equivalent) is always considered a major fund.
- Other individual governmental and enterprise funds should be reported in major columns based on the following criteria:
    - — Total assets, liabilities, revenues or expenditures/expenses of that individual fund are at least 10% of the corresponding total (assets, liabilities, revenues or expenditures/ expenses), and

- Total assets, liabilities, revenues, or expenditures/expenses of the individual fund are at least 5% of the corresponding total for all governmental and enterprise funds combined.
- In addition to these criteria, if the government believes that a particular fund not meeting the above criteria is important to financial statement readers, it may be reported as a major fund. (In other words, nonmajor funds are reported in a single column. If a government desires to break out a nonmajor fund separately, it should treat that fund as a major fund.)
- In applying the 5% and 10% criteria above to governmental funds, it should be noted that revenues do not include other financing sources and expenditures do not include other financing uses.
- In applying the 5% and 10% criteria above to enterprise funds, it should be noted that both operating and nonoperating revenues and expenses should be considered.
- Blended component units of the component unit should be evaluated to determine whether they must be reported as major funds.
- The major fund determination is done using the combined fund type amounts, regardless of any reconciling items to the government-wide financial statements. In addition, the analysis is done using amounts as reported under generally accepted accounting principles—the budgetary basis of accounting (if different from generally accepted accounting principles) should not be used.

The following are the required financial statements for the various fund types:

Governmental funds

- Balance sheet
- Statement of revenues, expenditures, and changes in fund balances

Proprietary funds

- Statement of net assets or balance sheet
- Statement of revenues, expenses, and change in fund net assets or fund equity
- Statement of cash flows

Fiduciary funds

- Statement of fiduciary net assets
- Statement of changes in fiduciary assets

In preparing these fund financial statements, the following significant guidance of GASBS 34 should be considered:

- A reconciliation of the governmental fund activities in the government-wide financial statements with the governmental fund financial statements should be prepared. A summary reconciliation to the government-wide financial statements should be presented at the bottom of the fund financial statements or in an accompanying schedule. If the aggregation of reconciling information obscures the nature of the individual elements of a particular reconciling item, a more detailed explanation should be provided in the notes to the financial statements.
- General capital assets and general long-term debt are not reported in the fund financial statements.
- GASBS 34 requires activities to be reported as enterprise funds if any one of the following criteria is met:
  - The activity is financed with debt that is secured solely by a pledge of the net revenues from fees and charges of the activity.
  - Laws or regulations require that the activity's costs of providing services, including capital costs, be recovered with fees and charges, rather than with taxes or similar revenues.
  - The pricing policies of the activity establish fees and charges designed to recover its costs, including capital costs.

Budgetary Comparison Schedules

GASBS 34 requires that certain budgetary comparison schedules be presented in required supplementary information (RSI). This information is required only for the general fund and each major special revenue fund that has a legally adopted annual budget. Governments may elect to report the budgetary comparison information in a budgetary comparison statement as part of the basic financial statements, rather than as RSI.

The budgetary comparison schedules must include the originally adopted budget, as well as the final budget. The government is given certain flexibility in the format in which this information is present. For example, the comparisons may be made in a format that resembles the budget document instead of being made in a way that resembles the financial statement presentation. Of important note, the actual information presented is to be presented on the budgetary basis of accounting, which for many governments differs from generally accepted accounting principles. Regardless of the format used, the financial results reported in the budgetary comparison schedules must be reconciled to GAAP-based fund financial statements.

INTRA-ENTITY TRANSACTIONS—
GOVERNMENT-WIDE FINANCIAL STATEMENT

GASBS 34 provides guidance for handling internal balances and transactions when preparing the government-wide financial statements. The following paragraphs summarize this guidance.

Statement of Net Assets

GASBS 34 prescribes that eliminations should be made in the statement of activities to minimize the grossing-up effect on assets and liabilities within the governmental and business-type activities columns of the primary government. Amounts reported as interfund receivables and payables should be eliminated within the governmental and business-type activities columns of the statement of net assets, except for residual amounts due between the governmental and business-type activities, which should be presented as internal balances. Amounts reported in the funds as receivable from or payable to fiduciary funds should be included in the statement of net assets as receivable from or payable to external parties. This is consistent with the nature of fiduciary funds as more external than internal. All internal balances should be eliminated in the total primary government column.

Statement of Activities

GASBS 34 prescribes that eliminations should also be made in the statement of activities to remove the doubling-up effect of internal service fund activity. The effect of similar internal events that are in effect allocation of overhead expenses from one function to another or within the same function should also be eliminated.

The effect of interfund services provided and used between functions should not be eliminated in the statement of activities because doing so would misstate the expenses of the purchasing function and the program revenues of the selling function.

Intra-Entity Activity

GASBS 34 prescribes that resource flows between the primary government and blended component units should be reclassified as internal activity of the reporting entity and treated as interfund activity is treated. Resource flows (except those that affect only the balance sheet) between a primary government and its discretely presented component units should be reported as if they were external transactions. Amounts payable and receivable between the primary government and its discretely presented component units or between those component units should be reported on a separate line.

INTERFUND TRANSACTIONS—FUND FINANCIAL STATEMENTS UNDER GASBS 34

GASBS 34 also redefines reporting of interfund transactions, which it describes as follows:

> *Interfund activity within and among the three fund categories (governmental, proprietary, and fiduciary) should be classified and reported as follows:*
>
> a.   **Reciprocal interfund activity** *is the internal counterpart to exchange and exchange-like transactions. It includes*
>
>   *(1)*   **Interfund loans**—*amounts provided with a requirement for repayment. Interfund loans should be reported as interfund receivables in lender funds and interfund payables in borrower funds. This activity should not be reported as other financing sources or uses in the fund financial statements. If repayment is not expected within a reasonable time, the interfund balances should be reduced and the amount that is not expected to be repaid should be reported as a transfer from the fund that made the loan to the fund that received the loan.*
>
>   *(2)*   **Interfund services provided and used**—*sales and purchases of goods and services between funds for a price approximating their external exchange value. Interfund services provided and used should be reported as revenues in seller funds and expenditures or expenses in purchaser funds. Unpaid amounts should be reported as interfund receivables and payables in the fund balance sheets or fund statements of net assets.*

b.   ***Nonreciprocal interfund activity*** *is the internal counterpart to nonexchange transactions. It includes*

(1)   *Interfund transfers—flows of assets (such as cash or goods) without equivalent flows of assets in return and without a requirement for repayment. This category includes payments in lieu of taxes that are not provided. In governmental funds, transfers should be reported as other financing uses in the funds making transfers and as other financing sources in the funds receiving transfers. In proprietary funds, transfers should be reported after nonoperating revenues and expenses.*

(2)   ***Interfund   reimbursements***—*repayments from the funds responsible for particular expenditures or expenses to the funds that initially paid for them. Reimbursements should not be displayed in the financial statements.*

Note and Other Disclosures

GASBS 34 contains a number of disclosure requirements specifically related to its new requirements. GASBS 34 prescribes the following disclosures, where applicable, to be included in the note to the financial statements which includes a summary of significant accounting policies:

- A description of the government-wide financial statements, noting that neither fiduciary funds nor component units that are fiduciary in nature are included
- The measurement focus and basis of accounting used in the government-wide statements
- The policy for eliminating internal activity in the statement of activities
- The policy for applying FASB pronouncements issued after November 30, 1989, to business-type activities and to enterprise funds of the primary government
- The policy for capitalizing assets and for estimating the useful lives of those assets (used to calculate depreciation expense)
- Governments that choose to use the modified approach for reporting eligible infrastructure assets should describe that approach
- A description of the types of transactions included in program revenues and the policy for allocating indi-

rect expenses to functions in the statement of
activities
- The government's policy for defining operating and
nonoperating revenues of proprietary funds
- The government's policy regarding whether to first
apply restricted or unrestricted resources when an expense is incurred for purposes for which both restricted and unrestricted net assets are available

GASBS 34 also requires governments to provide additional information in the notes to the financial statements
about the capital assets and long-term liabilities. The disclosures should provide information that is divided into the major
classes of capital assets and long-term liabilities as well as
those pertaining to governmental activities and those pertaining to business-type activities. In addition, information about
capital assets that are not being depreciated should be disclosed separately from those that are being depreciated.

Required disclosures about major classes of capital assets include

- Beginning- and end-of-year balances (regardless of
whether beginning-of-year balances are presented on
the face of the government-wide financial statements),
with accumulated depreciation presented separately
from historical cost
- Capital acquisitions
- Sales or other dispositions
- Current period depreciation expense, with disclosure
of the amounts charged to each of the functions in the
statement of activities

Required disclosures about long-term liabilities (for both debt
and other long-term liabilities include

- Beginning- and end-of-year balances (regardless of
whether prior year data are presented on the face of
the government-wide financial statements)
- Increases and decreases (separately presented)
- The portions of each item that are due within one year
of the statement date
- Which governmental funds typically have been used
to liquidate other long-term liabilities (such as compensated absences and pension liabilities) in prior
years

In addition, GASBS 34 requires governments that report
enterprise funds or that use enterprise fund accounting and financial reporting report certain segment information for those
activities in the notes to the financial statements. GASB 34
defines a segment for these disclosure purposes as

. . .an identifiable activity reported as or within an enterprise fund or another stand-alone entity for which one or more revenue bonds or other revenue-backed debt instruments (such as certificates of participation) are outstanding. A segment has a specific identifiable revenue stream pledged in support of revenue bonds or other revenue-backed debt, and business-related expenses, gains and losses, assets, and liabilities that can be identified.

GASBS 34 specifies that disclosure requirements be met by providing condensed financial statements and other disclosures as follows in the notes to the financial statements:

1. Type of goods or services provided by the segment
2. Condensed statement of net assets

   a. Total assets—distinguishing between current assets, capital assets, and other assets. Amounts receivable from other funds or component units should be reported separately.

   b. Total liabilities—distinguishing between current and long-term amounts. Amounts payable to other funds or component units should be reported separately.

   c. Total net assets—distinguishing among restricted (separately reporting expendable and nonexpendable components); unrestricted; and amounts invested in capital assets, net of related debt.

3. Condensed statement of revenues, expenses, and changes in net assets

   a. Operating revenues (by major source)

   b. Operating expenses. Depreciation (including any amortization) should be identified separately.

   c. Operating income (loss)

   d. Nonoperating revenues (expenses)—with separate reporting of major revenues and expenses

   e. Capital contributions and additions to permanent and term endowments

   f. Special and extraordinary items

   g. Transfers

   h. Change in net assets

   i. Beginning net assets

   j. Ending net assets

4. Condensed statement of cash flows
   a. Net cash provided (used) by
      (1) Operating activities
      (2) Noncapital financing activities
      (3) Capital and related financing activities
      (4) Investing activities
   b. Beginning cash and cash equivalent balances
   c. Ending cash and cash equivalent balances

COMPREHENSIVE ANNUAL FINANCIAL REPORT

As described in the beginning section of this chapter, the basic financial statements and required supplementary information (BFS) constitute a significant component of a state or local government's comprehensive annual financial report (CAFR). The BFS, however, represent only one part of the CAFR. The CAFR contains additional sections that are important components of a government's external financial reporting.

CAFR Requirements

What should constitute a government's annual financial report—a CAFR or that part of the CAFR known as the BFS? The GASB concludes that, while no governmental financial statements are actually *required*, the annual financial report of a government should be presented as a comprehensive annual financial report—a CAFR.

The GASB does not preclude a government, however, from issuing basic financial statements separately from the CAFR. BFS are often issued for inclusion in official statements on bond offerings and are sometimes used for wide distribution to users who require less detailed information about a government's finances than is contained in the CAFR. A transmittal letter from the government accompanying the separately issued BFS should inform users of the availability of the CAFR for those requiring more detailed information.

The CAFR should encompass all funds of the primary government, including its blended component units. The CAFR also encompasses all of the discretely presented component units of the reporting entity.

The CAFR should contain

- The basic financial statements and required supplementary information
- Combining and individual statements for the nonmajor funds of the primary government, including its blended component units, nonmajor discretely presented component units, and fiduciary funds.

- Introductory, supplementary, and statistical information
- Schedules needed to demonstrate compliance with finance-related legal and contractual provisions

The general outline and minimum content of the CAFR specified by the GASB Codification are as follows:

I.   Introductory section—includes table of contents, letter of transmittal, and other material deemed appropriate by management

II. Financial section—includes the following:

— Auditor's report
— Basic financial statements
— Nonmajor combining and individual funds statements and schedules

III. Statistical tables

The 2001 GAAFR provides much more detailed information on each of these sections of the CAFR. These requirements are beyond the scope of this Field Guide.

Statistical tables. The third section of the CAFR is the statistical section. The statistical section provides both financial and nonfinancial information that is often very useful to investors, creditors, and other CAFR users. The statistical section presents certain information on a trend basis; that is, summary information is provided for each year in a ten-year period.

NCGAS 1 and other authoritative guidance issued by the GASB describe fifteen individual statistical tables that should be included in the statistical section of the CAFR. The 2001 GAAFR provides the financial statement preparer with additional information useful in describing how these statistical schedules should be presented.

The following are the statistical tables and a brief description of each. In cases where a table is clearly not applicable to a government, the table should be omitted from the statistical section.

- Government-wide expenses by function (optional)
- Government-wide revenues (optional)
- General governmental expenditures by function, last ten fiscal years
- General government revenues by source, last ten fiscal years
- Property tax levies and collections, last ten fiscal years
- Assessed and estimated actual value of taxable property, last ten fiscal years

- Property tax rates: all overlapping governments, last ten fiscal years
- Principal taxpayers
- Special assessment billings and collections, last ten fiscal years
- Computation of the legal debt margin
- Ratio of net general bonded debt to assessed value and net bonded debt per capita, last ten fiscal years
- Ratio of annual debt service for general bonded debt to total general expenditures, last ten years
- Computation of overlapping debt
- Revenue bond coverage, last ten fiscal years
- Demographic statistics
- Property value, construction, and bank deposits, last ten fiscal years
- Miscellaneous statistics

While the above list of statistical tables presents a "bare minimum" approach to meeting the requirements for the CAFR, governments should review the content of the tables in light of their own environments and operations to determine whether additional information could be added to the statistical tables to make them more meaningful to the readers of the CAFR.

CASH FLOW STATEMENT PREPARATION AND REPORTING

The cash flow statement prepared by governments differs from those of a commercial enterprise in two basic ways.

- Not all of the fund types that are reported by the governmental entity are required to prepare a cash flow statement. A cash flow statement of a commercial enterprise would include all of the operations of the enterprise.
- Differences exist in the categorization of cash receipts and cash disbursements and in some of the related disclosure requirements.

The following paragraphs provide detailed guidance on when a cash flow statement is required and how a cash flow statement for a governmental entity is prepared.

When Is a Cash Flow Statement Required?

A cash flow statement is required for each period that an operating statement is presented in the government's financial statements. However, not all of the fund types must be included in the statement of cash flows. Statements of cash flows must be prepared for proprietary funds and governmental entities that use proprietary fund accounting, such as public benefit corporations and authorities, governmental utilities, and governmental hospitals and other health care providers. Public employee retirement systems (PERS) and pension trust funds are exempt from the requirement to present a statement of cash flows. PERS and pension trust funds are not precluded, however, from presenting a statement of cash flows.

For purposes of this book, the entities that are required to prepare a statement of cash flows will be referred to as *governmental enterprises*. This is for convenience, but also for consistency with GASB Statement 9 (GASBS 9), *Reporting Cash Flows of Proprietary and Nonexpendable Trust Funds and Governmental Entities That Use Proprietary Fund Accounting*.

Objectives of the Statement of Cash Flows

In presenting a statement of cash flows, the preparer of the government's financial statements should keep in mind the purpose of the statement of cash flows. GASBS 9 highlights that the information about cash receipts and disbursements presented in a statement of cash flows is designed to help the reader of the financial statements assess (1) an entity's ability to generate future net cash flows, (2) its ability to meet its obligations as they come due, (3) its needs for external financing, (4) the reasons for differences between operating income or net income, if operating income is not separately identified on the operating statement, and (5) the effects of the entity's financial position on both its cash and its noncash investing, capital, and financing transactions during the period.

Cash and *Cash Equivalents* Definitions

While a statement of cash flows refers to and focuses on cash, included in the definition of the term *cash* for purposes of preparing the statement are cash equivalents. Cash equivalents are short-term, liquid investments that are so close to cash in characteristics that for purposes of preparing the statement of cash flows, they should be treated as if they were cash.

GASBS 9 provides specific guidance as to what financial instruments should be considered cash equivalents for the purposes of preparing a statement of cash flows. *Cash equivalents* are defined as short-term, highly liquid investments that are

- Readily convertible to known amounts of cash
- So near their maturity that they present insignificant risk of changes in value because of changes in interest rates

In general, only those investments with original maturities of three months or less are considered in GASBS 9 to meet this definition. *Original maturity* means the maturity to the entity holding the investment. Under GASBS 9, both a three-month US Treasury bill and a three-year Treasury note purchased three months from maturity qualify as cash equivalents. On the other hand, if the three-month US Treasury note was purchased three years ago, it does not become a cash equivalent as time passes and it only has three months left until maturity.

Common examples of cash equivalents are Treasury bills, commercial paper, certificates of deposit, money-market funds, and cash management pools. When these cash equivalents are purchased and sold during the year as part of the entity's cash management practices, these purchases and sales are not reported as cash inflows or outflows on the statement of cash flows. To do so would artificially inflate inflows and outflows of cash that are reported.

The total amount of cash and cash equivalents at the beginning and end of the period shown in the statement of cash flows should be easily traceable to similarly titled line items or subtotals shown in the statement of financial position as of the same dates. Cash and cash equivalents are included in the statement of cash flows regardless of whether there are restrictions on their use. Accordingly, when comparing the cash and cash equivalents on the statement of financial position with the statement of cash flows, both restricted and unrestricted cash and cash equivalents on the statement of financial position must be considered.

The governmental enterprise should establish an accounting policy on which securities will be considered cash equivalents within the boundaries established above. In other words, a governmental entity may establish an accounting policy that is more restrictive than that permitted by GASBS 9 regarding what is considered a cash equivalent. The accounting policy should be disclosed in the notes to the financial statements.

Classification of Cash Receipts and Cash Disbursements

A statement of cash flows should classify cash receipts and disbursements into the following categories:

- Cash flows from operating activities
- Cash flows from noncapital financing activities
- Cash flows from capital and related financing activities
- Cash flows from investing activities

Gross and net cash flows. In applying the categorization of cash flows into these classifications, governmental enterprises should consider that the GASB concluded that reporting gross cash receipts and payments during a period is more relevant than information about the net amount of cash receipts and payments. However, the net amount of cash receipts and disbursements provides sufficient information in certain instances that GASBS 9 permits "net" reporting rather than displaying the gross amounts of cash receipts and cash payments. These specific instances are as follows:

- Transactions for the purchase and sale of cash equivalents as part of the cash management activities of the governmental enterprise may be reported as net amounts.
- Where the governmental enterprise elects to use the "indirect" method of determining net cash provided or used by operations qualifies for net reporting. (This method will be more fully discussed later in this chapter.)
- Items that qualify for net reporting because of their quick turnovers, large amounts, and short maturities are cash receipts and disbursements relating to investments (other than cash equivalents), loans receivable, and debt, provided that the original maturity of the asset or liability is three months or less. (Amounts that are due on demand meet the requirement of having a maturity of three months or less.)
- In certain circumstances, governmental enterprises may report the net purchases and sales of their highly liquid investments rather than report the gross amounts. These requirements are somewhat onerous and one would not expect many governmental enterprises to meet this circumstance when net reporting would be permitted. Such net reporting is allowed if both of the following conditions are met:
  - During the period, substantially all of the governmental enterprise's assets were highly liquid investments, such as marketable securities and other assets for which a market is readily determinable.

— The government enterprise had little or no debt, based on average debt outstanding during the period, in relation to average total assets.

The following paragraphs provide guidance on classifying transactions into these categories and provide examples of the types of cash inflows and outflows that should be classified.

Cash flows from operating activities. Operating activities generally result from providing services and producing and delivering goods. On the other hand, operating activities include all transactions and other events that are not defined as capital and related financing, noncapital financing, or investing activities, and therefore could be viewed as a "catch-all" for transactions that don't meet the definition of the other cash flow classifications. Cash flows from operating activities are generally the cash effects of transactions and other events that enter into the determination of operating income. Although *operating income* is not defined in the literature for governments, it is generally agreed to represent operating revenues less operating expenses.

GASBS 9 provides the following examples of cash inflows from operating activities:

- Cash inflows from sales of goods and services, including receipts from collection of accounts receivable and both short- and long-term notes receivable arising from those sales
- Cash receipts from quasi-external operating activities with other funds
- Cash receipts from grants for specific activities considered to be operating activities of the grantor government (A grant agreement of this type is considered to be essentially the same as a contract for services.)
- Cash receipts from other funds for reimbursement of operating transactions
- All other cash receipts that do not result from transactions defined as capital and related financing, noncapital financing, or investing activities

Some examples of cash outflows from operating activities are the following:

- Cash payments to acquire materials for providing services and manufacturing goods for resale, including principal payments on accounts payable and both short- and long-term notes payable to suppliers for those materials or goods

- Cash payments to other suppliers for other goods or services
- Cash payments to employees for services
- Cash payments for grants to other governments or organizations for specific activities considered to be operating activities of the grantor government
- Cash payments for taxes, duties, fines, and other fees or penalties
- Cash payments for quasi-external operating transactions with other funds, including payments in lieu of taxes
- All other cash payments that do not result from transactions defined as capital and related financing, noncapital financing, or investing activities

In addition to the cash flows described above, the government may also need to consider some of its loan programs as having cash flows from operations if the loan programs themselves are considered part of the operating activities of the governmental enterprise. For example, program-type loans such as low-income housing mortgages or student loans are considered part of a governmental enterprise's program in that they are undertaken to fulfill a governmental enterprise's responsibility. Accordingly, the cash flows from these types of loan activities would be considered operating activities, rather than investing activities, the category in which loan cash flows are included.

Cash flows from noncapital financing activities. As its title indicates, cash flows from noncapital financing activities include borrowing money for purposes other than to acquire, construct, or improve capital assets and repaying those amounts borrowed, including interest. This category should include proceeds from all borrowings, including revenue anticipation notes not clearly attributable to the acquisition, construction, or improvement of capital assets, regardless of the form of the borrowing. In addition, this classification of cash flows should include certain other interfund and intergovernmental receipts and payments.

GASBS 9 provides the following examples of cash inflows from noncapital financing activities:

- Proceeds from bonds, notes, and other short- or long-term borrowing not clearly attributable to the acquisition, construction, or improvement of capital assets
- Cash receipts from grants or subsidies (such as those provided to finance operating deficits), except those specifically restricted for capital purposes and specific

activities that are considered to be operating activities of the grantor government

- Cash received from other funds except (1) those amounts that are clearly attributable to acquisition, construction, or improvement of capital assets, (2) quasi-external operating transactions, and (3) reimbursement for operating transactions
- Cash received from property and other taxes collected for the governmental enterprise and not specifically restricted for capital purposes

Examples of cash outflows for noncapital purposes include the following:

- Repayments of amounts borrowed for purposes other than acquiring, constructing, or improving capital assets
- Interest payments to lenders and other creditors on amounts borrowed or credit extended for purposes other than acquiring, constructing, or improving capital assets
- Cash paid as grants or subsidies to other governments or organizations, except those for specific activities that are considered to be operating activities for the grantor government
- Cash paid to other funds, except for quasi-external operating transactions

Special considerations are needed to properly classify grants made by a governmental enterprise (the grantor). For the grantor's classification purposes, it is irrelevant whether the grantee uses the grant as an operating subsidy or for capital purposes. The grantor should classify all grants as noncapital financing activities, unless the grant is specifically considered to be part of the operating activities of the grantor governmental enterprise.

Cash flows from capital and related financing activities. This classification of cash flows includes those cash flows for (1) acquiring and disposing of capital assets used in providing services or producing goods, (2) borrowing money for acquiring, constructing, or improving capital assets and repaying the amounts borrowed, including interest, and (3) paying for capital assets obtained from vendors on credit.

GASBS 9 includes the following examples of cash inflows from capital and related financing activities:

- Proceeds from issuing or refunding bonds, mortgages, notes, and other short- or long-term borrowing clearly attributable to the acquisition, construction, or improvement of capital assets

- Receipts from capital grants awarded to the governmental enterprise
- Receipts from contributions made by other funds, other governments, and the cost of acquiring, constructing, or improving capital assets
- Receipts from sales of capital assets and the proceeds from insurance on capital assets that are stolen or destroyed
- Receipts from special assessments or property and other taxes levied specifically to finance the construction, acquisition, or improvement of capital assets

Examples of cash outflows for capital and related financing activities include the following:

- Payments to acquire, construct, or improve capital assets
- Repayments or refundings of amounts borrowed specifically to acquire, construct, or improve capital assets
- Other principal payments to vendors who have extended credit to the governmental enterprise directly for purposes of acquiring, constructing, or improving capital assets
- Cash payments to lenders and other creditors for interest directly related to acquiring, constructing, or improving capital assets.

Cash flows from investing activities. The final category of cash flows is cash flows from investing activities. Investing activities include buying and selling debt and equity instruments and making and collecting loans (except loans considered part of the governmental enterprise's operating activities, as described above.)

GASBS 9 provides the following examples of cash inflows from investing activities:

- Receipts from collections of loans (except program loans) made by the governmental enterprise and sales of the debt instruments of other entities (other than cash equivalents) that were purchased by the governmental enterprise
- Receipts from sales of equity instruments and from returns on the investments in those instruments
- Interest and dividends received as returns on loans (except program loans), debt instruments of other en-

tities, equity securities, and cash management or investment pools
- Withdrawals from investment pools that the governmental enterprise is not using as demand accounts

Examples of cash outflows that should be categorized as cash flows from investing activities include the following:

- Disbursements for making loans (except program loans) made by the governmental enterprise and payments to acquire debt instruments of other entities (other than cash equivalents)
- Payments to acquire equity instruments
- Deposits into investment pools that the governmental enterprise is not using as demand accounts

Direct Method of Reporting Cash Flows from Operating Activities

GASBS 34 requires governmental enterprises to report cash flows from operating activities by the direct method. The direct method reports the major classes of gross cash receipts and gross cash payments; the sum (the total receipts less the total payments) equals the net cash provided by operating activities.

Format of the Statement of Cash Flows

The statement of cash flows should report net cash provided or used by each of the four categories described above. The total of the net effects of each of the four categories should reconcile the beginning and ending cash balances reported in the statement of financial position.

SUMMARY

This chapter provides a broad summary of the financial reporting requirements of governments. The level and extent of the detailed reporting requirements included in governments' CAFRs is extensive and presents a challenge to financial statement preparers and auditors. Specific information about accounting and reporting for individual fund types is provided in Chapters 7-11 and should be used in conjunction with the overview requirements presented in this chapter.

6 DEFINITION OF THE REPORTING ENTITY

INTRODUCTION

One of the challenges facing the preparer of financial statements for a governmental entity is to determine what entities should be included in the reporting entity of the government. Governments typically have related governmental entities and not-for-profit organizations that are so closely related to the government that their financial position and results of operations should be included with those of the government. These may also be for-profit organizations that should be included in the reporting entity of a government.

Unlike the consolidation principles used by private enterprises, there are no "ownership" percentages in the governmental and not-for-profit environments that the accountant can examine to determine what entities should be consolidated with that of the government. GASB Statement 14 (GASBS 14), *The Financial Reporting Entity,* provides guidance on inclusion in the government's reporting entity. While GASBS 14's guidance has proven effective in helping governments determine the proper reporting entity, there is still a significant degree of judgment needed to define a government's reporting entity.

This chapter provides a discussion of the detailed requirements of GASBS 14 and includes some practical guidance on applying its principles.

BACKGROUND

Governments often create separate legal entities to perform some of the functions normally associated with or performed by government. These separate entities may themselves be governmental entities or they may be not-for-profit or for-profit organizations. Sometimes these separate organizations are created to enhance revenues or reduce debt service costs of governments. Other times, these separate organizations are created to circumvent restrictions to which the state or local government would be subject.

The types and purposes of these entities continue to expand as governments seek to facilitate operations and to enter new service areas needed by their constituents.

ACCOUNTABILITY FOCUS

In developing new accounting principles relative to defining the reporting entity for state and local governments, the GASB focused on the concept of "accountability." As described in Chapter 2, the GASB has defined *accountability* as the cornerstone of governmental financial reporting, because the GASB believes that financial reporting plays a major role in fulfilling government's responsibility to the public.

Despite the outward appearance of autonomy, the organizations described above are usually administered by governing bodies appointed by the elected officials of the state or local government or by the government's officials servicing in *ex officio* capacities of the created entities. These officials of the state or local government are accountable to the citizens of the government. These officials are accountable to the citizens for their public policy decisions, regardless of whether they are carried out by the state or local government itself or by the specially created entity. This broad-based notion of the accountability of government officials led the GASB to the underlying concept of the governmental financial reporting entity. GASBS 14 states that "Governmental organizations are responsible to elected governing officials at the federal, state, or local level; therefore, financial reporting by a state or local government should report the elected officials' accountability for those organizations."

Because one of the key objectives of financial reporting as defined by the GASB is accountability, it became logical for the GASB to define the financial reporting entity in terms of the accountability of the government officials (and ultimately to the elected officials that appointed these government officials). The GASB also concluded that the users of financial statements should be able to distinguish between the financial information of the primary government and its component units (these terms are discussed in more detail below).

To accomplish the objectives and goals described above, the reporting entity's financial statements should present the fund types and account groups of the primary government (including certain component units whose financial information is blended with that of the primary government, because in substance, they are part of the primary government) and provide an overview of the other component units, referred to as discretely presented component units.

FINANCIAL REPORTING ENTITY DEFINED

The GASBS 14 definition of the financial reporting entity is as follows:

> *...the financial reporting entity consists of (a) the primary government, (b) organizations for which the primary government is financially accountable, and (c) other organizations for which the nature and significance of their relationship with the primary government are such that exclusion would cause the reporting entity's financial statements to be misleading or incomplete.*

Primary Government

The *primary government* is defined as a separately elected governing body; that is, one that is elected by the citizens in a general, popular election. A primary government is any state or local government (such as a municipality or county). A primary government may also be a special-purpose government, such as a department of parks and recreation or a school district, if it meets all of the following criteria:

- It has a separately elected governing body
- It is legally separate (defined below)
- It is fiscally independent of other state and local governments (defined below)

A primary government consists of all of the organizations that make up its legal entity. This would include all funds, organizations, institutions, agencies, departments, and offices that are not legally separate. If an organization is determined to be part of the primary government, its financial information should be included with the financial information of the primary government.

It is important to note that a governmental organization that is not a primary government (including component units, joint ventures, jointly governed organizations, or other stand-alone governments) will still be the nucleus of its own reporting entity when it issues separate financial statements. Although GASBS 14 addresses reporting issues for primary governments, these other organizations should apply the guidance of GASBS 14 as if they were a primary government when issuing separate financial statements.

NOTE: An example of this latter point of an entity other than a primary government being the nucleus of its own reporting entity might clarify this situation.

Assume that a city located on a major river establishes a separate legal entity to manage its port operations and foster shipping and other riverfront activities. The port authority is a separate legal entity, although its governing board is appointed by the city's mayor, that is, the governing board is not elected. The port authority is not a primary government.

However, assume the port authority itself sets up two additional separate legal entities: an economic development authority (to promote economic activity on the riverfront) and a souvenir shop (to raise funds as well as to publicize the riverfront activities). If these two separate entities meet the tests described in the chapter to be considered component units of the port authority, they would be included in the port authority's reporting entity, even though the port authority is not a primary government.

Separate legal standing. GASBS 14 provides specific guidance to determine whether a special-purpose government qualifies as legally separate, which is one of the three criteria for consideration as a primary government.

An organization has separate legal standing if is created as a body corporate or a body corporate and politic, or if it otherwise possesses the corporate powers that would distinguish it as being legally separate from the primary government. Corporate powers generally give an organization the capacity to, among other things

- Have a name
- Have the right to sue or be sued in its own name and without recourse to a state or local governmental unit
- Have the right to buy, sell, lease, and mortgage property in its own name

Financial statement preparers should look to the organization's charter or the enabling legislation that created the organization to determine what its corporate powers are. A special-purpose government (or other organization) that is not legally separate should be considered for financial reporting purposes as part of the primary government that holds the corporate powers described above.

Determining fiscal independence or dependence. A special-purpose government must also demonstrate that it is fiscally independent of other state or local governments to be considered a primary government. A special-purpose government is considered to be fiscally independent if it has the ability to complete certain essential fiscal events without substantive approval by a primary government. A special-purpose government is fiscally independent if it has the authority to do all of the following:

- Determine its budget without another government's having the authority to approve and modify that budget
- Levy taxes or set rates or charges without approval by another government
- Issue bonded debt without the approval of another government

The approvals included in these three criteria refer to substantive approval and not mere ministerial or compliance approvals. GASBS 14 offers the following examples of approvals that are likely to be ministerial- or compliance-oriented rather than substantive:

- A requirement for a state agency to approve local government debt after review for compliance with certain limitations, such as a debt margin calculation based on a percentage of assessed valuation
- A requirement for a state agency such as a department of education to review a local government's budget in evaluating qualifications for state funding
- A requirement for a county government official such as a county clerk to approve tax rates and levy amounts after review for compliance with tax rate and levy limitations

A special-purpose government subject to substantive approvals should not be considered a primary government. An example of a substantive approval is if a government has the authority to modify a special-purpose government's budget.

In determining fiscal independence using the criteria listed above, the financial statement preparer must be careful in determining whether approval is required or the special-purpose government is legally authorized to enter into a transaction. For example, consider a special-purpose government that would otherwise meet the criteria for fiscal independence, but is statutorily prohibited from issuing debt. In this case, special-purpose government's fiscal independence is not precluded because its issuance of debt is not subject to the approval of another government. Rather, it is simply prohibited from issuing debt by statute.

Another situation may be encountered in which a primary government is temporarily placed under the fiscal control of another government. A common example of this would be when a state government temporarily takes over the fiscal oversight of a school district. A primary government temporarily under the fiscal control of another government is still considered fiscally independent for purposes of preparing its financial statements as a primary government under the criteria of GASBS 14. The reason is that the control of the primary government is only temporary and fiscal independence will be restored in the future.

Component units. Component units are organizations that are legally separate from the primary government for which the elected officials are financially accountable. A component unit may be a governmental organization (except a governmental organization that meets the definition of a primary government), a not-for-profit organization, or even a for-profit organization. In addition to qualifying organizations that meet the "financial accountability" criteria (described more fully below), a component unit can be another type of organization whose relationship with the primary government requires its inclusion in the reporting entity's financial statements. As will be more fully described later in this chapter, once it is determined that the organization is a component unit included in the reporting entity, the financial statement preparer decides whether the component unit's financial information should be "blended" with that of the primary government or "discretely presented." Exhibit 1 presents a decision-tree flowchart adapted from GASBS 14 which will assist the reader in applying the tests to determine whether a related entity is a component unit.

Financial accountability. The GASB is careful to distinguish accountability from financial accountability. Elected officials are accountable for an organization if they appoint a voting majority of the organization's governing board. However, these appointments are sometimes not substantive because other governments, usually at a lower level, may have oversight responsibility for those officials. GASBS 14 uses the term *financial accountability* to describe the relationship that is substantive enough to warrant the inclusion of the legally separate organization in the reporting entity of another government. The criteria for determining whether a legally separate organization is financially accountable to a government, and therefore must be considered a component unit of the government's reporting entity, are

- The primary government is financially accountable if it appoints a voting majority of the organization's governing body, and (1) it is able to impose its will on that organization or (2) there is a potential for the organization to provide specific financial benefits to, or impose specific financial burdens on, the primary government. (In determining whether the primary government appoints a majority of the organization's board, the situation may be encountered where the members of the organization's governing body consist of the primary government's officials serving as required by law, that is, as ex officio members. While not technically "appointed" [because the individuals serve on the organization's board because their positions make them board members by law], this situation should be treated as if the individuals were actually appointed by the primary government for purposes of determining financial accountability.)

• The primary government may be financially accountable if an organization is fiscally dependent on the primary government regardless of whether the organization has (1) a separately elected governing board, (2) a governing board appointed by a higher level of government, or (3) a jointly appointed board.

In applying these principles, there are several matters to more carefully define. GASBS 14 clarifies the meaning of a number of terms to assist in their application, as follows.

Appointment of a voting majority. A primary government generally has a voting majority if it appoints a simple majority of the organization's governing board members. However, if more than a simple majority of the governing board is needed to approve financial decisions, the criterion for appointing the majority of the board to determine accountability has not been met.

The primary government's ability to appoint a voting majority of the organization's governing board must have substance. For example, if the primary government must appoint the governing board members from a list or slate of candidates that is very narrow and controlled by another level of government or organization, it would be difficult to argue that the primary government actually appointed a voting majority of a governing board, since the freedom of choice is so limited. A primary government's appointment ability would also not be substantive if it consisted only of confirming candidates to the governing board that were actually selected by another individual or organization.

Imposition of will. If, in addition to its ability to appoint a voting majority of an organization's governing board, a primary government is able to impose its will on the organization, the primary government is financially accountable for the organization. GASBS 14 provides guidance on when a primary government can impose its will on another organization. Generally, a primary government has the ability to impose its will on an organization if it can significantly influence the programs, projects, activities, or level of services performed or provided by the organization. Imposition of will can be demonstrated by the existence of any one of the following conditions:

- The ability to remove appointed members of the organization's governing board
- The ability to modify or approve the budget of the organization
- The ability to modify or approve rate or fee changes affecting revenues, such as water usage rate increases
- The ability to veto, overrule, or modify the decisions (other than the budget and rates or fee changes listed above) of the organization's governing body
- The ability to appoint, hire, reassign, or dismiss those persons responsible for the day-to-day operations or management of the organization

GASBS 14 acknowledges that there are other conditions that may exist that also indicate that the primary government has the capability to impose its will on another organization. As with the previously described tests, the focus should be on substantive instances where the primary government's will can be imposed, rather than on insignificant or ministerial approvals.

Financial benefit to or burden on the primary government. As described above, financial accountability for another organization can be demonstrated by a primary government if the primary government appoints a majority of the organization's governing board and imposes its will on the organization. In addition to these tests, there is another test that a government can use to demonstrate financial accountability for another organization. If the primary government appoints a voting majority of the organization's governing board and there is a potential for the organization to either provide specific financial benefits to or impose specific financial burdens on the primary government, the primary government is financially accountable for the organization.

The benefit or burden to the primary government may be demonstrated in several ways, such as legal entitlements or obligations or reflection of the benefit or burden in decisions made by the primary government or agreements between the primary government and the organization.

Other Organizations That Are Included in the Reporting Entity

In applying the criteria and conditions that indicate financial accountability, a significant amount of judgment is required on the part of the financial statement preparer, because the breadth of variation in the "typical" governmental reporting entity is wide. In addition, GASBS 14 specifies that certain organizations should be included in the reporting entity of a primary government even if the financial accountability test is not met. These organizations should be included as component units if the nature and significance of their relationships with the primary government are such that exclusion from the financial reporting entity of the primary government would make the primary government's financial statements incomplete or misleading. Clearly, a significant amount of judgment is required for compliance with this provision by the primary government. GASBS 14 provides some guidance and examples on applying this provision.

Organizations should be evaluated as potential component units if they are closely related to the primary government. Organizations affiliated with governmental units, agencies, colleges, universities, hospitals, and other entities may need to be included based on the closeness of their relationships. For example, a not-for-profit organization whose purpose is to raise funds for a governmental university may have such a close relationship with the governmental university that it should be included in the reporting entity.

As another example, authorities with state-appointed boards may be created to provide temporary fiscal assistance to a local government. The authority should be evaluated as a potential component unit of the local government. If the authority issues debt on behalf of the local government and serves as a conduit for receiving dedicated revenues of the local government designated for repayment of the debt, the nature and significance of the relationship between the authority and the local government would warrant including it as a component unit. The temporary nature of the state authority emphasizes that the debt and revenues are, in substance, the debt and revenues of the local government.

DISPLAY OF COMPONENT UNITS

The issue of which organizations should be included in the financial reporting entity of a state or local government is the first of a two-step process in addressing the financial statements of a state or local government. After determining which component units to include in the financial reporting entity of the government, the second step is to determine how the financial information of those component units (and their related disclosures) will be presented. This section addresses this second step of presenting the financial information of the component units as part of the financial statements of the reporting entity of the state or local government.

Overview of Reporting Component Units

An objective of the financial statements of the reporting entity should be to provide an overview of the entity based on financial accountability, while at the same time allowing financial statement users to distinguish among the financial information of the primary government and the financial information of the component units. As will be more fully described later in this chapter, some component units are so closely related to the primary government that their information is blended with that of the primary government. Other component units, which generally comprise the majority of component units, should be presented discretely from the primary government.

One other factor to consider in this overview of financial reporting is that a component unit of a reporting entity may itself have component units. To further an example presented earlier, a not-for-profit organization that raises funds for a governmental university may be a component unit of that governmental university. At the same time, the governmental university may be a component unit of the state government to which it is financially accountable. While the not-for-profit organization is not a component unit of the state, its financial information will be included in the state's reporting entity, because in treating the governmental university as a component unit of the state, all of the component units of the governmental university are included with the financial information of the governmental university included in the state's reporting entity.

In addition, the determination of whether an organization is a component unit and whether it should be blended or discretely presented is a process independent of the considerations that governments make in reporting fiduciary funds. There may be organizations that do not meet the definition for inclusion in the financial reporting entity. These organizations should be reported as fiduciary funds of the primary government if the primary government has a fiduciary responsibility for them. For example, pension funds or deferred compensation plans are not evaluated as component units. Rather, they are included in a government's reporting entity because of the government's fiduciary role and responsibility.

Discrete Presentation of Component Units

Most component units will be included in the financial statements of the reporting entity using discrete presentation. GASBS 14 defines *discrete presentation* as "The method of reporting financial data of component units in a column(s) separate from the financial data of the primary government.

GASBS 34's requirements for providing information in the basic financial statements about component units of a reporting entity government can be met in one of three ways (note that these requirements do not apply to component units that are fiduciary in nature).

1. Present each major component in a separate column in the reporting government's statement of net assets and activities
2. Include combining statements of major component units in the reporting government's basic financial statements after the fund financial statements
3. Present condensed financial statements of the major component units in the notes to the reporting government's financial statements

If the third option is chosen by a reporting government, GASBS 34 specifies the following condensed financial statement information to be included in the notes to the financial statements:

1. Condensed statement of net assets

    a. Total assets—distinguishing between capital assets and other assets. Amounts receivable form the primary government or from other component units should be reported separately.
    b. Total liabilities—distinguishing between long-term debt outstanding and other liabilities. Amounts payable to the primary government or to other component units should be reported separately.
    c. Total net assets—distinguishing between restricted, unrestricted, and amounts invested in capital assets, net of related debt

2.   Condensed statement of activities

    a.   Expenses (by major functions and for depreciation expense, if separately reported)

    b.   Program revenues (by type)

    c.   Net program (expense) revenues

    d.   Tax revenues

    e.   Other nontax general revenues

    f.   Contributions to endowments and permanent fund principal

    g.   Special and extraordinary items

    h.   Change in net assets

    i.   Beginning net assets

    j.   Ending net assets

Blended Component Units

The preceding discussion focused on the presentation and disclosures required for discretely presented component units. This section will focus first on the determination of whether a component unit's financial information should be "blended" with that of the primary government. Then, the presentation and disclosure requirements for component units that are determined to be blended component units are discussed.

Why blend some component units? One of the objectives of the financial reporting for the reporting entity described earlier was to be able to distinguish the financial information of the primary government from its component units. A question arises of why this objective seems to be abandoned in order to blend certain component units so that they are less distinguishable from the primary government. The answer to this is that the GASB concluded that there are component units that, despite being legally separate from the primary government, are so intertwined with the primary government that they are, in substance, the same as the primary government. It is more useful to report these component units as part of the primary government. These component units should be reported in a manner similar to the balances and transactions of the primary government itself, a method known as "blending."

Determination of blended component units. GASBS 14 describes two circumstances in which a component unit should be blended, as follows:

- The component unit's governing board is substantively the same as the governing body of the primary government. *Substantively the same* means that there is sufficient representation of the primary government's entire governing body on the component unit's governing body to allow complete control of the component unit's activities. For example, the board of a city redevelopment authority may be composed entirely of the city council and the mayor, serving in an *ex officio* capacity. The primary government is, essentially, serving as the governing body of the component unit. On the other hand, if the mayor and city council have three seats on the governing board of a public housing authority that has a governing board of ten seats, the housing authority's governing board would not be substantively the same as the primary government's. GASBS 14 also states that this criterion will rarely, if ever, apply to a state government because of the impracticality of providing sufficient representation of the state's entire governing body.

- The component unit provides services entirely (or almost entirely) to the primary government, or otherwise exclusively (or almost exclusively) benefits the primary government even though it does not provide services directly to it. The nature of this type of arrangement is similar to that of an internal service fund. The goods and services are provided to the government itself, rather than to the individual citizens. GASBS 14 provides the example of a building authority created to finance the construction of office buildings for the primary government. If the component unit provides services to more than just the primary government, it should still be blended if the services provided to others are insignificant to the overall activities of the component unit. Other component units that should be blended are those that exclusively (or almost exclusively) benefit the primary government by providing services indirectly. GASBS 14 provides the example of a primary government that establishes a component unit to administer its employee benefit programs. In this case, the component unit exclusively benefits the primary government, even though the component unit provides services to the employees of the primary government, rather than to the primary government itself.

In some cases, the component units that are to be blended with the primary government have funds of different fund types. For example, a component unit may have a general fund and a capital projects fund. In this case, the fund types (and account groups, if applicable) should be blended with those of the primary government by grouping them with the appropriate other funds of the primary government. However, since the primary government's general fund is usually the main operating fund of the reporting entity and is a focal point for users of the financial statements, the primary government's general fund should be the only general fund for the reporting entity. The general fund of a blended component unit should be reported as a special revenue fund.

Other reporting entity issues. In addition to the basic issues of determining a state or local government's reporting entity and providing guidance on presenting blended and discretely presented component units, GASBS 14 addresses several other issues related to the government's reporting entity, including

- Investments in for-profit corporations
- Reporting periods
- Note disclosures
- Separate and stand-alone financial statements
- Reporting organizations other than component units

The following section discusses each of these reporting entity issues that should be understood by financial statement preparers.

Investments in for-profit corporations. Sometimes governments own a majority of the voting stock of a for-profit corporation. The government should account for an investment in a for-profit corporation based on the government's intent for holding the stock. For example, GASBS 14 uses the example of a government that buys all of the outstanding voting stock of a major supplier of concrete so that it can control the operations of the corporation as a source of supply. In this case, the government has bought the stock for something other than an investment—it bought the stock to ensure the supply of concrete that the government needs for capital projects. In this case, the for-profit subsidiary should be considered a component unit of the government because the intent of the government in obtaining the company is to directly enhance its ability to provide governmental services. The criteria for determining whether the component unit should be blended with the primary government or discretely presented should be determined using the criteria described in this chapter. On the other hand, if the government purchases the stock of a for-profit corporation as an investment, rather than to directly aid in providing government services, the government should report the stock as an investment and not treat the corporation as a component unit.

Reporting periods. The primary government and its component units are likely to have different fiscal year-ends. GASBS 14 encourages a common fiscal year-end for the primary government and its component units, although full compliance with this is difficult, particularly when there are a large number of component units that have existed for a long time. The financial statement preparers of the primary government should encourage new component units to adopt the same fiscal year-end as the primary government.

If a common fiscal year-end cannot be achieved, the reporting entity (which uses the same fiscal year-end as the primary government) should incorporate the financial statements for the component unit's fiscal year ending during the reporting entity's fiscal year. If the component unit's fiscal year ends within the first quarter of the reporting entity's subsequent year, it is acceptable to incorporate that fiscal year of the component unit, rather than the fiscal year ending during the reporting entity's fiscal period. Of course, this should be done only if timely and accurate presentation of the financial statements of the reporting entity is not adversely affected.

Another problem arises when there are transactions between the primary government and its component units or between component units that have different year-ends. These different year ends may result in inconsistencies in amounts reported as due to or from, transfer to or from, and so forth. The nature and amount of those transactions should be disclosed in the notes to the financial statements. The fiscal year of the component units included in the reporting entity should be consistent from year to year, and changes in fiscal years should be disclosed.

Note disclosures. The notes to the financial statements of the reporting entity should include a brief description of the component units of the financial reporting entity and their relationship to the primary government. The notes should include a discussion of the criteria for including the component units in the financial reporting entity and how the component units are reported. The note should also include information about how the separate financial statements of the individual component units may be obtained.

Separate and stand-alone financial statements. A primary government may find it necessary or useful to prepare financial statements that do not include the financial information of its component units. When these primary government-only statements are issued, the statements should acknowledge that they do not include the financial data of the component units necessary for a fair presentation of the financial statements in accordance with GAAP.

In addition, component units themselves may issue separate financial statements. These separate financial statements should use a title that indicates that the entity is a component unit of a primary government. Unlike those of the primary government, the separate financial statements of the component unit can be issued in accordance with GAAP, provided that the component unit's financial reporting entity includes all of its own component units. The component unit itself can serve as a financial reporting "nucleus" and itself be considered a primary government that includes its own component units. The notes to the separately issued financial statements should identify the primary government in whose financial reporting entity it is included and describe the component unit's relationship with the primary government.

GASBS 14 also addresses "other stand-alone government financial statements." Other stand-alone governments are legally separate governmental organizations that do not have a separately elected governing body and do not meet the definition of a component unit of a primary government. These types of governments might include special-purpose governments, joint ventures, jointly governed organizations, and pools. Although the nucleus of a financial reporting entity is usually a primary government, another stand-alone government serves as the nucleus of its reporting entity when it issues financial statements. The financial reporting entity in this case consists of the stand-alone government and all component units for which it is financially accountable, and other organizations for which the nature and significance of their relationship with the stand-alone government are such that exclusion would cause the reporting entity's financial statements to be misleading or incomplete. In addition, any stand-alone government with a voting majority of its governing board appointed by another government should disclose that accountability relationship in its financial statements.

Reporting organizations other than component units. Sometimes primary government officials may appoint some or all of the governing board members of organizations that are not included as component units in a primary government's reporting entity. These organizations can fall into one of the following three categories:

1. Related organizations
2. Joint ventures and jointly governed organizations
3. Component units of another government with characteristics of a joint venture or jointly governed organization

The following paragraph describes the proper treatment of related organizations, followed by the accounting and financial reporting for joint ventures and jointly governed organizations.

Related organizations. Organizations for which a primary government is accountable because that government appoints a voting majority of the governing board but is not financially accountable are termed "related organizations." The primary government should disclose the nature of its accountability for related organizations in the notes to its financial statements. Groups of related organizations with similar relationships with the primary government may be summarized for the purposes of the disclosures. Therefore, related organizations are not considered component units. Their financial information is not included with that of the primary government. The only requirement is footnote disclosure of the relationship with the related organization that is described above. In addition, the related organization should disclose its relationship with the primary government in its own financial statements.

Joint ventures and jointly governed organizations. As mentioned above, a primary government may appoint some or all of the governing board members of organizations that are not included as component units of the primary government's reporting entity. Two classifications for these organizations are joint ventures and jointly governed organizations. (Jointly governed organizations are discussed later in this chapter.) This section describes the accounting and financial reporting requirements for organizations that fall into these categories.

Joint ventures. A *joint venture* is defined by GASBS 14 as

> . . . *a legal entity or other organization that results from a contractual arrangement and that is owned, operated, or governed by two or more participants as a separate and specific activity subject to joint control, in which the participants retain (a) an ongoing financial interest or (b) an ongoing financial responsibility.*

Joint ventures are generally established to pool resources and share the costs, risks, and rewards of providing goods or services to the joint venture participants directly, or for the benefit of the general public or specific recipients of service. What distinguishes a joint venture from a "jointly governed organization" is that a jointly governed organization is jointly controlled by the participants, but the participants do not have an ongoing financial interest or ongoing financial responsibility for it.

The "joint control" of a jointly governed organization means that no single participant has the ability to unilaterally control the financial or operating policies of the joint venture.

Financial reporting for joint ventures. The financial accounting and reporting for joint ventures is determined by whether the participating governments have an equity interest in the joint venture. An equity interest in a joint venture may be in the form of ownership of shares of joint venture stock or otherwise having an explicit, measurable right to the net resources of a joint venture (usually based on an investment of financial or capital resources by a participating government). The equity interest may or may not change over time as a result of an interest in the net income or losses of the joint venture. An equity interest in a joint venture is explicit and measurable if the joint venture agreement stipulates that the participants have present or future claim to the net resources of the joint venture and sets forth the method to determine the participant's shares of the joint venture's net resources.

The definition of an equity interest in a joint venture should not be interpreted to mean that it is the same as a government's residual interest in assets that may revert to the government on dissolution for lack of another equitable claimant. GASBS 14 relates this type of interest to an escheat interest, in which the reversion of property to a state results from the absence of any known, rightful inheritors to the property.

If it is determined that a participating government has an equity interest in a joint venture, that equity interest should be reported as an asset of the fund that has the equity interest. Differences in reporting this asset of a fund will result depending on whether the fund holding the equity interest in the joint venture is a proprietary fund or a governmental fund.

- Proprietary fund. A proprietary fund that has an equity interest in a joint venture would record the investment as an asset in an account usually entitled "Investment in joint venture." The initial investment in the joint venture should be recorded at cost. If the joint venture agreement provides that the participating governments share in the net income or loss of the joint venture, the investment account should be adjusted for the participating governments' share of the net income or loss of the joint venture. This adjustment would be similar to what a commercial enterprise would record for an investment accounted for by the equity method. In recording this adjustment, the financial statement preparer should determine whether there are any operating profits or losses recorded by the joint venture on transactions between the proprietary fund and the joint venture. If there are operating profits or losses on transactions between the fund and the joint venture, these amounts should be eliminated before recording the adjustment for the share of the profits and losses of the joint venture. For financial statement display purposes, the investment in the joint venture and the fund's share of the joint venture's net income or loss should be reported as single amounts in the balance sheet and operating statement. In other words, the participating government does not record *pro rata* shares of each of the joint venture's assets, liabilities, revenues, and expenses.

- Governmental funds. The accounting for investments in joint ventures for governmental funds is different from that of proprietary funds because the equity interest in the joint venture does not meet the definition of a financial resource and would not be recorded as an asset of the fund. Rather, the equity investment in the joint venture should be reported only on the government-wide statement of net assets. The amount that should be reported is the total equity interest adjusted for any portion of the equity interest included in the balance sheet of the governmental fund. For instance, if the general fund reports an amount payable to or receivable from the joint venture, the investment account in the government-wide statement of net assets should be adjusted by that amount. This should result in the combination of accounts reported in the government-wide statement of net assets equaling the total equity interest in the net assets of the joint venture.

Differences also arise in a governmental fund's recording of the operating activities of a joint venture. Governmental fund operating statements should report changes in joint venture equity interests only to the extent that the amounts received or receivable from the joint venture or the amounts paid or payable to the joint venture satisfy the revenue or expenditure recognition criteria for governmental funds. For amounts receivable from the joint venture, while the "measurable" criteria for revenue recognition may be readily met, the "available" criteria will generally only be met if the joint venture distributes the fund's share of the joint venture's net income soon after the fund's fiscal year-end so that the fund has the cash available to pay for its current obligations. The recording of the operating activities of a joint venture is in the government-wide statement of activities.

Disclosure requirements—equity interest and nonequity interests. While GASBS 14 only requires the recording of amounts for joint ventures in the financial statements of participating governments when they have an equity interest in the joint venture, it does prescribe disclosure requirements for joint ventures regardless of whether there is an equity interest.

Other joint organization issues. In addition to the common joint venture type agreement that is discussed above, there are any number of additional joint relationships that may have to be evaluated by a government in determining its reporting entity and the proper accounting for joint ventures. GASBS 14 addresses several of these unique cases that provide additional guidance to the financial statement preparer. While a detailed discussion of each is beyond the scope of this field guide, they are listed for purposes of completeness.

- Joint building or finance authorities.
- Jointly governed organizations.
- Component units and related organizations with component joint venture characteristics.
- Pools.
- Undivided interests.
- Cost-sharing arrangements.

GASBS 14 describes several types of agreements that may have some of the characteristics of a joint venture, but that are not joint ventures for various overriding reasons. For example

- Cost-sharing projects (such as highway projects financed by federal, state, and local governments) should not be considered joint ventures because the participating governments do not retain an ongoing financial interest or responsibility for the projects.
- Joint purchasing agreements, in which a group of governments agree to purchase a commodity or service

over a specified period and in specified amounts, should not be considered joint ventures.

- Multiemployer public employee retirement systems should also not be considered joint ventures.
- Investment pools, which are more fully described in Chapter 15, should not be considered joint ventures.

SUMMARY

Defining the reporting entity for a state or local government or other governmental unit can be a difficult task because of the variety of relationships in which governments typically are involved. Applying the concepts described above under GASBS 14 should enable governments to effectively define the reporting entity and accomplish financial reporting objectives.

7 GENERAL FUND AND SPECIAL REVENUE FUNDS

INTRODUCTION

The general fund and special revenue funds are distinct. This chapter examines them together because many of the accounting and reporting aspects of these two fund types are the same. To enable the financial statement preparer to understand how and when these funds should be used, this chapter examines the following topics:

- Basis of accounting and measurement focus
- Nature and use of the general fund
- Nature and use of special revenue funds
- Accounting for certain revenues and expenditures of general and special revenue funds
- Accounting for assets, liabilities, and fund balances of general and special revenue funds

Additional information regarding the budgets and display of these types of funds in a government's financial statements is found in Chapters 4 and 5 respectively.

BASIS OF ACCOUNTING AND MEASUREMENT FOCUS

The general and special revenue funds are governmental funds. As such, they use the modified accrual basis of accounting and the current financial resources measurement focus.

Under the modified accrual basis of accounting, revenues and other general and special revenue fund revenues are recognized in the accounting period in which they become susceptible to accrual. *Susceptible to accrual* means that the revenues are both measurable and available. *Available* means that the revenues are collectible within the current period or soon enough thereafter to be used to pay liabilities of the current period. In applying the susceptibility to accrual criterion, judgment must be used to determine materiality of the revenues involved, the practicality of determining the accrual, and the consistency in application of accounting principles.

Under the modified accrual basis of accounting, expenditures are recognized when the liability is incurred. Goods and services received prior to the end of the fiscal year of the government are recognized in the period that a liability for the goods or services is incurred, generally when the goods and services are received. (As described later in this chapter, an exception to the general rule is that inventories and prepaid items may be recognized as expenditures when they are used instead of when they are received.)

The general fund and the special revenue funds use the current financial resources measurement focus. The measurement focus determines what transactions are recognized in the funds, in contrast to the basis of accounting, which determines when transactions are recognized in the funds.

Under the current financial resources measurement focus, the emphasis is on increases and decreases in the amount of spendable resources during the reporting period. Thus, as a generalization, long-term assets and liabilities are not recorded in general and special revenue funds. Rather, these long-term assets and liabilities are recorded in the general fixed asset account group and the general long-term debt account group, along with the long-term assets and liabilities of the other governmental fund types.

NATURE AND USE OF THE GENERAL FUND

The general fund is the chief operating fund of a government. A government is permitted by GAAP to report only one general fund. Essentially, the general fund is used to account for all financial resources of the government, except for those financial resources that are required to be accounted for in another fund. There should be a compelling reason for a government to account for financial resources in a fund other than the general fund. The 1994 GAAFR provided three examples of compelling reasons that might justify accounting for resources in a fund other than the general fund.

Since the general fund is a "catchall" fund, it would make no sense for a government to have more than one general fund. As mentioned earlier, a government is prohibited from having multiple general funds for accounting and financial reporting. However, two situations require special treatment.

NATURE AND USE OF SPECIAL REVENUE FUNDS

Special revenue funds are used to account for the proceeds of specific revenue sources that are legally restricted to expenditure for specific purposes. Governments should not use special revenue funds to account for expendable trusts or major capital projects.

The creation and use of special revenue funds is optional. (Of course, if a special revenue fund is created because a blended component unit has its own general fund, creation of the special revenue fund in this case is not really optional, it would be required to conform to GAAP.)

In the absence of a legal requirement to create one or more special revenue funds, governments should carefully consider whether the creation of special revenue funds is really needed. Keep in mind that GAAP for governments prescribes a minimum number of funds.

The "legal restrictions" that encourage use of a special revenue fund may be from external or internal sources. For example, a grant that a government receives may require that a special revenue fund be established to account for the grant revenue and related expenditures. In another example, a law that establishes a new tax to provide funds for a specific purpose may require that a special revenue fund be established to account for the revenue and the related expenditures.

On the other hand, a government may find it convenient to establish a special revenue fund to account for a revenue source that it internally restricts for a specific purpose. For example, the government's own governing body may establish a new tax to pay for a specific type of expenditure, but the governing body that establishes the tax may not actually require that the revenue and related expenditures be accounted for in a special revenue fund.

When a government decides that it will use special revenue funds, it must then decide how many special revenue funds it should create. On one hand, particularly when the government is electing on its own to establish special revenue funds, only one special revenue fund may be established. This would then account for all of the types of special revenues and their related expenditures.

On the other hand, if there are laws, regulations, or contractual agreements that require that particular designated revenues and their expenditures be accounted for in their own funds, the government will need to establish as many separate special revenue funds as it is legally or otherwise required to have.

ACCOUNTING FOR CERTAIN REVENUE AND EXPENDITURES OF GENERAL AND SPECIAL REVENUE FUNDS

The following pages review in detail the types of revenue transactions typically accounted for by both the general fund and special revenue funds. Many of the revenues recorded by the general and special revenue funds are nonexchange transactions that are described in Chapter 14.

Special program considerations—Food stamps. Specific guidance on accounting and financial reporting for food stamps was provided by GASBS 24. State governments should recognize distributions of food stamp benefits as revenues and expenditures in the general fund or in a special revenue fund, whether the state government distributes the benefits directly or through agents, to the ultimate individual recipients regardless of whether the benefits are in paper or electronic form. Expenditures should be recognized when the benefits are distributed to the individual state government or its agents. Revenue should be recognized at the same time. When food stamps are distributed using an electronic benefit transfer system, distribution (and accordingly, expenditure and revenue recognition) takes place when the individual recipients use the benefits.

State governments should report food stamp balances held by them or by their agents at the balance sheet date as an asset offset by deferred revenue. Revenues, expenditures, and balances of food stamps should be measured based on the face value of the food stamps.

Special Assessments

Some capital improvements or services provided by local governments are intended to benefit a particular property owner or group of property owners rather than the general citizenry. Special assessments for capital improvements are discussed in Chapter 8. Special assessments for special services, however, are generally accounted for in the general fund or in a special revenue fund, and therefore are included in this chapter.

Service-type special assessment projects are for operating activities and do not result in the purchase or construction of fixed assets. The assessments are often for services that are normally provided to the public as general governmental functions that are otherwise financed by the general fund or a special revenue fund. Examples of these services include street lighting, street cleaning, and snow plowing. Financing for these routine services typically comes from general revenues. However, when routine services are extended to property owners outside the normal service area of the government or are provided at a higher level or more frequent intervals than for the general public, a government sometimes levies a special assessment on those property owners who are the recipients of the higher level of service.

Special assessments used to be accounted for in a special fund type known as special assessment funds. GASB Statement 6 (GASBS 6), *Accounting and Financial Reporting for Special Assessments*, eliminated this separate fund type and directed that these arrangements be accounted for in a general fund, special revenue fund, capital projects fund, or debt service fund, depending on the nature of the special assessment.

The general fund or special revenue funds should be used to account for special service-type assessments. Without special legal restrictions to create a separate fund, the general fund is usually a good choice to account for these activities and the related revenue. Service-type special assessment revenues should be treated in a manner similar to user fees and should be recorded in accordance with the modified accrual basis of accounting. The related expenditures should also be accounted for similarly to other expenditures of the general fund and special revenue fund. Accounting for expenditures of these funds is discussed in a later section of this chapter.

Miscellaneous Revenues

In addition to the major categories of revenues described above, the general and special revenue funds are used to account for various miscellaneous revenues that the government receives. Examples of these miscellaneous revenues include fines and forfeitures, golf and swimming fees, inspection charges, parking fees, and parking meter receipts. These miscellaneous revenues should theoretically be accounted for using the modified accrual basis of accounting in the funds and the accrual basis of accounting in the government-wide financial statements. However, sometimes these are de minimis amounts and recording these types of revenues on the cash basis may be acceptable since the difference between the cash basis and the modified accrual and accrual basis would be very small.

Expenditures

The measurement focus of governmental fund accounting is on expenditures rather than expenses. Expenditures in the general and special revenue funds result in net decreases in financial resources. Since most expenditures and transfers out of the fund are measurable, they should be recorded when the related liability is incurred.

General and special revenue funds should therefore generally record expenditures when a liability is incurred. In the simplest example, goods and services received prior to the end of the fiscal year should be accrued as expenditures because the liability for the goods or services has been incurred. The special nature of the current financial resources measurement focus used by governmental funds results in eight different types of expenditures to not be recognized when the liability is incurred. These types of expenditures (and the chapter in which they are addressed) are as follows:

- Compensated absences (Chapter 17)
- Judgments and claims (Chapter 20)
- Unfunded pension contributions (Chapter 18)
- Special termination benefits (Chapter 19)
- Landfill closure and postclosure costs (Chapter 22)
- Debt service (Chapter 9)
- Supplies inventories and prepaids (discussed below)
- Operating leases with scheduled rent increases (Chapter 21)

The exceptions referred to above arise because governmental funds such as the general fund and special revenue funds record expenditures when a liability is incurred, but only record the liability for the fund when the liability will be liquidated with expendable available financial resources. In addition, the focus on current financial resources means that the accounting for the purchase of long-term assets is different than that encountered in commercial organizations. These concepts are more fully discussed below and in Chapter 3.

NOTE: For governments that have fund-raising activities, readers should be aware of the guidance of AICPA Statement of Position 98-2, **Accounting for Costs of Activity of Not-for-Profit Organizations and State and Local Governmental Entities That Include Fund-Raising.**

ACCOUNTING FOR ASSETS, LIABILITIES, AND FUND BALANCES OF GENERAL AND SPECIAL REVENUE FUNDS

The balance sheets of the general fund and special revenue funds should contain only assets that are current financial resources and the liabilities that those current financial resources will be used to pay.

On the asset side of the balance sheet, the following are the typical assets normally found on general and special revenue fund balance sheets, along with the location in this Guide where the accounting and financial reporting requirements are discussed:

- Cash and investments (Chapter 15)
- Receivables (discussed with related revenue accounts in this chapter and Chapter 14)
- Interfund receivables (Chapter 13)
- Inventories and prepaids (discussed below)

On the liability side of the balance sheet, the following are the typical liabilities normally found on general and special revenue fund balance sheets, along with the location in this Guide where the accounting and financial reporting requirements are discussed:

- Accounts payable and accrued expenses (addressed with related expenditure recognition in this chapter)
- Interfund payables (Chapter 13)
- Deferred revenues (discussed with the related revenue accounts in this chapter)
- Revenue anticipation notes and tax anticipation notes (Chapter 13)

As can be seen from the previous paragraphs, there are limited accounts and balances that are reported on the balance sheets of the general fund and special revenue funds. Two areas that are not covered elsewhere in this Guide relating to the balance sheets of these fund types are the accounting and financial reporting for inventories and prepaids and the classification of fund balances. These two topics are discussed in the following sections.

Inventories and Prepaids

There are alternative expenditure and asset recognition methods at the final financial statement level for materials and supplies and prepaids.

- Inventory items, such as materials and supplies, may be considered expenditures when purchased (referred to as the *purchase method*) or when used (referred to as the *consumption method*). However, when a government has significant amounts of inventory, it should be reported on the balance sheet. The credit amount that offsets the debit recorded on the balance sheet for inventories is "reserved fund balance," discussed in the following section on fund balance reservations. A similar reservation of fund balance is recorded when prepaid items are recorded as assets on the balance sheet.
- Expenditures for insurance and similar services extending over more than one accounting period need

not be allocated between or among accounting periods, but may be accounted for as expenditures in the period of acquisition.

For accounting for inventories at the government-wide financial statement level, the consumption method would be used. In addition, there would be no restriction on net assets to correspond to the reservation of fund balance recorded above.

Fund Balances

The equity (assets less liabilities) of the general fund and any special revenue funds is reported as fund balance. In governmental funds, reserves of fund balance are used in connection with financial assets that are not yet spendable (such as a longer-term receivable or an amount equal to the amount of inventory reported as an asset on the balance sheet). Reserves of the general fund balance or the fund balance of any special revenue fund used are also used to reflect legal restrictions on the use of assets reported on the balance sheet.

SUMMARY

This chapter discusses appropriate uses of the general fund and special revenue funds, when the government is required or elects to establish special revenue funds. It also addresses some of the more common types of revenues, expenditures, assets, and liabilities found in the general fund and special revenue funds. This guidance should be used in conjunction with the other specialized accounting treatments for various types of transactions and balances discussed throughout this guide.

8 CAPITAL PROJECTS FUNDS

INTRODUCTION

Governments often use the capital projects fund type to account for and report major capital acquisition and construction activities. NCGAS 1 describes the purpose of capital projects funds as "to account for financial resources to be used for the acquisition or construction of major capital facilities (other than those financed by proprietary funds and trust funds)."

BASIS OF ACCOUNTING

As a governmental fund type, capital projects funds use the modified accrual basis of accounting. Revenues are recorded when they are susceptible to accrual (that is, they are accrued when they become measurable and available). Expenditures are recorded when the liability is incurred. The expenditure recognition exceptions (inventories, prepaid items, judgments and claims, etc.) described in Chapter 7 relating to general and special revenue funds would also apply to capital projects funds.

MEASUREMENT FOCUS

As a governmental fund type, capital projects funds use the current financial resources measurement focus. The operating statement of the capital projects fund reports increases and decreases in spendable resources. Increases in spendable resources are reported in the operating statement as "revenues" and "other financing sources," while decreases in spendable resources are reported as "expenditures" or "other financing uses." As such, it is worthy to note that while capital projects funds are used to account for resources used in major acquisition or construction projects, the resulting assets are not reported as assets of the capital projects fund. Rather, these assets are reported in the government-wide financial statements. The capital projects fund accounts for the acquisition and construction of assets as expenditures.

WHEN ARE CAPITAL PROJECTS FUNDS USED?

In most cases, governments are permitted, but not required, to establish capital projects funds to account for resources used for major acquisition and construction of assets. The majority of governments use one or more capital projects funds to account for these activities. As seen in the following discussion, the significance of the dollar amounts that flow through the capital projects fund to the general fund might well result in an overshadowing of the general governmental activities reported in the general fund. Capital projects funds are also used to account for special revenues that relate to capital projects as well as capital improvements financed by special assessments. A later section of this chapter describes the accounting and financial reporting when special assessment debt is issued to finance capital projects.

There is one instance where GAAP requires that a government establish and use a capital projects fund. NCGAS 2, *Grants, Entitlement, and Shared Revenue Accounting by State and Local Governments,* requires that capital grants or share revenues restricted for capital acquisitions or construction (other than those associated with enterprise and internal service funds) be accounted for in a capital projects fund.

Once a government determines that it desires to establish a capital projects fund (or is required by GAAP to establish one), the government needs to decide how many capital projects funds should be established. A government may well determine that it can adequately account for and manage its capital projects with one capital projects fund. This serves to simplify financial reporting and provide the government with the opportunity to utilize its accounting system to track and manage individual projects within its capital projects funds.

On the other hand, a government may decide that establishing a number of capital projects funds will better serve its accountability and financial management needs. While governmental financial statement preparers will certainly have their own views on when using multiple capital projects funds is appropriate, it would seem that when there are two to five major capital projects that dominate the major asset acquisition or construction activities of the government, using an individual capital projects fund for each of these few significant capital projects would be appropriate.

REVENUES AND OTHER FINANCING SOURCES

The number of categories and types of revenues and other financing sources that are typically found in capital projects funds are usually far fewer than those found in the general and special revenue funds. Since governments typically finance major acquisitions and construction of capital assets through the use of debt, the issuance of debt is typically the most significant source of resources for capital projects funds, and it is reported as an "other financing" source. In addition, capital projects funds may account for receipt of resources from federal, state, or other aid programs, transfers from other funds, such as the general fund, and capital leases. The following paragraphs describe some of the accounting issues that governments may encounter in accounting for these resources in capital projects funds.

Proceeds from Debt Issuance

This section describes the appropriate accounting for the proceeds from debt issuance. In addition to the general concept of accounting for debt proceeds in the capital projects fund, specific guidance that relates to bond anticipation notes, demand bonds, special assessment debt, and arbitrage rebate considerations are discussed.

Basic journal entries to record the issuance of debt. As mentioned above, proceeds from the sale of debt to finance projects accounted for by the capital projects funds should be recorded as an other financing source of the capital projects fund. To illustrate the proper accounting within the capital projects fund, assume that a government issues debt with a face amount of $100,000. The basic journal entry that would be recorded is

Cash	100,000	
Other financing sources—		
Proceeds from the sale of bonds		100,000
To record the sale of bonds.		

However, the simplicity of this journal entry is rarely encountered in practice. For example, when bonds are issued, there are underwriter fees, attorney fees, and other costs that are typically deducted from the proceeds of the bonds. Assume in the above example that such fees are $5,000. A government has two ways to account for these fees. It can record the proceeds from the bonds net of the issuance costs and fees, or it can record the proceeds of the debt at the gross amount and record an expenditure for the issuance fees and costs. The latter method is the recommended method, in which an expenditure is recorded for the issuance fees and costs. Using this recommended approach, the following journal entry would be recorded:

Cash	95,000	
Expenditures—Bond issuance costs	5,000	
Other financing sources—		
Proceeds from the sale of bonds		100,000
To record the issuance of bonds and the payment of bond issuance costs.		

There are two other instances that represent a departure from the simplified first journal entry provided above. These instances are when bonds are issued at a premium or a discount.

Bonds are issued at a discount when the prevailing market interest rate at the time of issuance is higher than the stated or coupon rate of interest for the particular bonds being issued. If the $100,000 of face-amount bonds were actually sold for $97,500 and there was still $5,000 of issuance costs, the recommended journal entry is

Cash	92,500	
Expenditures—Bond issuance costs	5,000	
Other financing sources—		
Proceeds from the sale of bonds		97,500

To record the sale of bonds at a discount, net of issuance costs and fees.

If the prevailing market rate of interest is lower than the stated or coupon rate of interest of the specific bonds being issued, the bonds would be sold at a premium. Assuming the same facts as in the previous journal entry, except that the bonds were sold at a $2,500 premium instead of a $2,500 discount, the following journal entry would be recorded:

Cash	97,500	
Expenditures—Bond issuance costs	5,000	
Other financing sources—		
Proceeds from the sale of bonds		102,500

To record the sale of $100,000 face-amount bonds at a premium, net of bond issuance costs and fees.)

Note that no further journal entries to amortize the premium or discount would be required by the capital projects fund. Because the measurement focus of the capital projects fund is on current financial resources, the fund simply records the bond proceeds (that is, the current financial resources received) which will likely reflect premium or discount. Since the debt is not recorded in the capital projects fund, there is no need to record amortization of the premium or discount. Chapter 9 describes a situation where debt may be issued at a deep discount or super premium, in which case the amounts of the discount or premium are reflected in the general long-term debt account group and accreted or decreted over the life of the debt. The debt service on these bonds is likely to be paid out of a debt service fund (or less likely out of the general fund). Entries to record debt service are fully addressed in Chapter 9.

Arbitrage Rebate Accounting

The interest paid by state and local governments on debt issued for public purposes is generally not subject to federal taxation. Since this interest is not subject to federal taxes, the interest rates at which the government is able to issue debt is generally lower than the interest rate required for comparable debt whose interest payments are taxable to the debtholder.

Accordingly, a government has the opportunity for "arbitrage" earnings on the spread between its tax-exempt interest rate and the rate that it is able to earn on taxable investments purchased in the open market. Subject to certain safe-harbor requirements in which the bond proceeds are disbursed within a limited period, the state or local government is required to "rebate" these arbitrage earnings to the federal government. Typically, arbitrage rebate payments must be made to the federal government every five years and within sixty days of the related debt's financial maturity.

Although a government may not be required to remit the arbitrage rebate payments until several years have passed, the government should recognize a liability for rebatable arbitrage as soon as it is both probable and measurable that a liability has been incurred. In determining the amount of the liability, it must be considered that the excess arbitrage earnings earned in one year may be offset by lesser earnings in a subsequent year. Therefore, the liability recognized for the year should be only that portion of the estimated future payment that is attributable to earnings of the current period. In other words, the government should take into consideration whether its earnings on the same investments in subsequent years will offset excess earnings in the first year, for example, so that it is not necessarily required to record a liability for the full amount of any excess earnings in the first or beginning years of a debt issue.

The accounting treatment for rebatable arbitrage is to treat it similar to a judgment or claim. In this approach, all interest income, regardless of whether it is rebatable, would be reported as revenue of the capital projects fund. The liability for the rebatable arbitrage rebate would then be reported in the general long-term debt account group until it is due to be paid.

At the close of construction, both the liability for rebatable arbitrage and related assets are typically removed from the capital projects fund and reported in the debt service fund.

SUMMARY

Governments often establish capital projects funds to account for the major acquisition and construction of capital assets. This chapter focuses on the basic accounting for the typical transactions of the capital projects fund and also on some unique areas of accounting, which primarily involve the issuance of debt providing the funds for capital projects. The reader should also consider the information in Chapters 9-11 which describe the accounting and reporting for debt service funds, the general long-term debt, and capital assets for additional information on transactions that affect the accounts of the capital projects fund.

9 DEBT SERVICE FUNDS

INTRODUCTION

Governments often issue long-term debt to finance various governmental projects. Generally, this long-term debt is repaid from a governmental fund called a debt service fund. In other cases, although not legally required, a government may choose to establish a debt service fund to account for the accumulation of resources that will be used for debt service.

This chapter discusses the following topics in relation to the establishment and use of debt service funds:

- Situations in which a debt service fund is required or desirable
- Basis of accounting and measurement focus
- Expenditure recognition for debt service payments
- Accounting for the advance refunding of long-term debt

In addition to the above topics, useful information relative to a government's issuance and repayment of long-term debt is provided in Chapters 8 and 13.

SITUATIONS WHEN A DEBT SERVICE FUND IS REQUIRED OR DESIRABLE

NCGAS 1 describes the purpose of a debt service fund as to account for the accumulation of resources for, and the payment of, general long-term debt principal and interest.

In deciding to establish one or more debt service funds, a government should first determine whether it is required to establish such a fund or funds. The first requirement to consider is whether there are any laws that require the government to use a debt service fund. In addition to any legal requirements that might be established through the legislative process of the government, another potential source of legal requirement is the bond indenture agreements executed when long-term obligations are issued and sold. These agreements may require that debt service funds be used for the protection of the bondholders. The requirement to establish debt service funds as an accounting and financial reporting mechanism is different from the requirement in many bond indentures or similar agreements that establish reserve funds or other financial requirements. These other requirements may well be met through other mechanisms, such as restricted cash accounts, rather than the establishment of a debt service fund. Financial statement preparers should review these legal requirements carefully to ensure compliance with the requirements, which does not automatically lead to the use of a debt service fund.

In addition to the legal requirements described above, GAAP require the use of a debt service fund if financial resources are being accumulated for principal and interest payments maturing in future years. This requirement might be interpreted to mean that if a government has resources at the end of a fiscal year to use to pay debt service in the following year, a debt service fund would be required. This would result in almost all governments with long-term debt outstanding to be required to establish a debt service fund. In practice this requirement is interpreted more narrowly. An accumulation is only deemed to have occurred for determining whether a debt service fund is required if the government has accumulated resources for debt service payments in excess of one year's worth of principal and interest payments.

As is consistent with GAAP, the number of funds established should be kept to the minimum either required to be established by law, or considered necessary by the government for the appropriate financial management of its resources. When considering these two instances, the government also needs to determine whether it is required to establish one or more debt service funds. Ideally, in keeping with the goal of minimizing the number of funds that a government uses, a government would establish one debt service fund. This one fund should provide an adequate mechanism for the government to use to account for the accumulation of resources and payment of long-term debt. However, the legal requirements of the government itself or the bond indentures mentioned above may actually result in more than one debt service fund, perhaps even a separate debt service fund for bond issues of the government.

It should be noted that the debt service fund should be used to account for the accumulation and payment of debt service. There are other long-term obligations, such as those for capital leases, judgments and claims, and compensated absences, considered to be nondebt long-term obligations. The payments of these obligations should be reported in the fund that budgets for their payment, which is most often the general fund. The debt service fund should only be used for the accumulation of resources and payment of debt service for long-term obligations that are considered to be debt, and not for other nondebt long-term obligations.

BASIS OF ACCOUNTING AND
MEASUREMENT FOCUS

As a governmental fund, the debt service fund should use the modified accrual basis of accounting and the current financial resources measurement focus. Revenues are recorded when they are susceptible to accrual. That is, they are accrued when they become measurable and available. Expenditures are recorded when the liability is incurred. However, recognition of expenditures for debt service principal and interest payments are unique for debt service funds. The recognition criteria for debt service payments are discussed in the following section of this chapter.

As a governmental fund type, the debt service fund uses the current financial resources measurement focus. The operating statement of the debt service fund reports increases and decreases in spendable resources. Increases in spendable resources are reported in the operating statement as "revenues" and "other financing sources," while decreases in spendable resources are reported as "expenditures" or "other financing uses."

In applying these accounting principles to debt service funds, the financial statement preparer may encounter the situation where a specific revenue source, such as property taxes or sales taxes, is restricted for debt service on general long-term debt. Assuming that the government has established a debt service fund, the government must determine whether these restricted tax revenues should be recorded directly into the debt service fund, or whether they should be recorded as revenues of the general fund, and then recorded as a transfer to the debt service fund.

When taxes are specifically restricted for debt service, generally they should be reported directly in the debt service fund, rather than as a transfer from the general fund to the debt service fund. However, circumstances such as a legal requirement to account for all of the restricted taxes in the general fund may sometimes require that restricted taxes be reported first in the general fund. In this case, an operating transfer from the general fund to the debt service fund would be recorded for the amount of the specific tax.

NOTE: In many cases, the taxes that are restricted to debt service may only present a portion of the total of the particular tax reported as revenue for the reporting entity as a whole. For example, a city may collect $100 million of property taxes, required to be pledged to cover the city's annual debt service payments of $40 million. Once the $40 million of debt service requirements *are collected, the balance of the property tax revenue, or $60 million, is available for the government's general use. It may be that the government's full $100 million of property tax revenue is budgeted in the general fund, along with a transfer of $40 million to the debt service fund for debt service. In this case, it may be more appropriate to record the $100 million of property tax revenue in the general fund and then record an operating transfer of $40 million from the general fund to the debt service fund to reflect the transfer for debt service.*

EXPENDITURE RECOGNITION FOR DEBT SERVICE PAYMENTS

As stated above, debt service funds should use the modified accrual basis of accounting and recognize expenditures when the liability is incurred. NCGAS 1, as subsequently amended by GASBS 6, provides a significant exception to this recognition criterion for debt service payments. The exception relates to unmatured principal and interest payments on general long-term debt, including special assessment debt for which the government is obligated in some manner.

Financial resources are usually appropriated in other funds for transfer to a debt service fund in the period in which maturing debt principal and interest must be paid. Theoretically, these amounts are not current liabilities of the debt service fund because their settlement will not require expenditure of existing resources of the debt service fund. If the debt service fund accrued an expenditure and liability in one period but recorded the transfer of financial resources for debt service payments in a later period, it would result in an understatement of the fund balance of the debt service fund.

Thus, the NCGA and the GASB concluded that debt service payments are usually appropriately accounted for as expenditures in the year of payment. Therefore, there is no accrual of interest or principal payments prior to the actual payments. Principal and interest expenditures are essentially recognized in the debt service fund on a cash basis, with only disclosure of subsequent-year debt service requirements. The cash basis is a practical way to consider recognition of debt service expenditures, although there is an assumption that debt is paid when it is due. Technically, debt service expenditures are actually recognized when the expenditure is due. Therefore, if there is a default on the payment of debt service (or if debt service is not paid because a payee cannot be located) an expenditure and corresponding liability would be recorded in the debt service fund.

The above discussion is based on the premise that the resources to actually make the debt service payment are not transferred into the debt service fund until the time that the debt service payment is actually going to be made. There is an additional consideration that must be made when the government has transferred or provided the resources for debt service payments that are due in a subsequent period. Under GAAP, if the debt service fund has been provided the resources during the current year for the payment of principal and interest due early in the following year, the expenditure and the related liability may be recognized in the debt service fund. This consideration often arises when resources are provided to a paying agent before year end for debt due very early in the next fiscal year, such as when a fiscal year ends on June 30, and debt holders are entitled to an interest payment on July 1. In addition, the debt principal amount may be removed from the long-term debt account group.

It is important to note that the recognition of expenditures in the debt service fund for unmatured debt service principal and interest is optional for the government. Governments are not required to recognize debt service expenditures in debt service funds until they are due.

In instances where the government has an option to accrue debt service payment expenditures for unmatured debt service payments because resources have been provided in the current year for payments to be made early in the subsequent year, the 2001 GAAFR addresses the requirements that must be met in order to use. The 2001 GAAFR provides that the following three conditions must be met:

- The government uses a debt service fund to account for debt service payments.
- The advance provision of resources to the debt service fund is mandatory rather than discretionary.
- Payment is due within a short period of time—usually one to several days, and not more than one month.

The above conditions reflect GASB Interpretation 6, *"Recognition and Measurement of Certain Liabilities and Expenditures in Governmental Fund Financial Statements."*

Consistency is important in the selection of the option for early recognition because without consistency, the level of debt service expenditures would vary widely from year to year.

ACCOUNTING FOR THE ADVANCE REFUNDING
OF LONG-TERM DEBT

One of the more unique accounting transactions likely to be accounted for in a debt service fund is the advance refunding of long-term debt. While this topic is closely related to the requirements of GAAP as to when the refunded debt can be removed from the government-wide statement of net assets, it has an effect on the debt service fund as well, because it is the most likely place where refundings, including advance refundings, of long-term debt are reported. GASB Statement 7 (GASBS 7), *Advance Refundings Resulting in Defeasance of Debt*, provides significant background and accounting guidance for determining the appropriate accounting for these activities.

Because the benefits a government realizes from advance refunding debt are likely to be available before the debt is actually due or redeemable, it is necessary for a government to take the necessary steps to advance refund the debt. A government accomplishes an advance refunding by taking the proceeds of a new debt that is issued to refinance the old debt by placing the proceeds of the new debt in an escrow account that is subsequently used to provide funds to do the following, at minimum:

- Meet periodic principal and interest payments of the old debt until the call or maturity date
- Pay the call premium, if redemption is at the call date
- Redeem the debt at the call date or the maturity date

Most advance refunding transactions result in a defeasance of the debt, enabling the government to remove the amount of the old debt from the general long-term debt account group. A defeasance can be either legal or in-substance.

- A legal defeasance occurs when debt is legally satisfied based on certain provisions in the instrument, even though the debt is not actually repaid.
- An in-substance defeasance is the far more common type of defeasance. An in-substance defeasance occurs when debt is considered defeased for accounting purposes even though a legal defeasance has not occurred.

GASBS 7 prescribes the criteria that must be met before debt is considered defeased in substance for accounting and reporting purposes. The government must irrevocably place cash or assets with an escrow agent in a trust to be used solely for satisfying scheduled payments of both interest and principal of the defeased debt, and the possibility that the debtor will be required to make future payments on that debt is remote. The trust is restricted to owning only monetary assets that are essentially risk-free as to the amount, timing, and collection of interest and principal. The monetary assets should be denominated in the currency in which the debt is payable. GASBS 7 also prescribes that for debt denominated in US dollars, risk-free monetary assets are essentially limited to

- Direct obligations of the US government (including state and local government securities (SLGS) that the US Treasury issues specifically to provide state and local governments with required cash flows at yields that do not exceed the Internal Revenue Service's arbitrage limits)
- Obligations guaranteed by the US government
- Securities backed by US government obligations as collateral and for which interest and principal payments generally flow immediately through to the security holder.

The following describes the accounting treatment for advance refundings of debt in the debt service fund. Chapter 10 provides a significantly different model for accounting for advance refundings of the debt of proprietary funds. In addition, disclosure requirements for advance refundings are included in Chapter 13.

For advance refundings that result in defeasance of debt reported in the government-wide financial statements, the proceeds from the new debt should be reported as "other financing source—proceeds of refunding bonds" in the fund receiving the proceeds, which, for purposes of this Guide, is assumed to be the debt service fund. Payments to the escrow agent from resources provided by the new debt should be reported as "other financing use--payment to the refunded bond escrow agent." Payments to the escrow agent made from other resources of the entity should be reported as debt service expenditures.

Crossover Transaction and Refunding Bonds

A crossover refunding transaction is a transaction in which there is no legal or in-substance defeasance and the debt is not removed from the general long-term debt account group. In fact, both the new bonds that were issued and the original bonds that were refunded appear in the long-term debt account group. In a cross-over refunding transaction, the escrow account is not immediately dedicated to debt service principal and interest payments on the refunded debt. Instead, the resources in the escrow account are used to temporarily meet the debt service requirements on the refunding bonds themselves. At a later date, called the crossover date, the resources in the escrow account are dedicated exclusively to the payment of principal and interest on the refunded debt. While an in-substance defeasance does not occur when the refunding bonds are issued, an in-substance defeasance may occur at the crossover date if the in-substance defeasance requirements of GASBS 7 are met.

There are circumstances when refunding bonds are issued in a transaction that is not immediately accounted for as an in-substance or legal defeasance. In these circumstances, the assets in the escrow account would be accounted for in the debt service fund. In addition, the liability for the debt that is eventually refunded is not removed from the general long-term debt account group until the debt is actually repaid or defeased legally or in substance.

SUMMARY

Debt service funds provide a useful mechanism for governments to account for transactions relating to the payment of principal and interest on long-term debt. Governments should consider both their legal and financial management requirements in determining whether to use a debt service fund and how many funds are to be established.

In determining the proper accounting for debt service transactions, governments also need to consider transactions accounted for in the general fund and the government-wide statement of net assets.

10 PROPRIETARY FUNDS

INTRODUCTION

Proprietary funds are used to account for a government's ongoing organizations and activities that are similar to those found in the private sector. In other words, these activities resemble commercial activities performed by governments, and the basis of accounting and measurement focus of these funds reflect this resemblance. There are two types of proprietary funds—enterprise funds and internal service funds.

This chapter describes the basic characteristics and accounting for proprietary funds, both enterprise and internal service funds. The following specific topics are addressed:

- Basis of accounting and measurement focus for proprietary funds
- Enterprise funds

  — Background and uses
  — Specific accounting issues

    - Restricted assets
    - Debt
    - Contributed capital
    - Advance refundings of debt
    - Tap fees
    - Regulated industries
    - Fixed assets—Infrastructure and contributions of general fixed assets

- Internal service funds

  — Background and uses
  — Specific accounting issues

    - Duplications of revenues and expenses
    - Surpluses and deficits
    - Risk financing activities

While GASBS 34 does not affect the basis of accounting and measurement focus of proprietary funds (the same are used in both the government-wide and fund financial statements), it does affect certain aspects of how and when these funds are used. These points will be highlighted throughout the chapter.

BASIS OF ACCOUNTING AND MEASUREMENT
FOCUS FOR PROPRIETARY FUNDS

In general terms, proprietary funds use the same basis of accounting and measurement focus as commercial enterprises. Proprietary funds use the accrual basis of accounting and the economic resources measurement focus. Accordingly, proprietary funds recognize revenues when they are earned and recognize expenses when a liability is incurred. Revenue recognition is sometimes difficult to determine in the commercial accounting arena. However, the types of goods and services typically provided by governmental units through proprietary funds should make this difficulty rare.

For example, a municipal water utility would recognize revenue for water provided to customers at the time that it actually provides the water to the customers. In contrast to the modified accrual basis of accounting, the timing of the billing of the water customers does not enter into the revenue recognition criteria. Under the accrual basis of accounting, even if a water customer does not pay his or her bill for a year, the revenue is still recognized by the proprietary fund. Under the modified accrual basis of accounting, revenue not collected for a year after its billing will likely be determined not to meet the "available" criterion for revenue recognition.

For expenses recognition, the timing of the recognition of expenses (i.e., when the liability is incurred) is virtually the same as that for the modified accrual basis of accounting. The difference between "expenses" recognized by proprietary funds and "expenditures" recognized by governmental funds is in what "costs" are included in expenses and expenditures. This is determined by the different measurement focuses used by proprietary funds and governmental funds. Proprietary funds use the flow of economic resources measurement focus. Governmental funds use the current financial resources measurement focus, which recognizes as expenditures those costs that result in a decrease in current financial resources. Under the flow of economic resources measurement focus, costs are recognized when the related liability is incurred, including the recognition of depreciation expense. In addition to depreciation, the most significant differences in recognizing expenses in proprietary funds (compared with expenditures in governmental funds) are related to the recognition of the liability and expense for the longer-term portions of liabilities for vacation and sick leave, judgments and claims, landfill liabilities, and accrued interest expense. The accounting for these activities is specifically described either later in this chapter or in separate chapters of this guide; however, at this point it is important to understand the conceptual difference between the two. For example, a proprietary fund that incurs costs for vacation and sick leave will recognize an expense for these costs as it accrues a liability for vacation and sick leave pay, regardless of when these amounts will be paid. In contrast, a governmental fund would not record an expenditure for vacation and sick leave costs that will not be paid from current financial resources. Accordingly, governmental funds generally record expenditures for vacation and sick leave costs when these amounts are actually paid to the employees.

In addition to the long-term liabilities described above, a proprietary fund records long-term bonded debt and other notes as a fund liability. On the other side of the balance sheet, assets that are capitalized are recorded as long-term assets of the proprietary fund (net of accumulated depreciation), which would not be the case for governmental funds.

The equity section of a proprietary fund's balance sheet also differs significantly from that of a governmental fund. Under GASBS 34, proprietary fund net assets are categorized as invested in capital assets, net of related debt, restricted, and unrestricted. Capital contributions are not shown separately as a component of net assets.

NOTE: Under GASBS 34, the concept of "retained earnings" is essentially replaced by the net asset restricted versus unrestricted presentation. Furthermore, GASBS 34 states that there should be no "designations" of unrestricted net assets reported by proprietary funds on the face of the financial statements.

It is conceptually simple to state that proprietary funds should use the commercial accounting model. However, the actual application of this concept is much more difficult because some accounting principles and standards promulgated by the Financial Accounting Standards Board (FASB) for commercial enterprises may conflict with pronouncements promulgated by the GASB. A proprietary fund attempting to apply accounting principles applicable to commercial enterprises would be unclear as to which of the conflicting accounting principles should be applied.

Fortunately, the GASB issued Statement 20 (GASBS 20), *Accounting and Financial Reporting for Proprietary Funds and Other Governmental Entities That Use Proprietary Fund Accounting.* GASBS 20 applies to the accounting and financial reporting for proprietary activities. This includes proprietary funds and governmental entities that use proprietary fund accounting, such as public benefit corporations and authorities, governmental utilities, and governmental hospitals and other health care providers.

GASBS 20 requires that proprietary funds should apply all applicable GASB pronouncements, as well as the following pronouncements issued on or before November 30, 1989, unless those activities conflict with or contradict GASB pronouncements:

- FASB Statements
- FASB Interpretations
- Accounting Principles Board (APB) Opinions
- Accounting Research Bulletins (ARBs)

Proprietary funds have the option to apply all FASB Statements and Interpretations, APB Opinions, and ARBs issued after November 30, 1989, except for those that conflict with or contradict GASB pronouncements.

In applying the guidance of GASBS 20, there are several important matters that a government's financial statement preparer must consider, summarized in the following sections.

- GASBS 20 does not change the applicability to proprietary activities of any FASB pronouncements issued on or before November 30, 1989. For example, FASB Statement 87, *Employers' Accounting for Pensions*, is not applicable to proprietary activities.
- When a state or local governmental entity makes an election to apply the commercial accounting pronouncements issued after November 30, 1989, that do not conflict or contradict GASB pronouncements, this election must be made uniformly. That is, the entity cannot elect to apply some, but not all, of the applicable standards. The GASB explicitly states in its "Basis for Conclusions" to GASBS 20 that it wishes to prevent "picking and choosing" individual accounting standards.
- The basic financial statements of a governmental entity may include a number of proprietary activities, including component units. While GASBS 20 encourages the same application of FASB pronouncements to be used by all proprietary activities, including component units, in the basic financial statements it does not require it.

ENTERPRISE FUNDS

Background and Uses

Enterprise funds are used to account for operations that fall within two basic categories.

1. Operations that are financed and operated in a manner similar to private business enterprises, where the intent of the governing body is to finance or recover costs (expenses, including depreciation) of providing goods and services to the general public on a continuing basis primarily through user charges

2. Operations where the governing body has decided that periodic determination of revenues earned, expenses incurred, and/or net income is appropriate for capital maintenance, public policy, management control, accountability, or other purposes

Enterprise funds are primarily used to account for activities that are financed through user charges. However, the total cost of the activity does not have to be paid for by the user charges. The government (or other governmental entity) may subsidize a significant portion of the costs of the enterprise fund.

For example, a government may establish a water authority to provide water to its residential and commercial water users. In this case, the water rates are generally set to recover the full cost of the water authority's operations. On the other hand, there may be circumstances where public policy determinations result in the user charges not covering the total costs of the operations. For example, a transit authority might be established to provide public transportation by buses, trains, or subways. Often, fares charged to the customers of the transit means provided by transit authorities do not cover the full cost of operation the transit authority. Usually, the local government would subsidize the transit authority's operations. In addition, there may be state and federal mass transportation grants that help to subsidize the operations of the transit authority. These subsidies sometimes result in the transit fares covering a relatively small percentage of the total cost of the transit authority.

The decision to account for a particular operation as an enterprise fund is based both on whether the cost recovery through user charges is fundamental to the enterprise fund, and on whether the government finds it useful to have information on the total cost of providing a service to the government's citizens. This decision disregards the degree to which the charges to the users of the service cover the total cost of providing the service.

GASBS 34 continues the general guidance that an enterprise fund may be used to report any activity for which a fee is charged to external users as goods and services. However, GASBS 34 also specifies three situations where the use of an enterprise fund is required. The criteria are to be applied to the activity's principal revenue sources, meaning that insignificant activities where fees are charged would not automatically require the use of an enterprise fund. An enterprise fund is required to be used if one of the following criteria are met:

- The activity is financed with debt that is secured solely by a pledge of the revenues from fees and charges of the activity. If the debt is secured in part from its own proceeds, it is still considered to be payable solely from the revenues of the activity. In other words if a portion of the proceeds of a revenue bond issued is placed in a debt service reserve account, yet the revenue bond is payable solely from the revenues of the activity with the exception of the potential use of the reserve funds, this criterion is still met and the use of an enterprise fund would be required. On the other hand, if the debt is secured by a pledge of the revenues of the activity and the full faith and credit of a related primary government or component unit, it is not considered payable solely from the fees of the activity, even if it is not expected that the primary government or other component unit would actually make any payments on the debt. In this case, the criterion is not met and the use of an enterprise fund would not be required.
- Laws or regulations require that the activity's costs of providing services (including capital costs such as depreciation or debt service) be recorded from fees and charges, rather than taxes or similar revenues.
- The pricing policies of the activity establish fees and charges designed to recover its costs, including capital costs such as depreciation or debt service.

Specific Accounting Issues

Restricted assets. Typically, enterprise funds are used to issue long-term bonds to provide financing for their activities. The benefit of issuing bonds by the enterprise fund, rather than by the general government, is that there is typically a dedicated revenue stream in the enterprise fund that can be pledged to the service of the related debt. Often, this dedicated and pledged revenue results in a higher rating on the enterprise fund's long-term debt, resulting in a lower interest cost for the government. For example, a water utility may issue long-term debt to finance investments in water and sewer infrastructure, such as water filtration plants or sewage treatment plants. Water and sewer charges may represent a fairly constant source of revenue that may be judged by the investment community to be more reliable than general tax revenues. Accordingly, if the enterprise fund pledges its receipts for water and sewer charges to debt service, the related debt, commonly referred to a as a revenue bond, will probably carry a lower interest rate than the government's general long-term debt.

As a result of the high level of debt issuance typically found in enterprise funds, these funds can often be found to have restricted assets. These restricted assets normally represent cash and investments whose availability to the enterprise fund is restricted by bond covenant. The following are examples of commonly found restricted assets:

- Revenue bond construction (such as cash, investments, and accrued interest segregated by the bond indenture for construction)
- Revenue bond operations and maintenance (such as accumulations of resources equal to operating costs for a specified period)
- Revenue bond current debt service (such as accumulations of resources for principal and interest payments due within one year)
- Revenue bond future debt service (such as accumulations of resources for principal and interest payments beyond the subsequent twelve months)
- Revenue bond renewal and replacement (such as accumulations of resources for unforeseen repairs and maintenance of assets originally acquired from bond proceeds)

The reason that restricted assets may be a unique or important accounting concern for enterprise funds is that the recording of restricted assets may result in a restriction of retained earnings reported by the fund prior to implementation of GASBS 34. However, while retained earnings are often reserved in connection with restricted assets, the amount of reserved retained earnings is usually not equal to the amount of restricted assets. Reserved retained earnings should reflect only those restricted assets funded by operations, rather than by bond proceeds. If assets are obtained as a result of the operations of the enterprise fund, it is appropriate to report these amounts as reservations of retained earnings. On the other hand, if the source of the restricted assets is other than a result of operations (such as from the proceeds of bonds), it would not be appropriate to report these amounts as reservations of retained earnings.

One other form of restricted assets results from the enterprise fund holding deposits from its customers. Typically, the cash and investments related to these deposits are recorded as a restricted asset with a related offsetting liability that reflects the fact that the enterprise fund must return the deposits to its customers.

A similar concept applies upon implementation of GASBS 34. The amount of restricted net assets reported may not be equal to the amount of restricted assets that are reported on the statement of net assets and the fund's balance sheet.

Debt. As stated earlier in this chapter, long-term debt applicable to the financing of the activities of proprietary funds are recorded in the funds as a fund liability. Some enterprise debt may be backed by the full faith and credit of the government. Even though the debt may be a general obligation of the government, it should be reported as a liability of the enterprise fund if the debt was issued for enterprise fund purposes and is expected to be repaid from enterprise fund resources. Therefore, it is the expected source of repayment for the debt (rather than the security interest for the debt) that is the primary factor in determining whether a liability for debt is recorded as a liability of the enterprise fund.

An additional consideration relating to the issuance of long-term debt that will be repaid from the resources of an enterprise fund concerns the accounting for arbitrage rebate. As more fully described in Chapter 8, governments that earn excess interest on the proceeds resulting from the issuance of tax-exempt debt must rebate these arbitrage earnings after a period of time to the federal government.

Two methods may be used to report the liability for arbitrage rebates. The more common method records the amount of excess earnings to be rebated as a reduction of the interest income from investments made with the proceeds from the issuance of bonds. The second method treats the amount of the arbitrage liability similar to a judgment or claim liability and reports it as an expense and a liability with no reduction of interest revenue.

Under the first method, different timing in the recognition of the arbitrage rebate amount may result, where the government capitalizes interest costs related to the construction of assets recorded in the enterprise fund. Under the provisions of FASB Statement 62 (SFAS 62), *Capitalization of Interest Cost in Situations Involving Certain Tax-Exempt Borrowings and Certain Gifts and Grants*, the amount of capitalized interest is calculated by offsetting the interest expense and related interest revenue. Because this approach reduces interest revenue, it actually increases the amount of interest that will be capitalized. The effect of the revenue reduction method involving capitalized interest is to defer a portion of interest expense to future periods, where it eventually is recognized as depreciation expense, once the assets in question have been completed and placed in service.

As such, the same amount of expense will be reported in the operating statement under either the revenue reduction approach or the judgment and claims approach. However, the revenue reduction approach effectively spreads the effect of rebatable arbitrage over the life of the constructed asset, while the claims and judgments approach recognizes the full effect of rebatable arbitrage in the period in which it is incurred.

Under GASBS 34, the accounting for capital contributions to proprietary funds is changed significantly. There is no "contributed capital" classification of net assets for proprietary funds. Net assets are categorized as invested in capital assets, net of related debt (which would include within it the resulting net assets from capital contributions), restricted and unrestricted. Contributed capital would not be displayed separately on the face of the financial statements.

The more significant change under the new financial reporting model, however, is that capital contributions are not recorded directly as an increase in the net assets of the proprietary fund. Instead they flow through the statement of revenues, expenses, and changes in net assets, where they are reported separately from operating revenues and expenses. The following presents an example of an abbreviated operating statement that reflects how capital contributions would be reported under the new financial reporting model:

Operating revenues:
    (Details of operating revenues)   xxx
Operating expenses:
    (Details of operating expenses, including depreciation xxx
      on all depreciable fixed assets)
Operating income (loss)   xxx
Nonoperating revenues/expenses
    (Details of nonoperating revenues)   xxx
Income (loss) before other revenues (expenses, gains,
    losses, and transfers, if applicable)   xxx
Capital contributions   xxx
Increase (decrease) in net assets   xxx
Net assets—beginning of period   xxx
Net assets—end of period   xxx

Refundings of debt. The underlying background and general principles of refundings of debt for governments are fully described in Chapters 9 and 13. The GASB issued Statement 23 (GASBS 23), *Accounting and Financial Reporting for Refundings of Debt Reported by Proprietary Activities,* to specifically address the accounting issues related to advance refundings of debt for proprietary funds. Because these funds have an income determination focus, previous guidance resulted in the entire amount of the gain or loss being recognized for financial reporting purposes in the year of the advance refunding.

GASBS 23 applies to both current refundings and advance refundings of debt resulting in defeasance of debt reported by proprietary activities, which includes proprietary funds and other governmental entities that use proprietary fund accounting, such as public benefit corporations and authorities, utilities, and hospitals and other health care providers.

Refundings involve the issuance of new debt whose proceeds are used to repay previously issued, or old, debt. The new debt proceeds may be used to repay the old debt immediately, which is a current refunding. The new debt proceeds may also be placed with an escrow agent and invested until they are used to pay principal and interest on the old debt in the future, which is an advance refunding. An advance refunding of debt may result in the in-substance defeasance, provided that certain criteria (described in Chapter 13) are met. GASBS 23 applies to both current refundings and advance refundings that result in a defeasance of debt.

GASBS 23 requires that for current refundings and advance refundings resulting in a defeasance of debt reported by proprietary activities, the difference between the reacquisition price and the net carrying amount of the old debt should be deferred and amortized as a component of interest expense in a systematic and rational manner over the life of the old or new debt, whichever is shorter.

In applying the guidance of GASBS 23, two special terms need to be defined.

1. Reacquisition price. The reacquisition price is the amount required to repay previously issued debt in a refunding transaction. In a current refunding, this amount includes the principal of the old debt and any call premium incurred. In an advance refunding, the reacquisition price is the amount placed in escrow that, together with interest earnings, is necessary to pay interest and principal on the old debt and any call premium incurred. Any premium or discount and issuance costs pertaining to the new debt are not considered part of the reacquisition price. Instead, this premium or discount should be accounted for as a separate item relating to the new debt and amortized over the life of the new debt.

2. Net carrying amount. The net carrying amount of the old debt is the amount due at maturity, adjusted for any unamortized premium or discount and issuance costs related to the old debt.

On the balance sheet of the proprietary fund, the amount deferred should be reported as a deduction from or an addition to the new debt liability. The new debt may be reported net with either parenthetical or note disclosure of the deferred amount on refunding. The new debt may also be reported gross with both the debt liability and the related deferred amount present.

Two other situations involving prior refundings are also addressed by GASBS 23. For current refundings of prior refundings and for advance refundings of prior refundings resulting in the defeasance of debt, the difference between the reacquisition price and the net carrying amount of the old debt, together with any unamortized difference from prior refundings, should be deferred and amortized over the shorter of the original amortization period remaining from the prior refundings, or the life of the latest refunding debt. In other words, for a subsequent refunding of debt that was originally used to refund some other debt, add (or subtract) the remaining deferred gain or loss to the new gain or loss that would normally be calculated for the new refunding transaction. Amortize this combined amount over the shorter of the previous deferred amount's amortization period or the life of the new debt resulting from the new refunding transaction.

Tap fees. Tap fees refer to fees that new customers pay to a governmental utility to "tap into" or connect to the utility's existing system. They are also sometimes referred to as *connection fees* or *systems development fees*. The amount of the fee usually exceeds the actual cost to the utility to physically connect the new customer to the system. The excess profit that is built into tap fees is conceptually a charge to the new customers for their share of the costs of the existing infrastructure and systems of the governmental utility or a charge to offset a portion of the cost of upgrading the system.

The accounting issue relates to the treatment of the excess of the tap fee over the actual cost to the governmental utility to connect the new customer, which is considered an imposed nonexchange transaction. The 2001 GAAFR recommends that the portion of the tap fee that equals the cost of physically connecting the new customer be reported as operating revenue. This operating revenue then matches the operating expenses incurred in connecting the new customer. The amount charged in excess of the actual cost of physically connecting the new customer should be recorded by the governmental utility as nonoperating revenue as soon as the government has established an enforceable legal claim to the payment, usually upon connection. Prior to implementation of GASBS 34, these excess amounts are treated as contributed capital.

Customer and developer deposits. The AICPA *Audit and Accounting Guide for State and Local Government Units* describes the accounting treatment for deposits received from customers and developers by enterprises using proprietary accounting.

Utility-type and similar enterprise funds often require customers to pay a deposit to the enterprise fund to assure the timely payment for services. These deposits should be recorded by the enterprise fund as a current liability, until such time as the enterprise fund returns the deposit to the customers (such as when the service is terminated) or applies the deposit to an unpaid bill.

In some cases, land developers may also be required to make "good faith" deposits to finance the cost of the enterprise fund to extend utility service to the new development. These developer deposits are also recorded as current liabilities of the enterprise fund until such time as they are no longer returnable to the developer, at which time they should be recorded as revenue. That the subsequent use of these resources is legally restricted to capital acquisition or related debt service should be reflected as a restriction of net assets rather than as a deferral of revenue.

Regulated industries. The FASB provides guidance to commercial enterprises that are part of regulated industries. FASB Statement 71 (SFAS 71), *Accounting for the Effects of Certain Types of Regulation*, provided the initial guidance, which, with some minor subsequent revisions, is as follows:

- In certain circumstances, charges of the current period may be capitalized rather than expensed if they will be recovered through future rates.
- Rates that are levied in anticipation of future charges may not be recognized as revenue until the anticipated charge is incurred.
- If a gain reduces allowable costs and this reduction will be reflected in lower future rates for customers, then the gain itself should be amortized over this same period.

Enterprise funds are permitted, but not required, to follow the guidance of SFAS 71 for regulated industries if they meet all of the following criteria:

- Rates for regulated services or products are either established, or subject to approval, by

  — An independent, third-party regulator
  — The governing board itself, if it is empowered by statute or contract to establish rates that bind customers

- The regulated rates are designed to recover the specific enterprise's costs of providing regulated services or products.
- It is reasonable to assume that the regulated activity can set and collect charges sufficient to recover its costs.

Financial statement preparers and auditors should keep in mind that if an enterprise fund elects to follow the guidance of SFAS 71, this guidance modifies, but does not replace, the normal enterprise fund accounting and financial reporting requirements.

Fixed assets—Infrastructure and contribution of general fixed assets. Infrastructure assets are assets that are not movable and are of value only to the government. Proprietary funds are required to capitalize all of their assets, including infrastructure, even prior to the adoption of GASBS 34. For example, a water and sewer authority might have a grid of pipes and other connections that deliver water and collect waste water. The proprietary fund would be required to record these assets at their historical cost and depreciate them over their estimated useful lives.

INTERNAL SERVICE FUNDS

Background and Uses

Internal service funds are used to account for the financing of goods or services provided by one department or agency of a governmental unit to other departments or agencies of the same governmental unit on a cost-reimbursement basis. In some cases, blended component units are reported as internal service funds.

Because internal service funds use the flow of economic resources measurement focus and accrual basis of accounting (as discussed below), they allow the full cost of providing goods or services to other departments or agencies to be charged to the receiving department or agency. Were these activities to be accounted for using a governmental fund, the full cost of the goods or services would not be determinable because the governmental fund would focus on the effect on current financial resources, rather than the full cost of the goods or services.

As the main purpose of internal service funds is to identify and allocate costs of goods or services to other departments, it is generally recommended that governments use separate internal service funds for different activities. Although the use of internal service funds is not required by GAAP, it is logical that disparate activities be accounted for in separate internal service funds to more accurately determine the costs of the goods and services. It should be noted that GAAP does not require that internal service funds include the full cost of services that are provided. A government may chose to leave some of the related costs out of the internal service fund, such as a rent charge or utility charge.

For example, internal service funds are often used to determine and allocate the costs for activities as diverse as the following:

- Duplicating and printing services
- Central garages
- Motor pools
- Data processing
- Purchasing
- Central stores and warehousing

Clearly, combining the costs of providing motor pool services with the costs of providing data processing services in the same internal service fund will not result in a very useful basis on which to allocate costs. Establishing separate funds will result in a more effective cost-allocation process.

Governments generally use internal service funds to determine and allocate costs of goods and services to other agencies and departments within the governmental unit, but they may also be used for other purposes. For example, internal service funds may be used for goods and services provided on a cost-reimbursement basis to other governmental entities within the reporting entity of the primary government. In some cases, internal service funds are used for goods and services provided on a cost-reimbursement basis to quasi-governmental organizations and not-for-profit organizations. In these circumstances, the government may find it more appropriate to classify these activities as enterprise funds, rather than internal service funds, depending on the individual circumstances. In fact, GASBS 34 specifies that if the reporting government is not the predominant participant in the activity, the activity should be reported as an enterprise fund.

Specific Accounting Issues

The accounting issues described above for enterprise funds also generally pertain to internal service funds, and the above accounting and financial reporting guidance described above should be used as required in accounting for internal service funds.

Duplications of revenues and expenses. Many of the transactions between internal service funds and other funds take the form of quasi-external transactions. The funds receiving the goods or services from the internal service fund report an expenditure or an expense, while the internal service fund reports revenue. The consequence of this approach is that there is duplicate reporting of expenditures and expenses with the financial reporting entity of the government. For example, an internal service fund records an expense to recognize the cost of providing goods or services to another fund. This same expense is then duplicated in the other funds when the funds that received the goods or services are charged for their share of the cost. Revenue is also recognized in the internal service fund, based entirely on a transaction involving the funds of the government; in other words, an internal transaction. Because governments did not prepare consolidated financial statements, which would include eliminations prior to the implementation of GASBS 34, these duplicate transactions are not eliminated from the combined financial statements. However, GASBS 34 specifies that eliminations should be made in the statement of activities to remove the "doubling-up" effect of internal service activities.

While the duplication described above may seem like an important weakness in fund financial reporting, the weakness is offset by the fact that the duplicate transactions are recorded generally in one place—the internal service fund. Thus, the financial statement reader can readily identify where the duplicate expenses and expenditures are recorded and what the dollar amounts of the duplications actually are. The internal service fund has the advantage of isolating these duplicate transactions within a separate fund type, where their nature should be clear to the users of the financial statements.

Surpluses and deficits. Surpluses or deficits in internal service funds are likely to indicate that the other funds were not properly charged for the goods and services that they received. However, the government should take the view that internal service funds should operate on a breakeven basis over time. Surpluses or deficits in individual reporting periods may not necessarily indicate the need to adjust the basis on which other funds are charged for the goods or services provided by the internal service fund. It is only when internal service funds consistently report significant surpluses or deficits that the adequacy or inadequacy of charges made to other funds must be reassessed.

If it is determined that the charges made to other funds are either more or less than is needed to recover cost over a reasonable period, the excess or deficiency should be charged back to the participating individual funds. The 1994 GAAFR prescribes that it is not appropriate to report a material deficit in an internal service fund with the demonstrable intent and ability to recover that amount through future charges to other funds over a reasonable period.

In some cases, internal service funds use a higher amount of depreciation in determining charges to other funds than would ordinarily be calculated using acceptable depreciation methods in conjunction with historical cost. This is done so that the internal service fund accumulates enough resources from the other funds to provide for replacement of depreciable assets at what is likely to be a higher cost at the time of replacement. In this case, the surpluses recorded from the higher fees will eventually be offset by higher depreciation expense once the asset is replaced at a higher cost, and the higher cost is used in the depreciation expense calculation.

GASBS 34 has an interesting twist for reporting internal service fund asset and liability balances on the government-wide statement of net assets. Any asset or liability balances that are not eliminated would be reported in the governmental activities column. While one would expect that internal service fund balances would be reported in the business-type activities column, the rationale used by GASBS 34 is that the activities accounted for in internal service funds are usually more governmental than business-type in nature. However, if enterprise funds are the predominant or only participant in an internal service fund, the government would report the internal service fund's residual assets and liabilities within the business-type activities column in the statements of net assets.

Risk financing activities. Governments are required to use either the general fund or an internal service fund if they desire to use a single fund to account for all of their risk financing activities. Risk financing activities are fully described in Chapter 20. However, for purposes of understanding the use of internal service funds, the following brief discussion is provided.

If a government elects to use an internal service fund to account for its risk financing activities, interfund premiums are treated as quasi-external transactions, similar to external insurance premiums. In other words, the internal service fund would record an expense and a liability for the judgments and claims that are probable and measurable for the reporting period. However, it may charge a higher premium to the other funds (and record the higher amount as revenue). Because interfund premiums paid to external service funds are treated as quasi-external transactions rather than as reimbursements, their amounts are not limited by the amount recognized as expense in the internal service fund, provided that

- The excess represents a reasonable provision for anticipated catastrophe losses, or
- The excess is the result of a systematic funding method designed to match revenues and expenses over a reasonable period; for example, an actuarial funding method or a funding method based on historical cost

As will be more fully described in Chapter 20, deficits in risk-financing internal service funds must be charged back as expenditures or expenses to other funds if they are not recovered over a reasonable period. In addition, surplus retained earnings resulting from premiums charged for future catastrophe losses should be reported as a designation of retained earnings. This designation should be reported in the notes to the financial statements, rather than on the face of the financial statements. This is the sole instance where a designation of retained earnings is required by generally accepted accounting principles for a proprietary fund, although other designations are permitted and appropriate.

SUMMARY

The accounting and financial reporting for proprietary funds closely follows the accounting and financial reporting for commercial activities. However, there are some important differences and some unique accounting applications described in this chapter that distinguish this accounting from true commercial accounting. These differences must be understood by financial statement preparers to provide appropriate financial reports for proprietary activities.

11 FIDUCIARY FUNDS

INTRODUCTION

Governments are often required to hold or manage assets on behalf of others. NCGAS 1 recognized the need for fiduciary funds (known as *trust and agency funds* prior to GASBS 34), "to account for assets held by a governmental unit in a trustee capacity or as an agent for individuals, private organizations, other governmental units, and/or other funds."

GASBS 34 replaces the previous types of fiduciary funds with funds of different names, but similar functions.

1. Pension (and other employee benefit) trust funds
2. Investment trust funds
3. Private-purpose trust funds
4. Agency funds

The funds are reported under GASBS 34 only in fiduciary fund financial statements. They are not reported as part of the government-wide financial statements.

Each of these fund types is described below. In addition, Chapter 18 describes the accounting and financial reporting principles used by pension trust funds.

Deferred Compensation Plans

Many governments establish and offer participation to their employees in deferred compensation plans established under Section 457 of the Internal Revenue Code. These plans are often referred to as *Section 457 plans*. The laws governing these plans were changed so that as of August 20, 1996, new deferred compensation plans would not be considered eligible under Internal Revenue Code Section 457 unless all assets and income of the plan are held in trust for the exclusive benefit of the plan participants and their beneficiaries. For existing plans to remain eligible under Internal Revenue Code Section 457, this requirement was required to be met by January 1, 1999. Thus, the entire nature of the access to the assets of deferred compensation plans changed under the new requirements. The assets (and their related earnings) will no longer be accessible to the governmental entity and its creditors. They will be held in trust for the exclusive benefit of the plan participants and their beneficiaries.

In applying the requirements of GASBS 32, the first step for governments is to determine whether the Internal Revenue Code Section 457 plan should be included as a fiduciary fund of the reporting government. If the plan meets the criteria of NCGAS 1 for inclusion as a fiduciary fund, the plan would be reported after implementation of GASBS 34, if the same criteria are met, those plans would be reported as part of pension (and other employee benefit) trust funds. If the criteria of NCGAS 1 are not met, then the plan would not be included as a fiduciary fund of the reporting government.

NCGAS 1 defines fiduciary funds as "Trust and Agency funds to account for assets held by a governmental unit in a trustee capacity or as an agent for individuals, private organizations, other governmental units, and/or other funds." No additional guidance on when to report Internal Revenue Code Section 457 plans is provided by GASBS 32. The basis for conclusions of GASBS 32 indicates that the GASB's research indicated at the time of the statement issuance that most governments had little administrative involvement with their plans and did not perform the investing function for those plans. This is consistent with the practice that has emerged upon adoption of GASBS 32 of many governments not reporting their plans as fiduciary funds.

However, whether the plan is reported is a matter of professional judgment, and the extent of the governments activities relating to the plan, particularly in selecting investment alternatives and holding the assets in a trustee capacity needs to be evaluated.

Governments that report Internal Revenue Code Section 457 deferred compensation plans should apply the valuation provisions of GASB Statement 31 (GASBS 31), *Accounting and Financial Reporting for Certain Investments and for External Investment Pools*. In addition, all other plan investments should be reported at fair value. Thus, all of the investments of the plan will be reported at fair value.

GASBS 32 further provides that if it is impractical to obtain investment information from the plan administrator as of the reporting government's balance sheet date, the most recent report of the administrator should be used—for example, reports ending within the reporting government's fiscal year or shortly thereafter, adjusted for interim contributions and withdrawals.

AGENCY FUNDS

Agency funds are used to account for assets held solely in a custodial capacity. As a result, assets in agency funds are always matched by liabilities to the owners of the assets. The accounting for agency funds is the same before and after implementation of GASBS 34.

The accounting and financial reporting for agency funds are unique and do not really follow those of governmental funds or proprietary funds. Agency funds use the modified accrual basis of accounting for purposes of recognizing assets and liabilities, such as receivables and payables. However, agency funds do not have or report operations, and accordingly are said to not have a measurement focus.

In determining whether an agency fund or a trust fund is used to account for various types of transactions, there are no clear-cut distinctions for selecting the proper fund to account for a particular transaction. The degree of the government's management involvement and discretion over assets is generally much greater over trust fund assets than over agency fund assets. Expendable trust funds, for example, may require that a government's management identify eligible recipients, invest funds long- or short-term, or monitor compliance with regulations. Agency funds, on the other hand, typically involve only the receipt, temporary investment, and remittance of assets to their respective owners.

Agency funds are often used by school districts to account for student activity funds that are held by the school district but whose assets legally belong to the students. Another common use of agency funds is to account for taxes collected by one government on behalf of other governments. The collecting government has virtually no discretion on how the funds in the agency fund are to be spent. They are simply collected and then remitted to the government on whose behalf they were collected. In addition to this example, there are three instances where the use of an agency fund is mandated. These mandated uses are described in the following paragraphs.

Pass-Through Grants

GASB Statement 24 (GASBS 24), *Accounting and Financial Reporting for Certain Grants and Other Financial Assistance,* states that as a general rule, cash pass-through grants should be recognized as revenue and expenditures or expenses in a governmental, proprietary, or trust fund. GASBS 24 provides, however, that in those infrequent cases where a recipient government only serves as a cash conduit, the grant should be reported in an agency fund. The 1994 GAAFR, using the guidance of GASBS 24, recommends that an agency fund be used to account for grants meeting the following criteria:

- The government functions solely as an agent for some other government in collecting and forwarding funds
- The government undertakes no responsibility for subrecipient monitoring for specific requirements,
- The government is not responsible for determining the eligibility of recipients,
- The government has no discretion in the allocation of grant funds, and
- The government is not liable for grant repayments.

If a grant does not meet these criteria, it is required that the revenues and expenditures or expenses of the grant be accounted for and reported in one of the other fund types.

Special Assessments

The accounting and financial reporting for special assessments is described in Chapters 7 and 12. The use of an agency fund for special assessments is required when a government is not obligated in any manner for capital improvements financed by special assessment debt. GASBS 6 requires that "The debt service transactions of a special assessment issue for which the government is not obligated in any manner should be reported in an agency fund rather than a debt service fund, to reflect the fact that the government's duties are limited to acting as an agent for the assessed property owners and the bondholders."

When an agency fund is used for this purpose, any cash on hand from the special assessment would be shown on the agency fund's balance sheet. In addition, receivables would be reported for delinquent assessments. Only delinquent receivables would be reported as receivables on the agency fund's balance sheet, however. If the total receivables relating to the special assessment were shown, they would be offset by a liability that would essentially represent the special assessment debt. This would violate the requirement that special assessment debt for which the government is not obligated in any manner should not be displayed in the government's financial statements.

NOTE: In practice, agency funds are used by governments for the activities described above that are either repetitive or long-term. For infrequent transactions that will be settled within one or two years (for example, the asset will be received and the liability paid), many governments choose to simply use asset and liability accounts of the fund actually receiving the assets and paying the obligations rather than setting up a separate agency fund. Typically, these asset and liability accounts are set up in the government's general fund. The reason for using this approach, instead of setting up a large number of agency funds, is to avoid the administrative work involved in using a large number of agency funds.

PENSION TRUST FUNDS

Governments almost always offer pension benefits to their employees. The pension plans related to these benefits are reported as pension trust funds in the government's financial statements if either of the following criteria is met:

- The pension plan qualifies as a component unit of the government.
- The pension plan does not qualify as a component unit of the government, but the plan's assets are administered by the government.

Upon implementation of GASBS 34, this fund type, renamed "Pension (and Other Employee Benefit) Trust Funds, would be used to account for other employee benefit funds held in trust by a government, such as an Internal Revenue Code Section 457 Deferred Compensation Plan.

Pension trust funds use the flow of economic resources measurement focus and the full accrual basis of accounting, similar to nonexpendable trust funds and proprietary funds. A separate pension trust fund should be used for each separate plan. Separate pension trust funds are also sometimes established to account for supplemental pension benefits.

Governmental pension plans are usually administered by public employee retirement systems (PERS). The GASB has recently made significant changes to the accounting and financial reporting for both governmental employers that offer pension plans and the accounting and financial reporting of the plans themselves. Chapter 18 addresses the governmental employer accounting questions.

INVESTMENT TRUST FUNDS

A relatively new type of trust fund, the investment trust fund, will now be used by government that sponsor external investment pools and that provide individual investment accounts to other legally separate entities that are not part of the same financial reporting entity. The investment trust fund is required to be used in these circumstance by GASB Statement 31, *Accounting and Financial Reporting for Certain Investments and for External Investment Pools* (GASBS 31). The accounting for these funds is unchanged by GASBS 34.

Investment trust funds report transaction balances using the flow of economic resources measurement focus and the accrual basis of accounting. Accordingly, the accounting and financial reporting for investment trust funds is similar to that used by nonexpendable trust funds (and proprietary funds).

The two instances where GASBS 31 specifies that investment trust funds be used are as follows:

1.   External portion of external investment pools

      An external investment pool commingles the funds of more than one legally separate entity and invests on the participants' behalf in an investment portfolio. GASBS 31 specifies that the external portion of each pool should be reported as a separate investment trust fund. The external portion of an external investment pool is the portion of the pool that belongs to legally separate entities that are not part of the sponsoring government's financial reporting entity.

      In its financial statements, the sponsoring government should present for each investment trust fund a statement of net assets and a statement of changes in net assets. The difference between the external pool assets and liabilities should be captioned "net assets held in trust for pool participants." In the combined financial statements, investment trust funds should be presented in the balance sheet along with the other trust and agency funds. A separate statement of changes in net assets should be presented for the combined investment trust funds, although GASBS 31 permits that statement to be presented with similar trust funds, such as pension trust funds.

2.   Individual investment accounts

      GASBS 31 requires that governmental entities that provide individual investment account to other legally separate entities that are not part of the same financial reporting entity should report those investment in one or more separate investment trust funds. The way that individual investment accounts function, specific investments are acquired for individual entities and the income form and changes in the value of those investments affect only the entity for which they were acquired.

      The manner of presentation should be consistent with that described above for the external portion of external investment pools.

PRIVATE-PURPOSE TRUST FUNDS

Private-purpose trust funds are a type of fiduciary fund introduced by GASBS 34. They are used to report all trust arrangements (other than pension and other employee benefit, and investment trust funds), under which principal and income benefit individuals, private organizations, or other governments. Similar to other fiduciary funds, private-purpose trust funds cannot be used to support a government's own programs. It is important, therefore, to make sure that an activity is absent any public purpose of the government before it is accounted for as a private-purpose trust fund, even if individuals, private organizations, or other governments receive direct or indirect benefits from the activity.

SUMMARY

Governments frequently hold assets in a fiduciary capacity and should use the appropriate fiduciary fund to account for the assets and liabilities relating to these fiduciary responsibilities. The use of fiduciary funds provides the capability to improve accountability and control over these assets.

12 CAPITAL ASSETS

INTRODUCTION

Capital assets used in governmental activities under the pre-GASBS 34 financial reporting model were reported in the general fixed assets account group, which, as its name implies, is an account group and not a fund. GASBS 34 eliminates the use of the general fixed asset account group. Capital assets used in governmental activities are not reported in the fund financial statements, but are reported in the government-wide statement of net assets.

This chapter describes the accounting and financial reporting basics of GASBS 34 reporting of capital assets.

Information on recording fixed assets in proprietary funds is included in Chapter 10.

BASIC ACCOUNTING ENTRIES

Because of the nature of governmental financial reporting and operations, certain fixed assets are recorded in funds and others are recorded in the government-wide statement of net assets. Generally, fixed assets for the proprietary funds (the enterprise funds and the internal service funds) are recorded in the funds themselves.

Fixed assets other than those accounted for in the proprietary funds are considered capital assets used in governmental activities.

The reason that general fixed assets are not recorded in the governmental funds is that the measurement focus of the government's funds is the current financial resources measurement focus. General fixed assets do not represent current financial resources available for expenditure, but rather are considered items for which financial resources have been used and for which accountability should be maintained. Accordingly, they are considered not to be assets of the governmental funds, but are rather accounted for as assets of the government as a whole. NCGAS 1 determined that the primary purposes for governmental fund accounting are to reflect its revenues and expenditures (that is, the sources and uses of its financial resources) and its assets, related liabilities, and net financial resources available for appropriation and expenditure. To best meet these objectives, general fixed assets need to be excluded from the governmental fund accounts and instead be recorded in the general fixed assets account group. Note that conceptually GASBS 34 is similar, as will be described later in this chapter. Instead of recording these general fixed assets in an account group, however, they are recorded in the government-wide statement of net assets.

Capitalization Policy

In determining what assets to record in the government-wide financial statements, consideration of the government's policy for when assets are capitalized is key. Typically, this policy is based on a dollar threshold that ideally corresponds with the size of the government. For example, capital assets with a cost of more than $1,000 are capitalized and recorded in the government-wide statement of net assets. In addition, governments sometimes specify a minimum useful life to be used in conjunction with the dollar threshold. For example, capital assets with a cost of more than $1,000 and a useful life of five years or more are capitalized. The trend has been to increase capitalization thresholds, because abnormally low thresholds result in a significant increase in recordkeeping requirements that may be unnecessary to maintain control of the assets. Because governments are sometimes slow to act, many governments' capitalization thresholds have not kept up with inflation from a ten- or twenty-year perspective.

VALUATION OF ASSETS RECORDED, INCLUDING ACCUMULATED DEPRECIATION

As a general rule, fixed assets should be recorded in the government-wide financial statements at cost. *Cost* is defined as the consideration that is given or received, whichever is more objectively determinable. In most instances, cost will be based on the consideration that the government gave for the capital asset, because that will provide the most objective determination of the cost of the asset.

The cost of a fixed asset includes not only its purchase price or construction cost, but also any ancillary costs incurred that are necessary to place the asset in its intended location and in condition where it is ready for use. Ancillary charges will depend on the nature of the asset acquired or constructed, but typically include costs such as freight and transportation charges, site preparation expenditures, professional fees, and legal claims directly attributable to the asset acquisition or construction. An example of legal claims directly attributable to an asset acquisition is liability claims resulting from workers or others being injured during the construction of an asset, or damage done to the property of others as a direct result of the construction activities.

It is relatively easy to ascertain the costs of capital assets that are purchased currently. Contracts, purchase orders, and payment information are available to determine the acquisition or construction costs. The cost of a fixed asset includes not only its purchase price or construction cost, but also whatever ancillary charges are necessary to place the asset in its intended location and in condition for its intended use. Thus, among the costs that should be capitalized as part of the cost of a fixed asset are the following:

- Professional fees, such as architectural, legal, and accounting fees
- Transportation costs, such as freight charges
- Legal claims directly attributable to the asset acquisition
- Title fees
- Closing costs
- Appraisal and negotiation fees
- Surveying fees
- Damage payments
- Land preparation costs
- Demolition costs
- Insurance premiums during the construction phase
- Capitalized interest (discussed later in this chapter)

The reporting of capital assets by governments was not always common. As governments worked to adopt the requirements of NCGAS 1, they were faced with the task of establishing fixed asset records and valuation after many years of financial reporting without them. In these situations, many of the supporting documents and records that might contain original cost information were no longer available to establish the initial cost of these previously unrecorded assets.

Governments often found it necessary to estimate the original costs of these assets on the basis of such documentary evidence as may be available, including price levels at the time of acquisition, and to record these estimated costs in the appropriate fixed asset records. While this problem will diminish in size as governments retire or dispose of these assets with estimated costs, the notes to the financial statements should disclose the extent to which fixed asset costs have been estimated and the method (or methods) of estimation.

Governments sometimes acquire capital assets by gift. They should be recorded at their estimated fair value at the time of acquisition by the government.

To determine what assets will be treated as fixed assets (regardless of whether it is a capital asset used in governmental or business-type activities or a fixed asset of a proprietary fund) in practice, governments typically set thresholds for when assets may be considered for capitalization. For example, a government may determine that in order to be treated as a capitalized asset, an asset should cost at least $5,000 and have a useful life of five years. Note that this threshold applies only to items that are appropriately capitalizable by their nature. For example, a repair or maintenance expenditure of $7,000 would not be capitalized even if the threshold were $5,000. The threshold would apply to items that would normally be capitalized and is used to prevent too many small assets from being capitalized, which becomes difficult for governments to manage. Continuing the $5,000 threshold example, a personal computer purchased for $4,000 would not be capitalized. However, ten personal computers purchased as part of the installation of an integrated computer network would be eligible for capitalization in this example.

NOTE: Governments are notorious for having capitalization thresholds that, in the author's opinion, are far too low. Perhaps in their zeal to provide accountability for assets purchased with public resources, large governments exist that have capitalization thresholds of $100 to $500. Often, these thresholds have been in place for many years (sometimes from when the government first recorded general fixed assets) and have not been adjusted for inflation. This presents a waste of resources in accounting for the details of these numerous small assets. Governments should periodically review their capitalization thresholds to make sure that they make sense, given their significance to the government's financial statements. To address the accountability issue that is likely to arise in raising these thresholds, keep in mind that assets do not have to be recorded in the government-wide financial statements or in a proprietary fund to be safeguarded. In considering these accountability issues, the government must also consider that accountability standards may be imposed on the government from outside sources. For example, some federal and state contracts or grants may specify a capitalization level for tracking fixed assets that are acquired with funds provided under the contract or grant. Although this level must be adhered to for contract or grant management purposes, the level should not determine the capitalization threshold established for financial reporting purposes.

Depreciation

Governmental funds do not record depreciation expense. Governmental funds record the acquisition of capital assets as expenditures because acquiring these assets requires the use of the governmental funds' expendable financial resources. Conversely, governmental funds are provided with financial resources when general fixed assets are sold. Since depreciation expense is neither a source nor a use of governmental current financial resources, it is not proper to record it in the accounts of the governmental funds.

DEPRECIATION METHODS

Depreciation expense and the related accumulated depreciation are recorded in the government-wide statement of activities and in proprietary funds in a manner similar to that used by commercial entities.

In calculating depreciation, governments should follow the same acceptable depreciation methods used by commercial enterprises. There is actually very little authoritative guidance issued by the FASB and its predecessor standard-setting bodies. In fact, the financial statement preparer would need to go back to AICPA Accounting Research Bulletin 43 (ARB 43), *Restatement and Revision of Accounting Research Bulletins,* to find a definition of *depreciation accounting*, which is a system of accounting that aims to distribute the cost or other basic value of tangible capital assets, less any salvage value, over the estimated useful life of the unit (which may be a group of assets) in a systematic and rational manner. Viewed differently, depreciation recognizes the cost of using up the future economic benefits or service potentials of long-lived assets.

In addition to obtaining the original cost information described in the preceding section to this chapter, a government must determine the salvage value (if any) of an asset, the estimated useful life of the asset, and the depreciation method that will be used.

In practice, many governments usually assume that there will be no salvage value to the asset that they are depreciating. Governments tend to use things for a long time, and many of the assets that they record are useful only to the government, so there is no ready after-market for these assets. For example, what is the salvage value of a fully depreciated sewage treatment plant? Similarly, there is probably no practical use for used personal computer equipment, because governments are inclined to use these types of assets until they are virtually obsolete, which makes salvage value generally low. However, these governmental operating characteristics aside, if the government determines that there is likely to be salvage value for an asset being depreciated, the estimated salvage value should be deducted from the cost of the fixed asset to arrive at the amount that will be depreciated. (In certain accelerated depreciation methods, such as the double-declining balance method, salvage value is not considered.)

Next, the government should determine the estimated useful lives of the assets that will be depreciated. Usually assets are grouped into asset categories and a standard estimated life or a range of estimated lives is used for each class.

Following are some common depreciable asset categories:

- Buildings
- Leasehold improvements
- Machinery and equipment
- Office equipment
- Infrastructure, including roads, bridges, parks, etc.

Two areas to keep in mind are that land is not depreciated, because it is assumed to have an indefinite life. In addition, as will be discussed in Chapter 21, fixed assets that are recorded as a result of capital lease transactions are also considered part of the depreciable assets of a governmental organization.

The final component of the depreciation equation that a government needs to determine is the method that it will use. The most common method used by governments is the straight-line method of depreciation in which the amount to be depreciated is divided by the asset's useful life, resulting in the same depreciation charge each year.

Accelerated methods of depreciation, such as the sum-of-the-year's digits and the double-declining balance methods, may also be used. However, their use is far less popular than the straight-line method. Although proprietary funds do use a measurement focus and basis of accounting that result in a determination of net income similar to that of a commercial enterprise, there is less emphasis on the bottom line of proprietary activities than there would be for a publicly traded corporation, for instance. Reflecting this lower degree of emphasis, governments sometimes elect to follow the straight-line method of depreciation more for simplicity purposes, rather than for analyzing whether their assets actually do lose more of their value in the first few years of use.

Governments should also disclose their depreciation policies in the notes to the financial statements. For the major classes of fixed assets, the range of estimated useful lives that are used in the depreciation calculations should be disclosed.

The governmental organization should also disclose the depreciation method used in computing depreciation.

As described more fully in Chapter 10, governmental funds and entities that use proprietary accounting may elect to apply FASB statements and interpretations issued after November 30, 1989. Those entities that make this election must consider the requirements of FASB Statement 121, *Accounting for the Impairment of Long-Lived Assets and for Long-Lived Assets to Be Disposed Of* (SFAS 121) in accounting for their fixed assets.

SFAS 121 requires that long-lived assets and certain identifiable intangible assets that are held and used by an entity be reviewed for impairment whenever events or changes in circumstances indicate that the carrying amount of an asset may not be recoverable. First the entity determines whether an impairment loss has occurred by comparing the carrying amount of the asset with the estimated future cash flows (undiscounted and without interest charges) expected to result from the use of the asset and its eventual disposition. If an impairment loss is indicated because the estimated future cash flows are less than the carrying amount of the asset, the impairment loss is measured (and recognized) as the difference between the carrying amount and the fair value of the assets that are impaired.

NOTE: Governmental funds and entities applying SFAS 121 should be careful in determining whether an impairment of a long-lived asset has occurred. In many cases, enterprise funds or other public authorities charge fees that are not expected to recover the total cost of operations. The author believes that the anticipated operating subsidiaries from another fund or, if to a legally separate entity, from the government itself, should be taken into account when determining whether an impairment of an asset has occurred.

For example, it would not seem reasonable to determine that an impairment has occurred for assets of a transit system whose fares are only expected to cover half of its costs, using strictly the expected future cash flows from fares (which are the revenues generated by the assets of the transit system) without considering all of the federal and state operating subsidies that are received by the transit system.

SFAS 121 also requires, generally, that long-lived assets and certain identifiable intangibles to be disposed of be reported at the lower of the carrying amount of fair value less cost to sell. An exception to this requirement is for assets covered by APB 30, *Reporting the Results of Operations— Reporting the Effects of Disposal of a Segment of a Business,*

Extraordinary, Unusual and Infrequently Occurring Events and Transactions, in which case the assets to be disposed of are reported at the lower of the carrying amount or net realizable value.

Capitalization of interest on capital assets used in governmental activities is also not recorded under GASBS 34. It should be recorded, however, on fixed assets recorded in proprietary funds.

Interest cost is capitalized for assets that require an acquisition period to get them ready for use. The acquisition period is the period beginning with the first expenditure for a qualifying asset and ending when the asset is substantially complete and ready for its intended use. The interest cost capitalization period starts when three conditions are met.

- Expenditures have occurred
- Activities necessary to prepare the asset (including administrative activities before construction) have begun
- Interest cost has been incurred

The amount of interest cost capitalized should not exceed the actual interest cost applicable to the governmental fund that is incurred during the reporting period. To compute the amount of interest cost to be capitalized for a reporting period, the average cumulative expenditures for the qualifying asset during the reporting period must be determined. In order to determine the average accumulated expenditures, each expenditure must be weighted for the time it was outstanding during the reporting period.

To determine the interest rate to apply against the weighted-average of expenditures computed in the preceding paragraph, the government should determine if the construction is being financed with a specific borrowing. If it is, which in the governmental environment is fairly likely, then the interest rate of that specific borrowing should be used. In other words, this interest rate, multiplied by the weighted-average of expenditures on the qualifying assets, would be the amount of interest that is capitalized. If no specific borrowing is made to acquire the qualifying asset, the weighted-average interest rate incurred on other borrowings outstanding during the period is used to determine the amount of interest cost to be capitalized.

As stated above, the amount of interest capitalized should not exceed the interest cost of the reporting period. In addition, interest is not capitalized during delays or interruptions, other than brief interruptions, that occur during the acquisition or development phase of the qualifying asset.

Background

As described earlier in this chapter, the historical cost of acquiring an asset includes the costs incurred necessary to bring the asset to the condition and location necessary for its intended use. If an asset requires a period in which to carry out the activities necessary to bring it to that location and condition, the interest cost incurred during that period as a result of expenditures for the asset is part of the historical cost of the asset.

SFAS 34 states the objectives of capitalizing interest as the following:

- To obtain a measure of acquisition cost that more closely reflects the enterprise's total investment in the asset, and
- To charge a cost that relates to the acquisition of a resource that will benefit future periods against the revenues of the periods benefited.

Conceptually, interest cost is capitalizable for all assets that require time to get them ready for their intended use, called the *acquisition period*. However, SFAS 34 concludes that in certain cases, because of cost/benefit considerations in obtaining information, among other reasons, interest cost should not be capitalized. Accordingly, SFAS 34 specifies that interest cost should not be capitalized for the following types of assets:

- Inventories that are routinely manufactured or otherwise produced in large quantities on a repetitive basis
- Assets that are in use or ready for their intended use in the earnings activities of the entity
- Assets that are not being used in the earnings activities of the enterprise and are not undergoing the activities necessary to get them ready for use
- Assets that are not included in the balance sheet
- Investments accounted for by the equity method after the planned principal operations of the investee begin
- Investments in regulated investees that are capitalizing both the cost of debt and equity capital
- Assets acquired with gifts or grants that are restricted by the donor or the grantor to acquisition of those assets to the extent that funds are available from such gifts and grants (Interest earned from temporary investment of those funds that is similarly restricted should be considered an addition to the gift or grant for this purpose.)

- Land that is not undergoing activities necessary to get it ready for its intended use
- Certain oil- and gas-producing operations accounted for by the full cost method.

After consideration of the above exceptions, interest should be capitalized for the following types of assets, referred to as *qualifying assets*:

- Assets that are constructed or otherwise produced for an entity's own use, including assets constructed or produced for the enterprise by others for which deposits or progress payments have been made
- Assets that are for sale or lease and are constructed or otherwise produced as discrete projects, such as real estate developments
- Investments (equity, loans, and advances) accounted for by the equity method while the investee has activities in progress necessary to commence its planned principal operations, provided that the investee's activities include the use of funds to acquire qualifying assets for its operations.

Amount of Interest to Be Capitalized

The amount of interest cost to be capitalized for qualifying assets is intended to be that portion of the interest cost incurred during the assets' acquisition periods that could theoretically be avoided if expenditures for the assets had not been made, such as avoiding interest by not making additional borrowings or by using the funds expended for the qualifying assets to repay borrowings that already exist.

The amount of interest that is capitalized in an accounting period is determined by applying an interest rate (known as the capitalization rate) to the average amount of the accumulated expenditures for the asset during the period. (Special rules may apply when qualifying assets are financed with tax-exempt debt. These rules are discussed later in this chapter.) The capitalization rates used in an accounting period are based on the rates applicable to borrowings outstanding during the accounting period. However, if an entity's financing plans associate a specific new borrowing with a qualifying asset, the enterprise may use the rate on that specific borrowing as the capitalization rate to be applied to that portion of the average accumulated expenditures for the asset not in excess of the amount of the borrowing. If the average accumulated expenditures for the asset exceed the amounts of the specific new borrowing associated with the asset, the capitalization rate applicable to this excess should be a weighted-average of the rates applicable to the other borrowings of the entity.

SFAS 34 provides specific guidance on determining which borrowings should be considered in the weighted-average rate mentioned in the previous paragraph. The objective is to obtain a reasonable measure of the cost of financing the acquisition of the asset in terms of the interest cost incurred that otherwise could have been avoided. Judgment will likely be required to make a selection of borrowings that best accomplishes this objective in the particular circumstances of the governmental entity. For example, capitalized interest for fixed assets constructed and financed by revenue bonds issued by a water and sewer authority should consider the interest rate of the water and sewer authority's debt, rather than general obligation bonds of the government. The revenue bonds are likely to show a different, probably lower, rate than that of the general obligation bonds.

In addition to the above guidance on the calculation of the amount of capitalized interest, SFAS 34 specifies that the amount of interest that is capitalized in an accounting period cannot exceed the total amount of interest cost incurred by the entity in that period.

Capitalization Period

Generally, the capitalization period begins when the following three conditions are met:

1. Expenditures for assets have been made.
2. Activities that are necessary to get the asset ready for its intended use are in progress.
3. Interest cost is being incurred.

(The beginning of the capitalization period for assets financed with tax-exempt debt is described later in this chapter.)

Interest capitalization continues as long as the above three conditions continue to be met. The term *activities* is meant to be construed broadly according to SFAS 34. It should be considered to encompass more than physical construction. Activities are all the steps required to prepare the asset for its intended use, and might include

*   Administrative and technical activities during the pre-construction phase
*   Development of plans or the process of obtaining permits from various governmental authorities
*   Activities undertaken after construction has begun in order to overcome unforeseen obstacles, such as technical problems, labor disputes, or litigation

If the governmental entity suspends substantially all activities related to the acquisition of the asset, interest capitalization should cease until activities are resumed. However, brief interruptions, interruptions that are externally imposed, and delays inherent in the asset acquisition process do not require interest capitalization to be interrupted.

When the asset is substantially completed and ready for its intended use, the capitalization period ends. SFAS 34 specifically used the term *substantially complete* to prohibit the continuing of interest capitalization in situations in which completion of the asset is intentionally delayed. Interest cost should not be capitalized during periods when the entity intentionally defers or suspends activities related to the asset, because interest incurred during such periods is a holding cost and not an acquisition cost.

Capitalization of Interest Involving Tax-Exempt Borrowings and Certain Gifts and Grants

SFAS 62 amended SFAS 34 where tax-exempt borrowings are used to finance qualifying assets. Generally, interest earned by an entity is not offset against the interest cost in determining either interest capitalization rates or limitations on the amount of interest cost that can be capitalized. However, in situations where the acquisition of qualifying assets is financed with the proceeds of tax-exempt borrowings and those funds are externally restricted to finance the acquisition of specified qualifying assets or to service the related debt, this general principal is changed. The amount of interest cost capitalized on qualifying assets acquired with the proceeds of tax-exempt borrowings that are externally restricted as specified above is the interest cost on the borrowing less any interest earned on related interest-bearing investments acquired with proceeds of the related tax-exempt borrowings from the date of the borrowing until the assets are ready for their intended use.

In other words, when a specific tax-exempt borrowing finances a project, a governmental entity will earn interest income on bond proceeds that are invested until they are expended or required to be held in debt service reserve accounts. These interest earnings should be offset against the interest cost in determining the amounts of interest to be capitalized. Conceptually, the true interest cost to the government is the net of this interest income and interest cost. However, this exception to the general rule of not netting interest income against interest expense relates only to this specific exception relating to tax-exempt borrowings and where amounts received under gifts and grants are restricted to use in the acquisition of the qualifying asset.

Disclosures

In addition to the accounting requirements specified above, SFAS 34 contains two disclosure requirements relating to capitalized interest.

1. For an accounting period in which no interest cost is capitalized, the amount of interest cost incurred and charged to expense during the period should be disclosed.
2. For an accounting period in which some interest cost is capitalized, the total amount of interest cost incurred during the period and the amount thereof that has been capitalized should be disclosed.

GASBS 34 Reporting of Capital Assets

In the government-wide financial statements, capital assets should be reported at historical cost. Cost includes capitalized interest and ancillary costs (freight, transportation charges, site preparation fees, professional fees, etc.) necessary to place an asset into its intended location and condition for use.

One of the most significant aspects of GASBS 34 is its definition of what is included in capital assets: land, improvements to land, easements, buildings, building improvements, vehicles, machinery, equipment, works of art and historical treasures, infrastructure, and all other tangible and intangible assets that are used in operations and that have initial useful lives extending beyond a single reporting period. The GASBS 34 Implementation Guide defines land improvements to consist of betterments, other than building, that ready land for its intended use. Examples provided of land improvements include site improvements such as excavations, fill, grading, and utility installation; removal, relocation, or reconstruction of the property of others, such as railroads and telephone and power lines; retention walls; parking lots, fencing, and landscaping.

Included in this definition are infrastructure assets. Presently, governments have the option to capitalize infrastructure assets, and many, if not most, do not. (Infrastructure assets are defined by GASBS 34 as "long-lived capital assets that normally are stationary in nature and normally can be preserved for a significantly greater number of years than most capital assets.") Examples of infrastructure assets are roads, bridges, tunnels, drainage systems, water and sewer systems, dams, and lighting systems.

All governments will be required to report general infrastructure capital assets prospectively. Retroactive capitalization of infrastructure assets becomes more complicated.

- Phase 3 governments (governments with total annual revenues of less than $10 million) do not have to retroactively record infrastructure assets, although they are encouraged to do so.
- Phase 1 governments (governments with total annual revenues of $100 million or more) and Phase 2 governments (governments with total annual revenues of $10 million, but less than $100 million) are encouraged to retroactively report all major general infrastructure assets on the date that GASBS 34 is implemented.

NOTE: Chapter 1 provides GASBS 34 implementation information, which includes the definition of Phase 1, 2, and 3 governments.

However, Phase 1 governments must retroactively report all major general infrastructure assets for fiscal years beginning after June 15, 2005. Phase 2 governments must retroactively report all major general infrastructure assets for fiscal years beginning after June 15, 2006. At the general infrastructure transition date, Phase 1 and Phase 2 governments are required to capitalize and report major general fixed assets that were acquired in fiscal years ending after June 30, 1980, or that received major renovations, restorations, or improvements during that period.

NOTE: The determination of major infrastructure assets is made at the network or subsystem level as follows:

- *The cost or estimated cost of a subsystem is expected to be at least 5% of the total cost of all general capital assets reported in the first fiscal year ending after June 30, 1999.*
- *The cost or estimated cost of a network is expected to be at least 10% of the total cost of all general capital assets reported in the first fiscal year ending after June 15, 1999.*

Depreciation

Since the government-wide financial statements are prepared using the economic resources measurement focus, depreciation on capital assets is recorded. This is another highly controversial issue of GASBS 34. In response to commentary that infrastructure assets do not depreciate in value in the traditional sense, GASBS 34 allows a "modified approach" as to depreciation on qualifying infrastructure assets, as discussed below.

Basically, depreciation rules (aside from the modified approach) follow those currently used by proprietary funds, as well as by commercial enterprises. Capital assets are reported in the statement of net assets net of accumulated depreciation. (Capital assets that are not depreciated, such as land, construction in progress, and infrastructure assets using the modified approach, should be reported separately from capital assets being depreciated in the statement of activities.) Depreciation expense is recorded in the statement of activities. Capital assets are depreciated over their estimated useful lives, except for land and land improvements and infrastructure assets using the modified approach.

Depreciation expense may be calculated by individual assets or by classes of assets (such as infrastructure, buildings and improvements, vehicles, and machinery and equipment). In addition, depreciation may be calculated for networks of capital assets or for subsystems of a network of capital assets. A network of assets is composed of all assets that provide a particular type of service for a government. A network of infrastructure assets may be only one infrastructure asset that is composed of many components. A subsystem of a network of assets is composed of all assets that make up a similar portion or segment of a network of assets. The GASBS 34 Implementation Guide provides the example of a water distribution system of a government, which could be considered a network. The pumping stations, storage facilities, and distribution mains could be considered subsystems of that network.

NOTE: In implementing the capital asset requirements of GASBS 34, a number of implementation strategies and approaches have begun to develop, particularly for the retroactive capitalization of infrastructure assets. The use of various models and estimation techniques are being used by a number of governments in lieu of attempting to calculate specific, actual costs for specific assets. For example, to retroactively capitalize the cost of roads, a government may choose to refine one of the following general approaches:

- *The government estimates that it has 100 lane miles of road that it needs to capitalize. The current cost of constructing one lane mile of road is $1 million. The average age of a road is ten years, and the average estimated life of a road is twenty-five years. The average annual inflation rate for road construction projects over the last ten years is 4%. The government calculates that the current cost of constructing all of its roads is $100 million, which adjusted for ten years of inflation means that the average historical cost of a road is approximately $70 million. Using the straight-line depreciation method, accumulated depreciation is calculated at $28 million ($70 million divided by 25, multiplied by 10.)*

- *The government estimates that it spent $10 million each year on road construction over the last twenty years, for a total of $200 million. Each year it will capitalize the $10 million spent and depreciate 1/25 of the amount for the next twenty-five years, assuming the twenty-five-year estimated life. The calculation is repeated for each year of the prior twenty years, resulting in a total historical cost of $200 million and a cumulative amount of depreciation that would have been taken over the last twenty years.*

These examples are overly simplified to demonstrate their concepts. However, with the appropriate degree of refinement, they can result in historical cost and depreciation information that is acceptable under GASBS 34, auditable by the government's independent auditors, and not materially different from that which would be obtained by performing a complex inventory and analysis of road construction costs.

Modified Approach

Infrastructure assets that are part of a network or subsystem of a network are not required to be depreciated if two requirements are met.

1. The government manages the eligible infrastructure assets using an asset management system that has the following characteristics:

   a. An up-to-date inventory of eligible infrastructure assets is maintained

   b. Condition assessments of the eligible infrastructure assets are performed and summarized using a measurement scale

   c. An estimate is made each year of the annual amount to maintain and preserve the eligible infrastructure assets at the condition level established and disclosed by the government

2.   The government documents that the eligible infra-
     structure assets are being preserved approximately
     at or above a condition level established and dis-
     closed by the government. The condition level
     should be established and documented by adminis-
     trative or executive policy, or by legislative action.

*NOTE: Using the modified approach will certainly be one of the
more interesting implementation issues that will arise from
GASBS 34.   Governments are likely to have different
inventory/maintenance systems for different types of infrastructure assets, and determining whether each of these systems meets
these requirements will be important. Implementation guidance
from the GASB should be expected in this area. It is also an area
that will be important for independent auditors to focus on in order to determine the appropriate audit procedures that will be required to test compliance with these requirements.*

GASBS 34 requires that governments using the modified
approach should document that

1.   Complete condition assessments of eligible infra-
     structure assets are performed in a consistent man-
     ner at least every three years.
2.   The results of the most recent complete condition
     assessments provide reasonable assurance that the
     eligible infrastructure assets are being preserved
     approximately at or above the condition level es-
     tablished and disclosed by the government.

When the modified approach is used, GASBS 34 requires governments to present the following schedules, derived from asset management systems, as RSI for all eligible
infrastructure assets that are reported using the modified approach:

1.   The assessed condition, performed at least every
     three years, for at least the three most recent com-
     plete condition assessments, indicating the dates of
     the assessments
2.   The estimated annual amount calculated at the be-
     ginning of the fiscal year to maintain and preserve
     at (or above) the condition level established and
     disclosed by the government compared with the
     amounts actually expensed for each of the past five
     reporting periods.

The following are the GASBS 34 specified disclosures that should accompany this schedule:

1. The basis for the condition measurement and the measurement scale used to assess and report condition. For example, a basis for *condition measurement* could be distresses found in pavement surfaces. A *scale* used to assess and report condition could range from zero for failed pavement to 100 for a pavement in perfect condition.

2. The condition level at which the government intends to preserve its eligible infrastructure assets reported using the modified approach.

3. Factors that significantly affect the trends in the information reported in the required schedules, including any changes in the measurement scale, the basis for the condition measurement, or the condition assessment methods used during the periods covered by the schedules. If there is a change in the condition level at which the government intends to preserve eligible infrastructure assets, an estimate of the effect of the change on the estimated annual amount to maintain and preserve those assets for the current period also should be disclosed.

Failure to meet these conditions would preclude a government from continuing to use the modified approach.

NOTE: When the modified approach is used, depreciation expense is not recorded for the qualified infrastructure assets. Rather, all maintenance and preservation costs for those assets should be expensed in the period that they are incurred. Maintenance costs are those costs that allow an asset to continue to be used during its originally established useful life. Preservation costs (which would be capitalized if the modified approach was not being used) are considered to be those costs that extend the useful life of an asset beyond its originally estimated useful life, but do not increase the capacity or efficiency of the assets. Additions and improvements to assets that increase their capacity (i.e., the level of service provided by the assets) or efficiency (i.e., the level of service is maintained, but at a lower cost) are capitalized under both the modified approach and the depreciation approach.

SUMMARY

GASBS 34 significantly changes the way in which capital assets used in governmental activities of a government are reported. Reporting of infrastructure assets is a key requirement of GASBS 34 that must receive careful attention.

13 LONG-TERM OBLIGATIONS

OVERVIEW OF THE ACCOUNTING FOR THE GENERAL LONG-TERM DEBT ACCOUNT GROUP

Prior to the implementation of the financial reporting model for governments as promulgated by GASBS 34, long-term obligations related to governmental funds were accounted for in the general long-term debt account group. Under GASBS 34, long-term obligations are also not reported in the governmental funds. They are only reported as liabilities on the government-wide statement of net assets. This chapter describes the accounting for long-term debt and other long-term obligations, and several issues as to when certain obligations might be reported in governmental funds.

As indicated in its title, the general long-term debt account group is not a fund. As an "account group," it is actually a list of liabilities related to the governmental funds that are long-term in nature and are not recorded as liabilities of the applicable governmental funds.

This section of this chapter examines a government's accounting and financial reporting for the general long-term debt account group.

Other long-term liabilities typically found in the government-wide statement of net assets are specifically covered in other chapters of this guide. These liabilities (and the references to the related chapters) are as follows:

- Capital leases and operating leases with scheduled rent increases (Chapter 21)
- Compensated absences (Chapter 17)
- Judgments and claims (Chapter 20)
- Landfill closure and postclosure costs (Chapter 22)
- Pension-related liabilities (Chapter 18)

Readers should review these chapters to determine the appropriate recognition of these liabilities in the general long-term debt account group.

The following sections discuss the accounting for general long-term bonds and other debt that might be recorded only in the government-wide financial statements. A separate chapter (Chapter 21) discusses the accounting and reporting for capital leases and operating leases with scheduled rent increases. The balance of the amounts not recorded in the governmental funds, but only in the government-wide financial statements represents specific accrued liability-type items.

While specific requirements and calculation of these items is discussed in the chapters referred to above, a review of the overall accounting for accrued liabilities warrants special attention.

First, as a general rule, accrued liabilities should be automatically recorded in the governmental funds themselves, regardless of whether they will be liquidated with current resources. Usually, accrued liabilities for salaries and accounts payable for goods and services received prior to the end of the fiscal year, but paid in the following fiscal year, fall into this category. These typical, standard accruals, as mentioned, should be recorded in the governmental funds, which then become a part of the government-wide financial statements.

The only liabilities other than debt items that are excluded from being reported in the governmental funds are as follows:

- Judgments and claims
- Compensated absences
- Unfunded pension liabilities
- Special termination benefits
- Landfill closure and postclosure costs
- Capital lease obligation and operating leases with scheduled rent increases

In these cases, a liability should be recognized in only the government-wide financial statements to the extent that the liability would not "normally be liquidated with expendable available resources." The method of determining how a liability would normally be liquidated with expendable available resources is not provided in any GASB or NCGA pronouncement, although the 2001 GAAFR does provide some general practice guidance.

The 2001 GAAFR specifies that this practice should not affect the recognition of expenditures and fund liabilities, which would only be recognized as the related liability becomes due, regardless of the liability being advance-funded. This change is a result of GASB Interpretation 6, which is discussed more fully in Chapter 3.

Contrast the funded liability situation to the unfunded liability situation, where the government is not setting aside current resources to pay these unfunded liabilities. The government is relying on the resources of future periods to liquidate these liabilities when they become due. Accordingly, it can be concluded that these liabilities will not be liquidated with expendable available resources, even though the liabilities may be liquidated in the very near future. Unfunded liabilities will be paid with amounts that have not yet been provided as of the end of the fiscal year. Accordingly, unfunded liabilities for the special cases listed above should be reported in the general long-term debt account group, where they are appropriately offset by the balancing account described above: amount to be provided for the retirement for long-term debt.

The 1994 GAAFR uses the example of compensated absences to further demonstrate the unfunded example. Most governments report their entire liability for compensated absences in the general long-term debt account group. These same governments use the pay-as-you-go method for actually making the payments. For example, when a sick day or vacation time is paid, it is paid from the normal recurring payroll, while conceptually reducing the liability in the general long-term debt account group. Lump-sum payments are treated in a similar manner. However, compensated absences should be accrued in the fund for employees that have terminated service as of year-end but have not yet been paid for the vested compensated absences that are payable to them. The minority of governments that fund compensated absence liabilities by accumulating resources in the related governmental fund also report the liability for compensated absences in the same governmental fund.

The 1994 GAAFR emphasizes that the approach described above only applies to the specific items listed above. All other liabilities related to governmental funds must be reported in the funds themselves, regardless (1) of when they are expected to be paid and (2) of funding. In other words, a government could not report the accounts payable of its governmental fund in the general long-term debt group of accounts simply because it was behind on payments or because the amounts weren't actually due until a significant time after the fiscal year-end.

When determining whether a government funds one of the above special liabilities, it is important to consider that the criterion is based on whether a government "normally" liquidates the liability with expendable available financial resources. If a government ordinarily funds a certain type of liability, but fails to do so in a given year, the liability should continue to be reported in the governmental fund and the government-wide financial statements because it would normally be liquidated from expendable available financial resources based on the government's existing funding policies.

In addition, liabilities that are payable on demand as of the balance sheet date, other than those related to compensated absences, must be reported as fund liabilities, regardless of whether they are funded. For example, if a government settles a claim or receives a final judgment on a claim prior to the fiscal year-end, but does not actually pay the settlement or judgment until the next fiscal year, the fund from where judgments and claims are normally paid should record a liability for the settlement or judgment amount, regardless of whether it is funded.

The above approach to funded and unfunded liabilities represents the recommended approach in the 1994 GAAFR. A government may use other consistent approaches and still be in accordance with GAAP. For example, a government may establish a time period for expenditure and fund liability recognition, just as an availability period is used for recognition purposes. Were this alternative to be used, it should be consistently applied. In addition, the definition of a "current" liability should not be so broad as to include liabilities that extend for a long period. For example, a time period of twelve months would ordinarily not be appropriate because it is too long.

DEMAND BONDS

Demand bonds are debt instruments that create a potential call on a state or local government's current financial resources. The accounting question that arises is whether the liability for demand bonds should be recorded as a liability of the fund that receives the proceeds, or whether the debt should only be included in the government-wide statement of net assets. The GASB issued guidance through GASB Interpretation 1 (GASBI 1), *Demand Bonds Issued by State and Local Governmental Entities*, which is reflected in the discussion of the following accounting question.

Demand bonds are debt issuances that have demand provisions (termed "put" provisions) as one of their features that gives the bondholder the right to require that the issuer to redeem the bonds within a certain period, after giving some agreed-upon period of notice, usually thirty days or less. In some cases, the demand provisions are exercisable immediately after the bonds have been issued. In other cases, there is a waiting period of, for example, five years, until the put provisions of the bonds may be exercised by the bondholder. These provisions mean that the bondholder is less subject to risks caused by rising interest rates. Because the bondholder is assured that he or she can receive the par value of the bond at some future date, a demand bond has some features and advantages of a short-term investment for the bondholder, in addition to being a potential long-term investment. Accordingly, depending on the current market conditions, governments can issue these types of bonds at a lower interest rate than would be possible with bonds that did not have the demand bonds' put provision.

Because the issuance of demand bonds represents significant potential cash outlays by governments, steps are usually taken to protect the government from having to fund from its own cash reserves demand bonds redeemed by bondholders. First, governments usually appoint remarketing agents whose function is to resell bonds that have been redeemed by bondholders. In addition, governments usually obtain letters of credit or other arrangements that would make funds available sufficient to cover redeemed bonds.

To provide for long-term financing in the event that the remarketing agents are unable to sell the redeemed bonds within a specified period (such as three to six months), the government issuing demand bonds generally enters into an agreement with a financial institution to convert the bonds to an installment loan repayable over a specified period. This type of arrangement is known as a "take-out" agreement and may be part of the letter of credit agreement, or a separate agreement.

From the perspective of the government issuing debt in the form of demand bonds, the most important elements of the transaction are the standby liquidity agreement and the take-out agreement. The standby liquidity agreement assures the availability of short-term funds to redeem the bonds that are put by the bondholder pending resale by the remarketing agent. In addition, the take-out agreement is of equal or more importance because it provides assurance that the issuer will be able to repay any borrowings under the standby liquidity agreement and preserves the long-term nature of the basic debt.

As addressed by GASBI 1, demand bonds are those that by their terms have demand provisions that are exercisable at the balance sheet date or within one year from the date of the balance sheet. These bonds should be reported by governments in the general long-term debt account group, provided all of the following conditions delineated in GASBI 1 are met:

- Before the financial statements are issued, the issuer has entered into an arm's-length financing (take-out) agreement (an arm's-length agreement is an agreement with an unrelated third party, with each party acting in his or her own behalf) to convert bonds put

(but not resold) into some other form of long-term obligation.
- The take-out agreement does not expire within one year from the date of the issuer's balance sheet.
- The take-out agreement is not cancelable by the lender or the prospective lender during that year, and obligations incurred under the take-out agreement are not callable during that year.
- The lender, prospective lender, or investor is expected to be financially capable of honoring the take-out agreement.

Regarding the conditions above, if the take-out agreement is cancelable or callable because of violations that can be objectively verified by both parties and no violations have occurred prior to issuance of the financial statements, the demand bonds should be classified and recorded as long-term debt. If violations have occurred and a waiver has been obtained before issuance of the financial statements, the bonds should also be classified and recorded as long-term debt. Otherwise, the demand bonds should be classified and recorded as liabilities of the governmental fund.

If the take-out agreement is cancelable or callable because of violations that cannot be objectively verified by both parties, the take-out agreement does not provide sufficient assurance of long-term financing capabilities, and the bonds should be classified as liabilities of the fund.

If a government exercises a take-out agreement to convert demand bonds that have been redeemed into an installment loan, the installment loan should be reported in the general long-term debt account group.

If the above conditions are not met, the demand bonds should be recorded as a liability of a governmental fund, such as the capital projects fund. The selection of the fund to record the liability is determined by which fund receives the bond proceeds from the issuance of the demand bonds. Most often, this is the capital projects fund.

In addition, if a take-out agreement expires while its related demand bonds are still outstanding, the government should report a fund liability in the fund for the demand bonds that were previously reported in the general fixed asset account group. The liability is reported as a liability of the fund that originally reported the proceeds of the bond. A corresponding debit to "Other financing uses" would need to be made at this time to record the fund liability.

In addition to the accounting requirements relative to demand bonds, GASBI 1 requires that a number of disclosures be made about this type of bond and the related agreements. These disclosures are in addition to the normal disclosures required about debt and include the following:

- General description of the demand bond program
- Terms of any letters of credit or other standby liquidity agreements outstanding
- Commitment fees to obtain the letters of credit and any amounts drawn on them outstanding as of the balance sheet date
- A description of the take-out agreement, including its expiration date, commitment fees to obtain that agreement, and the terms of any new obligation under the take-out agreement
- The debt service requirements that would result if the take-out agreement were to be exercised

If a take-out agreement has been exercised converting the bonds to an installment loan, the installment loan should be reported as general long-term debt, and the payment schedule under the installment loan should be included as part of the schedule of debt service requirements to maturity.

Using the criteria and requirements of GASBI 1, the following is an illustrative footnote disclosure for demand bonds included in the general long-term debt account group. This disclosure can be modified for use when the demand bonds are not reported as a fund liability after implementation of GASBS 34.

ADVANCE REFUNDINGS

Accounting for transactions relating the advance refunding of long-term debt was described in Chapter 9. While that discussion focused on the flow of funds through a debt service fund when an advance refunding occurs, the critical accounting decision to be made for advance refundings of general long-term debt is whether the liability of the refunded debt is removed from the government-wide statement of net assets. That accounting decision and the related disclosure requirements for advance refundings is the focus of the following discussion.

GASBS 7, *Advance Refundings Resulting in Defeasance of Debt*, provides significant background and accounting guidance for determining the appropriate accounting for these activities.

There are several reasons why a government might desire to refund its debt in advance of the debt's maturity date. The following are some of these reasons a government may advance refund debt:

1. Most frequently, governments refinance debt to take advantage of more favorable interest rates. If interest rates have declined for similar securities, it is likely that the government can realize savings by advance refunding its older debt.
2. Governments may also refinance debt to change the structure of debt service payments, such as by shortening or lengthening the period.
3. Governments might also refinance debt to escape from unfavorable bond covenants, such as restrictions on issuing additional debt.

Because the benefits that a government may realize from the above reasons are likely to be available before the debt is actually due or redeemable, it is necessary for a government to advance refund the debt. A government accomplishes an advance refunding by taking the proceeds of the new debt issued to refinance the old debt and placing the proceeds in an escrow account that is subsequently used to provide funds to do the following, at minimum:

*   Meet periodic principal and interest payments of the old debt until the call or maturity date
*   Pay the call premium, if redemption is at the call date
*   Redeem the debt at the call date or the maturity date

Most advance refunding transactions result in a defeasance of the debt, enabling the government to remove the amount of the old debt from the general long-term debt account group. A defeasance can be either legal or in-substance.

*   A legal defeasance occurs when debt is legally satisfied based on certain provisions in the instrument, even though the debt is not actually repaid.
*   An in-substance defeasance is the far more common type of defeasance. An in-substance defeasance occurs when debt is considered defeased for accounting purposes even though a legal defeasance has not occurred.

GASBS 7 prescribes the criteria that must be met before debt is considered defeased for accounting and reporting purposes. The government must irrevocably place cash or assets with an escrow agent in a trust to be used solely for satisfying scheduled payments of both interest and principal of the defeased debt, and the possibility that the debtor will be required to make future payments on that debt is remote. The trust is restricted to owning only monetary assets that are essentially risk-free as to the amount, timing, and collection of interest and principal. The monetary assets should be denominated in the currency in which the debt is payable. GASBS 7 also prescribes that for debt denominated in US dollars, risk-free monetary assets are essentially limited to

- Direct obligations of the US government (including state and local government securities [SLGS] that the US Treasury issues specifically to provide state and local governments with required cash flows at yields that do not exceed the Internal Revenue Service's arbitrage limits)
- Obligations guaranteed by the US government
- Securities backed by US government obligations as collateral and for which interest and principal payments generally flow immediately through to the security holder

Determining the benefit of an advance refunding of long-term debt is not simply a matter of comparing the values of the old debt being refunded and the new debt that is being issued to provide the proceeds to accomplish the advance refunding. In fact, it may be necessary in a refunding to issue new debt in an amount greater than the old debt. In these cases, savings may result if the total new debt service requirements (principal and interest) are less than the old debt service requirements.

Although the difference in total cash flows between the old and the new debt service payments provides some indication of the effect of an advance refunding transaction, that transaction should also be examined from a time-value-of-money perspective. The value on a given date of a series of future payments is less than the sum of those payments because of the time value of money, commonly referred to as the present value of a future payment stream. The present value of the future payment stream provides a more meaningful measure of the savings or costs resulting from a refunding.

GASBS 7 defines the economic gain or loss on a refunding transaction as the difference between the present value of the new debt service requirements and the present value of the old debt service requirements. The interest rate used to determine the present value of these two payment streams should be an interest rate that reflects the estimate of the amount of earnings required on the assets placed in the escrow account, adjusted for any issuance costs that will result in a lower amount of funds actually being invested in the escrow account.

Determining the effective interest rate that is used to discount the cash flow streams on both the old and new debt service payments is an important component in determining the economic gain or loss on an advance refunding. As stated above, this rate is affected by costs that are allowable which will be paid out of the escrow account. The United States Treasury Department regulations limit the amount of earnings that a government may earn on funds from tax-exempt debt issuances that are invested by the government, including investments in escrow accounts that are used to pay debt service on the "old" debt in an advance refunding transaction.

NOTE: The purpose of the limitations are to prevent governments from issuing tax-exempt debt to obtain funds to invest in otherwise taxable securities. Because governments are not subject to income taxes, there would otherwise be a great opportunity to take advantage of these "arbitrage" earnings. For example, a government may be able to issue tax-exempt debt with an interest rate of 4%. At the same time, the government may be able to purchase US Treasury securities with a taxable interest rate of 6%. Since the government is not subject to income taxes, in this example it would have 2% more in earnings for every dollar it borrowed, ignoring debt issuance costs. The US Treasury requires that, after a complex set of calculations over a five-year period of time, arbitrage earnings be rebated to the US Treasury.

Because of the arbitrage rebate requirements, a government would generally be able to earn on its escrow funds an interest rate equal to the amount that it was paying in interest on the debt that it issued to obtain the funds to put in the escrow account. An adjustment to the interest rate allowed on the escrow funds can be made for certain advance refunding costs which the US Treasury Department deems "allowable," which means that they can be recouped in part through the escrow earnings. The term *allowable* used above relates to the fact that the US Treasury Department allows certain issuance costs to be deducted from bond proceeds before determining the maximum allowable yield of the escrow fund. Because the escrow fund is invested for a period shorter than the life of the bond, or at the time of the refunding, Treasury securities are yielding less than the escrow's legal maximum rate, not all allowable costs can be recovered. To the extent that these costs are recovered by escrow earnings, they effectively cost the issuing entity nothing, and are therefore ignored in computing the effective interest rate. If the costs cannot be recovered, they should be considered in the determination of the effective interest rate, as described above.

Having at least some of these costs allowable and eligible for recoupment from the escrow earnings means that a slightly higher rate would be allowed on the escrow earnings, which is clearly a benefit to a government in evaluating whether a particular advance refunding transaction would be favorable to it. The more that the escrow fund can earn, the smaller the escrow requirement. The smaller the escrow requirement, the less new debt a government must issue to accomplish the refunding transaction. One caveat to this benefit, however, is that the maximum allowable rate that can be earned on the escrow funds is simply that—a maximum rate. Market conditions may be such that a government may only be able to earn an interest rate on the escrow funds that is actually less than the maximum allowable rate.

NOTE: GASBS 7 provides three examples of the calculation of economic gains and losses in a nonauthoritative appendix that are helpful in understanding the components of the calculation. In practice, many governments will rely on underwriters or independent financial advisors to assist them in calculating these amounts. This is particularly true when there are numerous factors that are present in the refunding transaction, such as call dates for the old bonds, variability in coupon rates, etc.

GASBS 7 requires that governments that defease debt through an advance refunding provide a general description of the transaction in the notes to the financial statements in the year of the refunding. At a minimum, the disclosures should include (1) the difference between the cash flows required to service the old debt and the cash flows required to service the new debt and complete the refunding and (2) the economic gain or loss resulting from the transaction.

- When measuring the difference between the two cash flows, additional cash used to complete the refunding paid from resources other than the proceeds of the new debt (for example, for issuance costs or payments to the escrow agent) should be added to the new debt flows. Accrued interest received at the bond issuance date should be excluded from the new debt cash flows. If the new debt is issued in an amount greater than that required for the refunding, only that portion of debt service applicable to the refunding should be considered when determining these cash flows.

- As stated above, economic gain or loss is the difference between the present value of the old debt service requirements and the present value of the new debt service requirements, discounted at the effective interest rate and adjusted for additional cash paid, as described in the preceding paragraph.

The effective interest rate is the rate that when used to discount the debt service requirements on the new debt produces a present value equal to the proceeds of the new debt (including accrued interest), net of any premiums or discounts and any underwriting spread and issuance costs that are not recoverable through escrow earnings. Issuance costs include all costs incurred to issue the bonds, including, but not limited to, insurance costs (net of rebates from the old debt, if any), financing costs (such as rating agency fees), and other related costs (such as printing, legal, administrative, and trustee expenses).

In addition to these primary disclosures, GASBS 7 also provides additional disclosure guidance as follows:

- In all periods following an advance refunding for which debt that is defeased in substance remains outstanding, the amount, if any, of outstanding debt at the end of the reporting period should be disclosed. These disclosures should distinguish between the primary government and its discretely presented component units.
- The disclosures discussed in the preceding paragraphs should distinguish between the primary government's funds and account groups and its discretely presented component units. The reporting entity's financial statements should present the funds and account groups of the primary government (including its blended component units) and provide an overview of the discretely presented component units.

The reporting entity's financial statements should make those discretely presented component unit disclosures essential to the fair presentation of its general-purpose financial statements, fair presentation being a matter of professional judgment. Financial statement preparers should keep in mind that there are circumstances when aggregating disclosure information can be misleading. Reporting entities are not precluded from providing additional or separate disclosures for both the primary government and its discretely presented component units. For example, a significant loss in one fund may be offset by a significant gain in another fund. In this circumstance, additional or separate disclosure by fund should be made.

After implementation of GASBS 34, the accounting for the gain or loss from an advance refunding of debt needs to be considered in the government-wide financial statements. The gain or loss for accounting purposes is basically calculated as the difference between the carrying amount of the old and new debt. Any gain or loss is deferred in the government-wide statements and amortized over the life of the new debt, preferably by the effective interest method of amortization.

BOND, REVENUE, AND TAX ANTICIPATION NOTES

Bond, revenue, and tax anticipation notes are a mechanism for state and local governments to obtain financing in the form of a short-term note that the government intends to pay off with the proceeds of a long-term bond. Bond anticipation notes were discussed in Chapter 8 and are further discussed in the following paragraphs. Revenue and tax anticipation notes are also sources of short-term financing for governments. However, these short-term notes are not anticipated to be repaid from bond proceeds. They are expected to be paid from future collections of tax revenues, often real estate taxes, or other sources of revenue, often federal or state categorical aid. Therefore, these notes should be reported as a fund liability in the fund that receives that proceeds from the notes.

The accounting question for bond anticipation notes is whether the notes should be recorded as a short-term liability in the fund that received the proceeds of the notes (usually the capital projects fund), or whether certain prescribed conditions are met to enable the notes to be treated as a long-term obligation and recorded only in the government-wide financial statements. What distinguishes bond anticipation notes from revenue and tax anticipation notes is that the bond anticipation notes are expected to be paid with the proceeds of a long-term financing. If certain circumstances are met, the bond anticipation notes may be recorded only in the government-wide financial statements, instead of reporting them as a liability in the governmental fund that received their proceeds, most often the capital projects fund.

NOTE: Under GASBS 34, the same considerations are made as to whether the bond anticipation notes are recorded as a fund liability. In the government-wide statements, the liability will always be recorded; however, it must be determined whether the liability is reported as a current or noncurrent liability.

NCGA Interpretation 9 (NCGAI 9), *Certain Fund Classifications and Balance Sheet Accounts*, addresses the question of how bond, revenue, and tax anticipation notes should be reflected in the financial statements of a government, particularly how they should be accounted for by governmental funds. This guidance is particularly relevant for the capital projects fund, because this is the fund that usually receives the proceeds of bonds issued to finance major asset acquisitions or construction.

NCGAI 9 prescribes that if all legal steps have been taken to refinance the bond anticipation notes and the interest is supported by an ability to consummate refinancing the short-term notes on a long-term basis in accordance with the criteria set forth in FASB Statement 6 (SFAS 6), *Classification of Short-Term Obligations Expected to Be Refinanced* (see below), they should be shown as a fund liability, although they would be recorded as a liability on the government-wide statement of net assets. However, if the necessary legal steps and the ability to consummate refinancing criteria have not been met, then the bond anticipation notes should be reported as a fund liability in the fund receiving the proceeds.

The requirements of SFAS 6 referred to above are as follows:

> *The enterprise's intent to refinance the short-term obligation on a long-term basis is supported by an ability to consummate the refinancing demonstrated in either of the following ways:*
>
> a.   *Post-balance-sheet date issuance of long-term obligation or equity securities. After the date of an enterprise's balance sheet, but before that balance sheet is issued, a long-term obligation ... has been issued for the purpose of refinancing the short-term obligation on a long-term basis; or*
>
> b.   *Financing agreement. Before the balance sheet is issued, the enterprise entered into a financing agreement that clearly permits the enterprise to refinance the short-term obligation on a long-term basis on terms that are readily determinable, and all of the following conditions are met:*

   (i)   The agreement does not expire within
         one year (or operating cycle) from the
         date of the enterprise's balance sheet
         and during that period the agreement is
         not cancelable by the lender or the pro-
         spective lender or investor (and obliga-
         tions incurred under the agreement are
         not callable during that period) except
         for the violation of a provision with
         which compliance is objectively deter-
         minable or measurable.
   (ii) No violation of any provision of the fi-
         nancing agreement exists at the balance
         sheet date and no available information
         indicates that a violation has occurred
         thereafter but prior to the issuance of the
         balance sheet, or, if one exists at the
         balance sheet date or has occurred
         thereafter, a waiver has been obtained.
   (iii) The lender or the prospective lender or
         investor with which the enterprise has
         entered into the financing agreement is
         expected to be financially capable of
         honoring the agreement.

For purposes of applying the above provisions of SFAS
6, a "violation of a provision" is a failure to meet a condition
set forth in the agreement or breach or violation of a provision
such as a restrictive covenant, representation, or warranty,
whether or not a grace period is allowed or the lender is required to given notice. In addition, when a financing agreements is cancelable for violation of a provision that can be
evaluated differently by the parties to the agreement (for instance, when compliance with the provision is not objectively
determinable or measurable), it does not comply with the condition of b(ii) above.

*NOTE: To meet the above-described conditions to record short-
term bond anticipation notes as long-term debt, a government has
to either have completed the financing after the balance sheet
date but before the financial statements are issued, or must have a
solid agreement in place to obtain the long-term financing after
the financial statements are issued. This appears to be a fairly
narrow opening to avoid recording the financing as a long-term
liability in the general long-term debt account group. However,
the chance of complying with these conditions may be better than
it appears, because the requirements of the bond anticipation
notes themselves will likely require that concrete agreements to*

*issue the long-term bonds are in place before the lenders provide
the short-term financing through the bond anticipation notes.*

SPECIAL ASSESSMENT DEBT

As described in Chapter 8, the capital projects fund typically accounts for capital projects financed with the proceeds
of special assessment debt. More often than not, special assessment projects are capital in nature and are designed to enhance the utility, accessibility, or aesthetic value of the affected properties. The projects may also provide improvements or additions to a government's capital assets, including
infrastructure. Some of the more common types of capital
special assessments include streets, sidewalks, parking facilities, and curbs and gutters.

The cost of a capital improvement special assessment
project is usually greater than the amount the affected property owners can or are willing to pay in one year. To finance
the project, the affected property owners effectively mortgage
their property by allowing the government to attach a lien on
it so that the they can pay their *pro rata* share of the improvement costs in installments. To actually obtain funds for
the project, the government usually issues long-term debt to
finance the project. Ordinarily, the assessed property owners
pay the assessments in installments, which are timed to be due
based on the debt service requirements of the debt that was issued to fund the projects. The assessed property owners may
also elect to pay for the assessment immediately or at any
time thereafter, but prior to the installment due dates. When
the assessed property owners satisfy their obligations, the
government removes the liens from the respective properties.

GASB Statement 6 (GASBS 6), *Accounting and Reporting for Special Assessments*, defines *special assessment
debt* as those long-term obligations secured by a lien on the
assessed properties, for which the primary source of repayment is the assessments levied against the benefiting properties. Often, however, the government will be obligated in
some manner to provide resources for repayment of special
assessment debt in the event of default by the assessed property owners. It is also not uncommon for a local government
to finance an improvement entirely with the proceeds of a
general obligation debt and to levy special assessments
against the benefiting property owners to provide some of the
resources needed to repay the debt.

The primary source of funds for the repayment of special
assessment debt is the assessments against the benefiting

property owners. The government's role and responsibilities in the debt may vary widely. The government may be directly responsible for paying a portion of the project cost, either as a public benefit or as a property owner benefiting from the improvement. General government resources repay the portion of the debt related to the government's share of the project cost. These costs of capital projects would be expenditures of the capital projects fund. On the other hand, the government may have no liability for special assessment debt issues. Between these two extremes, the government may pledge its full faith and credit as security for the entire special assessment bond issue, including the portion of the bond issue to be paid by assessments against the benefiting property owners. (Further information on determining the extent of a government's responsibility for special assessment debt is provided below.)

If the government is obligated in some manner to assume the payment of related debt service in the event of default by the property owners, all transactions related to capital improvements financed by special assessments should be reported in the same manner, and on the same basis of accounting, as any other capital improvement and financing; that is, transactions of the construction phase of the project should be reported in a capital projects fund (or other appropriate fund), and transactions of the debt service phase should be reported in a debt service fund, if a separate fund is used.

At the time of the levy of a special assessment, special assessments receivable should be recorded in the capital projects fund, offset by the same amount recorded as deferred revenues. The government should consider the collectibility of the special assessment receivables and determine whether the receivables should be offset with a valuation allowance. The deferred revenue amount should then be decreased because revenues are recognized when they become measurable and available.

The extent of a government's liability for debt related to a special assessment capital improvement can vary significantly. The government may be primarily liable for the debt, as in the case of a general obligation bond, or it may have no liability whatsoever for the special assessment debt. Often, however, the government will be obligated in some manner for the special assessment debt because it provides a secondary source of funds for repayment of the special assessment debt in the event of default by the assessed property owners. The determination of whether the government is obligated in some manner for the debt is important because if so, the special assessment debt will be reported in the general long-term debt account group.

GASBS 6 provides guidance as to when a government is obligated in some manner for special assessment debt. A government is obligated in some manner for special assessment debt if (1) the government is legally obligated to assume all or part of the debt in the event of default or (2) the government may take certain actions to assume secondary liability for all or part of the debt, and the government takes, or has given indication that it will take, those actions. Conditions that indicate that a government is obligated in some manner include

1. The government is obligated to honor deficiencies to the extent that lien foreclosure proceeds are insufficient.

2. The government is required to establish a reserve, guarantee, or sinking fund with other resources.

3. The government is required to cover delinquencies with other resources until foreclosure proceeds are received.

4. The government must purchase all properties "sold" for delinquent assessments that were not sold at public auction.

5. The government is authorized to establish a reserve, guarantee, or sinking fund, and it establishes such a fund. If a fund is not established, the considerations in items 7. and 8. below may provide evidence that the government is obligated in some manner.

6. The government may establish a separate fund with other resources for the purpose of purchasing or redeeming special assessment debt, and it establishes such a fund. If a fund is not established, the considerations in items 7. and 8. below may provide evidence that the government is obligated in some manner.

7. The government explicitly indicates by contract, such as bond agreement or offering statement, that in the event of default it may cover deficiencies, although it has no legal obligation to do so.

8. Legal decisions within the state or previous actions by the government related to defaults on other special assessment projects make it probable that the government will assume responsibility for the debt in the event of default.

Given the broad nature of the situations when a government is obligated in some manner for the debt, GASBS 6 concludes that being "obligated in some manner" is intended to include all situations other than those in which (1) the government is prohibited (by constitution, charter, statute, ordinance, or contract) from assuming the debt in the event of default by the property owner or (2) the government is not legally liable for assuming the debt and makes no statement, or gives no indication, that it will, or may, honor the debt in the event of default.

Following are the accounting requirements for debt issued to finance capital projects that will be paid wholly or partly from special assessments against benefited property owners:

- General obligation debt that will be repaid in part from special assessments should be reported like any other general obligation debt.
- Special assessment debt for which the government is obligated in some manner should be reported in the government-wide statement of net assets, except for the portion, if any, that is a direct obligation of an enterprise fund or is expected to be repaid from operating revenues of an enterprise fund. (Note that the enterprise fund portion would also be included in the debt reported on the government-wide statement of net assets.)

  — The portion of the special assessment debt that will be repaid from property owner assessments should be reported as "special assessment debt with government commitment."
  — The portion of special assessment debt that will be repaid from general resources of the government (the public benefit portion, or the amount assessed against government-owned property) should be reported in the general long-term debt account group like other general obligation debt.

- Special assessment debt for which the government is not obligated in any manner should not be displayed in the government's financial statements. However, if the government is liable for a portion of that debt (the public benefit portion, or as a property owner), that portion should be reported in the general long-term debt account group.

GASBS 6 requires that when the government is obligated in some manner for special assessment debt, the notes to the financial statements should include the normal long-term disclosures about the debt. In addition, the government should describe the nature of the government's obligation, including the identification and description of any guarantee, reserve, or sinking fund established to cover defaults by property owners. The notes should also disclose that the amount of delinquent special assessment receivables are not separately displayed on the face of the financial statements.

In addition, the statistical section of the CAFR, if one is prepared, should present a schedule of special assessment billings and collections of those billings for the last ten years if the government is obligated in some manner for the related special assessment debt.

If the government is not obligated in any manner for special assessment debt, the notes to the financial statements should disclose the amount of the debt and the fact that the government is in no way liable for repayment but is only acting as agent for the property owners in collecting assessments, forwarding the collections to bondholders, and initiating foreclosure procedures, where appropriate.

SPECIAL TERMINATION BENEFITS

Special termination benefits typically arise when governments desire to reduce the number of employees on their payrolls or wish to change the composition of their workforce. Various cash and benefit incentives are offered to employees who either resign or retire early from their government service. In many cases, the benefits paid as special termination benefits are paid over a period of several years.

NCGA Interpretation 8, *Certain Pension Matters,* provides that the requirements of SFAS 74, *Accounting for Special Termination Benefits Paid to Employees,* relating to special termination benefits are applicable to state and local governmental employers. SFAS 74 requires an employer that offers short-period special termination benefits to employees to recognize a liability and an expense when the employees accept the offer and the amount of the special termination benefits can be reasonably estimated. The amount recognized should include any lump-sum payments and the present value of any expected future payments. Employers also need to consider the effect of special termination benefits on other employee benefits, such as pension benefits, because of differences between past assumptions and actual experience. If reliably measurable, the effects of any such changes on an employer's previously accrued expenses for those benefits that result directly from the termination of employees should be included in measuring the termination expense.

In applying the above requirements to governmental funds, the basis of accounting and measurement focus of governmental funds must be considered. Because governmental funds primarily emphasize the flow of current financial resources and use the modified accrual basis of accounting, the amount of special termination benefits recorded as expenditures in governments' funds should be the amount accrued during the year that would normally be liquidated with expendable available resources. Accordingly, the amount of the liability for special termination benefits for governmental funds that will not be liquidated with expendable available resources should not be recorded in the governmental fund. The liability for these benefits would always be recorded on the government-wide statement of net assets.

SUMMARY

This chapter summarizes the accounting and reporting for general long-term debt and other obligations. The financial statement preparer needs to consider not only the long-term debt that should be reported in a governmental fund or only in the government-wide financial statements. In addition, the relationship of certain debt-related issues, such as reporting special assessment debt and demand bonds, should be coordinated with the accounting for other governmental funds, particularly the capital projects fund and the debt service fund. The chapter also addresses the considerations that need to be made for accounting for long-term obligations under GASBS 34.

14 NONEXCHANGE TRANSACTIONS

The term *nonexchange transaction* has only recently gained wide use in government accounting and financial reporting, so governmental financial statement preparers may at first think that this chapter will not have broad applicability.

However, once the term is understood, it becomes clear that nonexchange transactions include accounting and financial reporting requirements for a significant part of a governmental entity's typical transactions.

GASB Statement 33, *Accounting and Financial Reporting for Nonexchange Transactions* (GASBS 33), divides all transactions into two categories.

1. Exchange transactions, in which each party to a transaction receives and gives up something of essentially the same value
2. Nonexchange transactions, in which a government gives or receives value without directly receiving or giving something equal in value in the exchange

As will be more fully described below, nonexchange transactions therefore include very significant items of revenues and expenditures for governmental activities, such as taxes (including property, sales, and income taxes) as well as revenues provided by federal and state aid programs.

NOTE: The GASB issued this Statement because there is very little professional guidance in existence for recognizing nonexchange transactions on an accrual basis, which the GASB correctly anticipated was needed when the accrual basis of accounting is used on a government-wide perspective under the new GASBS 34 financial reporting model. In addition, the GASB believed that the existing guidance for nonexchange transactions that are recorded on a modified accrual basis (which will continue at the fund level under the new financial reporting model) could also use some clarification and standardization.

Classes of Nonexchange Transactions

GASBS 33 identifies four classes of nonexchange transactions.

1. Derived tax revenues. These are transactions that result from assessments imposed by governments on exchange transactions. Included in this class are personal and corporate income taxes and sales taxes.

2. Imposed nonexchange revenues. These are transactions that result from assessments by governments on nongovernmental entities (including individuals) other than assessments on exchange transactions. Included in this class are property taxes, fines and penalties, and property forfeitures.

3. Government-mandated nonexchange transactions. These are transactions that occur when one government (including the federal government) at one level provides resources to a government at another level and requires that government to use them for a specific purpose (referred to as purpose restriction). The provider may also require that the resources be used within a specific time (referred to as a time restriction). Included in this class are federal aid programs that state and local governments are mandated to perform and state programs that local governments are mandated to perform. GASBS 33 identifies two significant characteristics of transactions in this class of nonexchange transactions.

    a. A government mandates that a government at another level (the recipient government) must perform or facilitate a particular program in accordance with the providing government's enabling legislation, and provides resources for that purpose.

    b. There is a fulfillment of eligibility requirements (including time requirements) in order for a transaction to occur.

4. Voluntary nonexchange transactions. These are transactions that result from legislative or contractual agreements, other than exchanges, entered into willingly by two or more parties. Included in this class are certain grants and entitlements and donations by nongovernmental entities. While these transactions are not imposed on the provider or the recipient, the fulfillment of purpose restrictions, eligibility requirements, and time requirements may be necessary for a transaction to occur.

Accounting and Financial Reporting Requirements

GASBS 33 has different accounting standards for revenue recognition under the accrual basis of accounting and the modified accrual basis of accounting. Under either basis of accounting, recognition of nonexchange transactions in the financial statements is required unless the transactions are not measurable (reasonably estimable) or are not probable (likely to occur) of collection. Transactions that are not recognizable because they are not measurable should be disclosed.

Accrual-basis requirements. In using the guidance of GASBS 33 for nonexchange transactions that are accounted for under the accrual basis of accounting, it is important to note that these are different standards for time requirements and purpose restrictions in determining whether a transaction has occurred.

- Time requirements—When a nonexchange transaction is government-mandated or voluntary, compliance with time requirements is necessary for the transaction to occur. Time requirements must be met for a provider to record a liability or expense and for a recipient to record a revenue and a receivable. For imposed nonexchange transactions, a government should recognize a receivable when it has an enforceable legal claim to the resources, but should not recognize revenue until the period when the use of the resources is required or first permitted.

- Purpose restrictions govern what a recipient is allowed to do with the resources once it receives them. Recognition of assets, liabilities, revenues, and expenses should not be delayed because of purpose restrictions. An exception arises in a grant or agreement in which the resource provider will not provide resources unless the recipient has incurred allowable expenditures under the grant or agreement. This is an eligibility requirement. In that case, there is no reward (i.e., no asset, liability, revenue, or expense) recognition until the recipient expenses the resources. (This exception relates to what was once referred to as *expenditure-driven revenue*.) Cash or other assets provided in advance should be reported as advances by providers and as deferred revenues by recipients.

In addition to these general requirements for the accrual basis of accounting, GASBS 33 provides specific guidance for each class of nonexchange transaction.

- Derived tax revenues—Assets from derived tax revenues are recognized as revenue in the period when the exchange transaction on which the tax is imposed occurs or when the resources are received, whichever occurs first. Resources received by a government in anticipation of an assessable exchange transaction should be reported as deferred revenue until the period of the exchange.

- Imposed nonexchange revenues—Assets from imposed nonexchange revenue transactions are to be recognized in the period when an enforceable legal claim to the assets arises or when the resources are received, whichever occurs first. For property taxes, this is generally (but not always) the date when the government has a right to place a lien on the property (the lien date).

  Revenues from imposed nonexchange revenue transactions should be recognized in the same period that the assets are recognized, unless the enabling legislation includes time requirements. If so, the government should report the resources as deferred revenues until the time requirements are met. This means that revenues from property taxes would be recognized in the period for which the taxes are levied, even if the lien date or the due date for payment occurs in a different period.

  *NOTE: The GASB issued an amendment to GASBS 33 to address a potential problem in applying this Statement in situations where a government shares its own derived tax revenues or imposed nonexchange transactions with other governments. This amendment, issued in the form of GASB Statement 36, **Recipient Reporting for Certain Shared Nonexchange Revenues—An Amendment of GASBS 33**, is discussed later in this chapter.*

- Government-mandated nonexchange transactions and voluntary nonexchange transactions—GASBS 33 provides that a transaction for these two classes of transactions does not occur (other than the provision of cash in advance) and should not be recognized until all eligibility requirements are met. In other words, the provider has not incurred a liability and the recipient does not have a receivable, and recognition of revenues and expenses for resources received or provided in advance should be deferred.

In April 2000, the GASB issued GASB Statement 36, *Recipient Reporting for Certain Shared Nonexchange Revenues—An Amendment of GASB Statement 33* (GASBS 36), which provides a technical correction of a requirement contained in GASBS 33. There are a number of circumstances in which a government may share its revenues

with another government. Under GASBS 33 as originally issued, a resource-providing government and a recipient government may have recognized these revenues at different
times. GASBS 36 supercedes paragraph 28 of GASBS 33 to
eliminate this potential discrepancy. Both the resource-
providing government and the recipient government should
comply with the requirements of GASBS 33, as amended, for
voluntary or government-mandated nonexchange transactions,
as appropriate. Because some recipient governments receive
these shared revenues through a continuing appropriation,
they may rely on periodic notification by the provider government of the accrual-basis information necessary for compliance. If the resource-providing government does not notify
the recipient government in a timely manner, the recipient
government should use a reasonable estimate of the amount to
be accrued. In this instance before amendment, GASBS 33
would have called upon the recipient government to record
these revenues on a basis of cash collections instead of using
an estimate.

The eligibility requirements are specified by GASBS 33
to comprise one or more of the following:

1. The recipient (and secondary recipients, if applica-
    ble) has the characteristics specified by the pro-
    vider.
2. If specified, the time requirements specified by the
    provider have been met. (That is, the period when
    resources are required to be used or when use is
    first permitted has begun.) If the provider is a non-
    governmental entity and does not specify a period,
    the applicable period is the first in which use is
    permitted. If the provider is a government and does
    not specify a period, the following requirements
    apply:

    a. The applicable period for both the provider
        and recipients is the provider's fiscal year and
        begins on the first day of that year. The entire
        amount of the provider's award should be rec-
        ognized at that time by the recipient as well as
        the provider.
    b. If the provider has a biennial budgetary pro-
        cess, each year of the biennium should be con-
        sidered a separate period, with proportional
        allocation of the total resources provided or to
        be provided for the biennium, unless the pro-
        vider specifies a different allocation.

3. The provider offers resources on a reimbursement basis, the related legislative or contractual requirements stipulate that the provider will reimburse the recipient for allowable expenditures, and the recipient has made allowable expenditures under the applicable program.
4. The provider's offer of resources is contingent on a specified action of the recipient and that action has occurred (applies only to voluntary nonexchange transactions).

Recipients should recognize assets and revenues from government-mandated or voluntary nonexchange transactions when all applicable eligibility requirements are met. If private donations to a government meet the above criteria, including promises to give, they should be recognized in the financial statements of the government.

Modified accrual basis. The preceding discussion describes the proposed transaction recognition criteria using the accrual basis of accounting. GASBS 33 also addresses revenue recognition using the modified accrual basis of accounting. Revenues from nonexchange transactions should be recognized in the accounting period when they become measurable and available. While this is consistent with current practice (except for the elimination of the "due date" criteria under GASBI 5, *Property Tax Revenue Recognition in Governmental Funds*), GASBS 33 provides the following guidance for each of the four classes of nonexchange transactions:

1. Derived tax revenues. Recipients should recognize revenues in the period when the underlying exchange transaction has occurred and the resources are available.
2. Imposed nonexchange revenues—property taxes. The guidance of GASBI 5 should be applied, which is current GAAP.
3. Imposed nonexchange revenues—other than property taxes. Revenues should be recognized in the period when an enforceable legal claim has arisen and the resources are available.
4. Government-mandated nonexchange transactions and voluntary nonexchange transactions. Revenues should be recognized in the period when all applicable eligibility requirements have been met and the resources are available.

Some examples of how some of the more common resources of governments would be recorded follow.

Property Taxes

Property taxes represent a significant source of revenue for many governments, particularly local governments. These governments, therefore, must make sure that they apply governmental accounting principles appropriately in reporting property tax revenues.

Property taxes recorded in a governmental fund should be accounted for as an imposed nonexchange revenue using the modified accrual basis. When a property tax assessment is made, it is to finance the budget of a particular period, meaning that the property taxes are intended to provide funds for the expenditures of that particular budget period. The revenue produced from any property tax assessment should be recognized in the fiscal period for which it is levied, provided that the "available" criterion of the modified accrual basis of accounting is met. (*Available* means that the property taxes are due to the government or past due and receivable within the current period, and are collected within the current period or expected to be collected soon enough thereafter to be used to pay current liabilities.) Property taxes that are due or past due must be collected within sixty days after the period for which they were levied.

NOTE: As a practical matter, some governments find that it is easier to use the two months following year-end for accruing this revenue, rather than a strict interpretation of sixty days. These governments find that their monthly closing process facilitates the recording of these revenue accruals, rather than attempting to cut off one or two days before the actual month end.

If unusual circumstances justify a period of greater than sixty days, the government should disclose the length of the period and the circumstances that justify its use. For example, in unusual circumstances, a government may be able to demonstrate that property taxes received after sixty days would be available to pay current liabilities if the current liabilities will be paid sometime after sixty days after year-end. Thus, there are two criteria that must be met before property tax revenue is to be recognized.

1. The property taxes are levied to finance the expenditures of the budget period reported.
2. The collections of these property taxes must take place no later than sixty days after the end of the reported period.

In 1997, the GASB issued Interpretation 5 (GASBI 5), *Property Tax Revenue Recognition in Governmental Funds.* GASBI 5 eliminated the former criteria that the property taxes must be due or past due within the reported period in order to be recognized. GASBI 5 became effective for financial statements for periods beginning after June 15, 2000, with earlier application encouraged.

In recording property taxes, there is a difference as to when a receivable is recorded for property tax revenue and when the related revenue is recognized. A receivable should be recorded on the balance sheet for property tax receivables (net of estimated uncollectible property taxes receivable) on the date that the property taxes are levied. To the extent that property taxes receivable exceed the amount of revenue that may be recognized under the "available" criterion, the difference should be recorded as deferred revenue. Accordingly, revenue should only be recognized for the amount of the property taxes receivable amount on the balance sheet at the end of the fiscal year for the amounts of the property tax receivable that were collected sixty days after the balance sheet date. The difference between the property tax receivable at the fiscal year-end and the amount recognized as property tax revenue should be recorded as deferred property tax revenue.

In addition, when property taxes are collected in advance of the year for which they are levied, the advance collections should be recorded as deferred revenue. These advance collections should not be recognized as revenue until the period for which they were levied is reached.

Unless they must be used to support a specific program, property taxes are reported as general revenues on the government-wide statement of activities. Converting the property tax revenue recorded in the governmental funds on a modified accrual basis to the accrual basis for purposes of accounting for the government-wide statements is fairly easy. Conceptually, the difference in the revenue between the two bases of accounting is the amount that was deferred as not collected within sixty days under the modified accrual method. The actual effect on the revenue recognized between the two methods would be the difference in the amounts deferred under the modified accrual basis from one year to the next, since the prior year entry would have been reversed.

Income and Sales Taxes, and Other Derived Tax Revenues

Income taxes usually represent a significant source of revenue to governments. Sales taxes are another common form of significant revenue provider that is used by governments to fund operations. In addition, other forms of derived taxes, such as cigarette taxes, provide revenues to many state and local governments. What these taxes have in common is that they are derived from taxes imposed on exchange transactions.

Most of these taxes were previously accounted for using the guidance of GASB Statement 22, *Accounting for Taxpayer-Assessed Tax Revenues in Governmental Funds* (GASBS 22).

GASBS 22 was superseded by GASBS 33. The scope of GASBS 22 focused on "taxpayer assessed" revenues, which were revenues that were the result of taxpayers calculating how much they owed by completing tax returns, remittance forms, etc. Included in this category of revenues were personal income taxes, corporate income taxes, and sales taxes, which also happen to be the same common taxes that GASBS 33 considers derived tax revenues.

On a modified accrual basis, the revenue from these taxes is fairly easy to determine because the availability criteria focus governments' attention on the collections from these taxes shortly after year-end. In practice, many governments have been using a one-month or two-month collection period after year-end (depending on the nature of the tax and how and when tax returns are filed) to determine the amounts that are recorded on the modified accrual basis. On the accrual basis, revenue recognition becomes more complicated in that estimates of what will be ultimately received for taxes imposed on exchange transactions occurring during the governments' fiscal year are required. Since many governments do not have fiscal years that match the calendar year and since many of these taxes are based on calendar-year tax returns, the calculations are further complicated.

Taxpayer-assessed revenues are difficult to measure for a number of reasons. First, the reporting period for these revenues is often a calendar year, and the majority of governments have a fiscal year that is other than the calendar year, and accordingly there are overlapping reporting periods. Second, the tax returns or remittance forms taxpayers use to remit these taxes are usually not due until several months after the calendar year-end and are subject to extension requests. Third, these types of taxes, particularly income taxes, are subject to estimated payment requirements throughout the year, and the final amount of the tax is determined when the tax return form is actually completed. Finally, since the revenues are taxpayer-assessed, it is sometimes difficult for the government to satisfactorily estimate the amount of tax it will ultimately receive based on historical information, because the taxes are generally based on the relative strength of the economy during the calendar year reported by the taxpayer. Historical information does not always have a direct correlation with the current status of the economy.

In some cases taxpayer-assessed revenues are collected by a level of government different from the government that is the actual beneficiary of the tax. For example, a state may be responsible for collecting sales taxes, although portions of the sales taxes collected are actually revenues of counties or cities located within the state. In these cases, the state will remit sales tax collections to the local governments (counties, cities, etc.) periodically. Similar situations exist where states collect personal income taxes imposed by major cities within the state.

The local governments receiving taxes collected by another level of government should apply the same criteria of recognizing these revenues (i.e., when they are measurable and available). If the collecting government remits the local government's portion of the taxes promptly, the local government is likely to recognize revenue in similar amounts to that which they would recognize if they collected the revenues themselves. On the other hand, if the collecting government imposes a significant delay until the time that it remits the portion of the collections due the local government to that local government, consideration must be given to when these revenues actually become available to the local government, given their delay in receiving the revenues from the collecting government.

NOTE: While the measurable criterion can usually be met by effective use of accounting estimates, the available criterion is more direct. For reporting on the modified accrual basis of accounting, some governments choose to use the same sixty-day criterion used for property taxes collected after year-end for determining the amount of these revenues that should be considered available. Before adopting this general rule, the government should ensure that the tax relates back to the fiscal year for which the estimate is being made. For example, sales tax returns are often due monthly following the month of the sale. Assume that a government with a June 30 year-end requires sales tax returns to be filed and taxes remitted by the twentieth day of the month following the date of the sales. In this case, sales taxes remitted with the July 20 sales tax returns would relate to sales in June and would appropriately be accrued back to the fiscal year that ended June 30. However, the sales taxes remitted with the August 20 sales tax returns would relate to sales in July of the new fiscal year and should not be accrued back to the fiscal year that ended on June 30, despite being collected within sixty days of the June 30 year-end.

In addition to accruing revenues for taxpayer-assessed taxes, governments must make the appropriate liability accruals for refunds that they are required to make based on tax returns that are filed. Governments should use actual refunds made after the fiscal year-end, combined with estimates for refunds made using a combination of historical experience and information about the economy of the fiscal year reported. When a government records this liability accrual, it should record the accrual as a reduction of the related tax revenue presented in the general or special revenue fund and as a liability of the fund. The liability should be recorded in the fund through a reduction of the related revenue rather than simply recording a refund liability in the general long-term debt account group. Tax refunds are likely to be a liability to be liquidated with current financial resources, and accordingly, a fund liability rather than a general long-term debt account group liability is recorded. Netting the tax refunds with the related tax revenues also provides a more accurate picture of the amount of tax revenues that should actually have been recorded by the government.

Adjustments for the Accrual Basis of Accounting

In order to report the derived revenues from the taxes described in the previous paragraphs on the accrual basis of accounting and economic resources measurement focus, the government needs to consider the taxes that will be collected after the availability period that is used for reporting these revenues on a modified accrual basis. The government needs to calculate how much revenue it "earns" during its fiscal year from exchange transactions that occurred during that fiscal year from exchange transactions that occurred during that fiscal year.

NOTE: Historically, when governments adopted GASBS 22 related to these taxpayer-assessed revenues, many set up a receivable and recognized revenue for the amounts that were measurable and available and recorded in a governmental fund using the modified accrual basis of accounting. An alternative approach would have been to estimate the ultimate amounts that were receivable (similar to the above calculation) and then record the total receivable, with revenue recognized for the amount of the receivable that was available and deferred revenue recorded for the difference between the total receivable and the amount recognized as revenue because it was available.

In adopting GASBS 34, governments that only recorded the amount of the receivable as equal to the amount of revenue recognized should consider changing to the alternative of recording the total receivable. In addition to being a more correct way of recording these amounts, recording the total receivable along with deferred revenue at the fund level makes conversion and reconciliation of the fund amounts with the government-wide amounts much easier. All the governments would need to do each year for the government-wide statements is reverse the amount of deferred revenue and recognizing revenue for this amount in the government-wide statements. Note that since a deferred revenue amount is also recorded in the prior year (and is the deferred revenue opening balance), the actual effect on revenue of adjusting to the accrual basis of accounting in the government-wide statements will be the change in the deferred revenue amounts from one year to the next. What makes this approach attractive is that the amount of the receivable for these derived revenues will be the same on the fund and government-wide financial statements. In addition, the reconciliation of the fund financial statements amounts to the government-wide amounts can be attributed to either the existence of the deferred revenue amount (on the statement of net assets) and the changes in the deferred revenue amount (on the statement of activities). In other words, these revenues would work essentially the same way that the property tax revenues described in the previous section are recorded.

Grants and Other Financial Assistance

State and local governments typically receive a variety of grants and other financial assistance. At the state level, this financial assistance may be primarily federal financial assistance. At the local government level, the financial assistance may be federal, state, or other intermediate level of local government. Financial assistance generally is legally structured as a grant, contract, or cooperative agreement. The financial assistance might take the form of entitlements, shared revenues, pass-through grants, food stamps, and on-behalf payments for fringe benefits and salary.

What financial assistance should be recorded? Governments often receive grants and other financial assistance that they are to transfer to or spend on behalf of a secondary recipient of the financial assistance. These agreements are known as *pass-through grants*. All cash pass-through grants should be reported in the financial statements of the primary recipient government and should be recorded as revenues and expenditures of that government.

There may be some infrequent cases when a recipient government acts only as a cash conduit for financial assistance. Guidance on identifying these cases is provided by GASB Statement 24 (GASBS 24), *Accounting and Financial Reporting for Certain Grants and Other Financial Assistance*. In these cases, the receipt and disbursement of the financial assistance should be reported as transactions of an agency fund. A recipient government serves as a cash conduit if it merely transmits grantor-supplied money without having administrative or direct financial involvement in the program. Some examples of a recipient government that would be considered to have administrative involvement in a program are provided by GASBS 24, as follows:

- The government monitors secondary recipients for compliance with program-specific requirements.
- The government determines eligibility of secondary recipients or projects, even if grantor-supplied criteria are used.
- The government has the ability to exercise discretion in how the funds are allocated.

A recipient government has direct financial involvement if, as an example, it finances some direct program costs because of grantor-imposed matching requirements or is liable for disallowed costs.

Revenue recognition of grants and other financial assistance. Grants, entitlements, or shared revenues recorded in the general and special revenue funds should be recognized as revenue in the accounting period in which they become susceptible to accrual (they are measurable and available). In applying these criteria, the financial statement preparer must consider the legal and contractual requirements of the particular financial assistance being considered.

Financial assistance in the form of shared revenues and entitlements is often restricted by law or contract more in form than in substance. Only a failure on the part of the recipient to comply with prescribed regulations would cause a forfeiture of the resources. Such resources should be recorded as revenue at the time of receipt, or earlier if the susceptibility to accrual criteria are satisfied. If entitlements and shared revenues are collected in advance of the period that they are intended to finance, they should be recorded as deferred revenue.

Grants are nonexchange transactions that would be classified as either government-mandated or voluntary nonexchange transactions. The accounting for both of these transactions is similar and is described earlier in this chapter. Many of the government-mandated grants that are received by governments are expenditure driven. These are covered later in this section. In many of the remaining grants, the key accounting component is when eligibility requirements are met, which determine when it is appropriate for the recipient government to recognize the grant as revenue. If the actual cash is received before the eligibility requirements have been met, the cash should be recorded as a deferred revenue until the eligibility requirements are met. On the other hand, if the eligibility requirements have been met and the cash has not yet been received by the recipient government, the recipient government would record a receivable and revenue for the grant revenue that it is owed. For recording this amount in a governmental fund on the modified accrual basis of accounting, the availability criteria should be examined to see if the revenue should be recognized or recorded as deferred revenue. In practice, grant revenue is usually received within a time frame where the availability criteria are met (this is also discussed later, in the expenditure-driven revenue section).

One of the more important eligibility requirements is the time requirement, where the time period in which a grant is to be spent is specified. For example, if a state government provides formula-based education aid to a local government or a school district and specifies that the aid is for the school year that begins in September and ends in June, that is the period of time for which the grant revenue would be recognized. Few, if any, differences between the modified accrual basis of accounting on the fund level and the accrual basis of accounting at the government-wide level should arise. However, if no time period is specified (and all other eligibility requirements are met) the total amount of the grant would be recognized as revenue immediately.

Expenditure-driven grants and other financial assistance revenue. Many grants and other financial aid programs are on a cost-reimbursement basis, whereby the recipient government "earns" the grant revenue when it actually makes the expenditures called for under the grant. This type of arrangement is described as "expenditure-driven" revenue, since the amount of revenue that should be recognized is directly related to the amount of expenditures incurred for allowable purposes under the grant or other contractual agreement. (Of course, the amount of revenue recognized under a grant or contract should not exceed the total allowable revenue for the period being reported, regardless of the amount of expenditures.) Updating the terminology for GASBS 33, making the expenditure is simply an eligibility requirement. To be eligible for the grant revenue, you must make the expenditure. The accounting for most expenditure-driven grants is likely to remain the same under GASBS 33 as it was prior to adoption of GASBS 33.

In accounting for expenditure-driven revenue, governments typically make the expenditures first and then claim reimbursement from the grantor or other aid provider. In this case, a receivable should be established, provided that the criteria for recording revenue under the modified accrual basis of accounting are satisfied. For expenditure-driven revenues, determining whether the "available" criterion is met is difficult for some grants and other sources of aid. First, there will be a time lag from when the government actually makes the expenditures under the grant, accumulates the expenditure information to conform with some predetermined billing period, and submits the claim for reimbursement to the grantor or other aid provider. Sometimes the grantors and other aid providers delay disbursing payments to the recipient organizations while they review the reimbursement claims submitted by the recipient organization. In some cases, the aid providers even perform some limited types of audit procedures on claims for reimbursement. Often, the actual receipt of cash for expenditure-driven revenues exceeds the period normally considered "available" to pay current obligations. Governments, however, do record the receivable from the grantor or other aid provider and the related grant revenue, despite it being unclear as to whether the "available" criterion will be met. The reason for not requiring that the available criteria be met is that the government has already recognized the expenditures for these grants and other aid programs. Without recognizing the related grant revenue, the governmental fund's operating statements will indicate that there was a use of resources for these grants and other programs, when in fact, these programs are designed to break even and result in no drain of financial resources on the government. As additional guidance, the 2001 GAAFR indicates that in practice, it is uncommon for the recognition of revenue related to reimbursement grants to be deferred based on the availability criterion of modified accrual accounting. Nevertheless, deferral ought to be considered in situations where reimbursement is not expected within a reasonable period. Financial statement preparers and auditors should consider this guidance on current practice in accounting for expenditure-driven revenue.

NCGA Statement 2 provides that when expenditure is the prime factor for determining eligibility for reimbursement, revenue should be recognized when the expenditure is made.

Effective Date

The requirements of GASBS 33 are effective for financial statements for periods beginning after June 15, 2000, with earlier application encouraged. In the first period that GASBS 33 is applied, accounting changes made to comply with the Statement should be treated as an adjustment of prior periods. Financial statements for the periods affected should be restated. If restatement of prior period financial statements is not practical, the cumulative effect of applying GASBS 33 should be reported as a restatement of beginning net assets (or equity or fund balance, as appropriate) for the earliest period restated.

NOTE: The provisions of GASBS 33 for accrual-basis revenue recognition cannot become effective for governmental activities until the provisions of GASBS 34 are adopted. Until GASBS 34 is adopted, the provisions of GASBS 33 that relate to the modified accrual basis of accounting would be used by governmental funds and expendable trust funds. The provisions of GASBS 33 that relate to the accrual basis of accounting would be used by proprietary funds, nonexpendable trust funds, pension trust funds, and investment trust funds.

15 CASH AND INVESTMENTS— VALUATION AND DISCLOSURES

INTRODUCTION

This chapter describes the accounting and financial reporting guidance for cash and investments held by governmental entities. Two significant GASB statements affect the accounting and financial reporting requirements for cash and investments.

- GASB Statement 3 (GASBS 3), *Deposits with Financial Institutions, Investments (Including Repurchase Agreements), and Reverse Repurchase Agreements*, focuses on disclosure requirements. Prior to its issuance, there were several instances where unwary governments suffered significant losses on a type of investment known as a *repurchase agreement*. GASBS 3 provided a good deal of background material on basic types of investments in an attempt to educate those responsible for the treasury and accounting functions of governments to attempt to minimize future losses resulting from governments not understanding the risks of the various types of investments in which they were participating. GASBS 3's disclosure requirements center on categorizing both cash deposits and investments in a way that would enable the financial statement reader to discern the types of risks inherent in the cash deposit balances and the investments of the government.
- GASB Statement 31 (GASBS 31), *Accounting and Financial Reporting for Certain Investments and for External Investment Pools*, was issued by the GASB to provide accounting guidance (really measurement guidance) for "certain" investments that are likely to comprise the majority of a government's investment holdings. Essentially, GASBS 31 requires many of the investments included within its scope to be measured and reported in the financial statements at fair value.

Each of these GASB statements was the subject of implementation guides issued by the GASB staff.

> — *Guide to Implementation of GASB Statement 3 on Deposits with Financial Institutions, Investments (Including Repurchase Agreements), and*

Reverse Repurchase Agreements: Questions and Answers (Implementation Guide 3)

— *Guide to Implementation of GASB Statement 31 on Accounting and Financial Reporting for Certain Investments and for External Investment Pools: Questions and Answers* (Implementation Guide 31)

Thus, with the issuance of GASBS 31 in March 1997, the GASB provided almost all of the basic accounting guidance that governmental financial statement preparers and auditors need to account for and report cash and investments. GASBS 31 provides guidance on the measurement and valuation of investments in the financial statements. GASBS 3 provides disclosure requirements for both cash and investments. (This assumes the obvious: that valuation guidance is not needed for cash.)

VALUATION OF INVESTMENTS

Prior to the issuance of GASBS 31, the authoritative literature related to the valuation of investments was found in the AICPA Audit and Accounting Guide (the AICPA Guide) *Audits of State and Local Governmental Units.* The AICPA Guide provided that governmental fund investments are generally reported at cost unless there are decreases in market value and the decline is not due to a temporary condition. This general requirement was sometimes difficult to apply in practice because many times it was difficult to determine whether the decline in the market value of the investment was temporary. In many cases, this decision was based on the government's intent and ability to hold securities until maturity. When securities were written down because of a decline in market value that was judged to be other then temporary, sometimes the market value of the security did recover. In this case, there was no basis in the professional accounting literature to write the investments back up to their previously recorded amounts.

The GASB issued GASBS 31 to address these concerns for most, but not all, of a government's investments. GASBS 31 takes into consideration movement of the Financial Accounting Standards Board toward the valuation of investments at fair value. For example, FASB Statement 115 (SFAS 115), *Accounting for Certain Investments in Debt and Equity Securities,* and FASB Statement 124 (SFAS 124), *Accounting for Certain Investments Held by Not-for-Profit Organizations* both result in investments generally being reported at fair value.

GASBS 31 establishes accounting and financial reporting standards for all investments held by governmental external investment pools. These standards for external investment pools will be discussed later in this chapter. For governmental entities other than external investment pools, defined benefit pension plans, and Internal Revenue Code Section 457 deferred compensation plans, GASBS 31 establishes accounting and financial reporting standards for investments in

- Interest-earning investment contracts (such as certificates of deposit with financial institutions, repurchase agreements, and guaranteed and bank investment contracts)
- External investment pools
- Open-end mutual funds
- Debt securities
- Equity securities (including unit investment trusts and closed-end mutual funds), option contracts, stock warrants, and stock rights that have readily determinable market values

The requirements of GASBS 31 for equity securities (which are described in the following bullet point of this section) apply only to equity securities with readily determinable fair values. The reader should not confuse this requirement with that of GASBS 31 for debt securities, which requires that all debt securities be reported at fair value, without consideration for whether their fair value is readily determinable.

One practical implementation problem for a financial statement preparer is how to determine fair value, when fair value is not readily determinable. Fair value for a debt security would not be readily determinable when the debt security is thinly traded or quoted market prices are not available. The GASB staff in Implementation Guide 31, question number 33, note that in these situations, the security's value should be estimated, which will require a degree of professional judgment on the part of the financial statement preparer.

The first consideration for estimating fair value is to consider the market prices for similar securities. This would take into consideration a particular debt security's coupon interest rate and credit rating of the issuer. Another common valuation technique for debt securities is determining fair value by the present value of expected future cash flows using a discount rate commensurate with the level of risk inherent in the debt security.

As the complexity of the features embodied in debt securities increases, valuation techniques may need to be expanded to consider matrix pricing estimates and options pricing models to consider these added complexities.

A technique referred to by Implementation Guide 31 as "fundamental analysis" may also be considered. This technique takes into consideration the assets, liabilities, operating statement performance, management, and economic environment of the entity that issued the debt security. These factors are then considered to determine the fair value of the security.

Implementation Guide 31 also advises financial statement preparers and auditors to exercise caution in accepting an estimate of fair value of a security from the issuer or broker of that security. An attempt should be made to confirm these fair value estimates with independent sources.

- An *equity security* is any security that represents an ownership interest in an entity, including common, preferred, or other capital stock; unit investment trusts; and closed-end mutual funds. The term *equity security* does not include convertible debt or preferred stock that either are required to be redeemed by the issuing entity or are redeemable at the option of the investor.

The following special types of securities are included in the scope of GASBS 31:

- Option contracts, which are contracts giving the buyer (owner) the right, but not the obligation, to purchase from (call option) or sell to (put option) the seller (or writer) of the contract a fixed number of items (such as shares of equity securities) at a fixed or determinable price on a given date or at any time on or before a given date.
- Stock warrants, which are certificates entitling the holder to acquire shares of stock at a certain price within a stated period. Stock warrants are often made part of the issuance of bonds or preferred or common stock.
- Stock rights, which are rights given to existing stockholders to purchase newly issued shares in proportion to their holdings on a specific date.

One other important definition contained in GASBS 31 is *fair value*, which has replaced the term *market value* in recent accounting pronouncements concerning investments. The reason for the new term is to indicate that an investment's fair value may be determined even if there is no actual, well-defined market (such as a stock exchange) for the investment. Fair value then represents "The amount at which a financial instrument could be exchanged in a current transaction between willing parties, other than in a forced or liquidation sale."

In determining whether equity and certain other securities are valued in the financial statements at fair value, there is an additional criterion that must be met. The fair value must be readily determinable. The fair value of equity securities, option contracts, stock warrants, and stock rights is readily determinable if sales prices or bid-and-asked quotations are currently available on a securities exchange registered with the US Securities and Exchange Commission (SEC) or in the over-the-counter market, provided that those prices and quotations for the over-the-counter market are publicly reported by the National Association of Securities Dealers Automated Quotations systems or by the National Quotation Bureau.

The fair value of equity securities, option contracts, stock warrants, and stock rights traded only in a foreign market is readily determinable if that foreign market is of a breadth and scope comparable to one of the US markets referred to in the preceding paragraph.

Specific Application of the Requirements of GASBS 31

Except as discussed in the following paragraphs, GASBS 31 requires that governmental entities, including governmental external investment pools, report investments at fair value in the balance sheet or statement of financial position. Fair value is the amount at which an investment could be exchanged in a current transaction between willing parties, other than in a forced liquidation or sale.

Generally, if a quoted market price is available for an investment, the fair value is calculated by multiplying the market price per share (or other trading unit) by the number of shares (or trading units) owned by the governmental entity. If an entity has purchased put option contracts or written call option contracts on securities, and it has those same securities among its investments, it should consider those contracts in determining the fair value of those securities to the extent that it does not report those contracts at fair value.

There are several exceptions to the general rule of reporting investments within the scope of GASBS 31 at fair value. These exceptions are described in the following paragraphs.

Interest-earning investment contracts. Valuation of investments in interest-earning investment contracts depends on whether the contracts held by the government are participating contracts or nonparticipating contracts.

- *Participating contracts* are investments whose value is affected by market changes that are tied to interest rate changes. If these contracts are negotiable or transferable, or if their redemption value considers market rates, they should be considered participating. Investments in participating contracts should generally be valued in the financial statements at fair value.
- *Nonparticipating contracts* are those such as nonnegotiable certificates of deposit, where the redemption terms do not consider market rates. Nonparticipating interest-earning investment contracts should be reported in the financial statements using a cost-based measure, provided that the fair value of those contracts is not significantly affected by the impairment of the credit standing of the issuer or other factors.

Money market investments. Money market investments generally should be reported in the financial statements at fair value. Money market investments that have a remaining maturity at the time of purchase of one year or less may be reported at amortized cost, provided that the fair value of the investment is not significantly affected by the impairment of the credit standing of the issuer or by other factors. This exception is similar to that described above for participating interest-earning investment contracts.

External investment pools. For investments in external investment pools that are not registered with the SEC, regardless of sponsorship by a governmental entity (such as bank short-term investment funds, which are nongovernmental pools not required to be registered with the SEC), fair value should be determined by the fair value per share of the pool's underlying portfolio, unless it is a 2a7-like pool, discussed below. Legally binding guarantees provided or obtained by the pool sponsor to support share value should be considered in determining the fair value of the participants' investments and should be evaluated in light of the creditworthiness of the sponsor. If a governmental entity cannot obtain information from a pool sponsor to allow it to determine the fair value of its investment, it should estimate the fair value of that investment and make the disclosures discussed later in this chapter.

A *2a7-like pool* is an external investment pool that is not registered with the SEC as an investment company, but has a policy that it operates in a manner consistent with the SEC's Rule 2a7 of the Investment Company Act of 1940. Rule 2a7 allows SEC-registered mutual funds to use amortized cost rather than market value to report net assets to compute share prices, if certain conditions are met. Those conditions include restrictions on the types of investments held, restrictions on the term-to-maturity of individual investments and the dollar-weighted average of the portfolio, requirements for portfolio diversification, requirements for divestiture considerations in the event of security downgrades and defaults, and required actions if the market value of the portfolio deviates from amortized cost by a specified amount. Investments positions in 2a7-like pools should be determined by the pool's share price.

FINANCIAL REPORTING REQUIREMENTS

All investment income, including changes in the fair value of investments, should be recognized as revenue in the operating statement (or other statement of activities). When identified separately as an element of investment income, the change in the fair value of investments should be captioned "net increase (decrease) in the fair value of investments." Consistent with reporting investments at fair value, interest income should be reported at the stated interest rate, and any premiums or discounts on debt securities should not be amortized.

NOTE: This was probably the most controversial aspect of GASBS 31 because changes in the fair value of investments are flowed through the operating statements. There were some conceptual differences with the GASB by some financial statement preparers as to whether this was appropriate in the governmental environment.

GASBS 31 specifies that realized gains and losses on sales of investments should not be displayed separately from the net increase or decrease in the fair value of investments in the financial statements. However, realized gains and losses may be separately displayed in the separate reports of governmental external investment pools, discussed later in this chapter. Realized gains and losses may also be displayed in the financial statements of investment pools that are reported as investment trust funds of a reporting entity.

Internal Investment Pools

Internal investment pools are arrangements that commingle or pool the moneys of one or more fund or component unit of the reporting entity. Investment pools that include participation by legally separate entities that are not part of the same reporting entity as the pool sponsor are not internal investment pools, but rather are considered to be external investment pools.

The equity position of each fund or component unit in an internal investment pool should be reported as an asset in those funds and component units.

Assignments of Interest

The asset reported should be an investment or a cash equivalent, not a receivable from another fund. In some cases, the income from investments associated with one fund is assigned to another fund because of legal or contractual provisions. In that situation, GASBS 31 specifies that the accounting treatment should be based on the specific language of the legal or contractual provisions. That is, if the legal and contractual provisions require a transfer of the investment income to another fund, the income should be reported in the fund that is associated with the assets, with an operating transfer to the recipient fund. However, if the legal or contractual provisions require that the investment income be that of another fund, no transfer of resources should be reported. Instead, the amount should be recognized in the recipient fund.

If the investment income is assigned to another fund for other than legal or contractual reasons, the income should be recognized in the fund that reports the investments. The transfer of that income to the recipient fund should be reported as an operating transfer.

The above provisions do not apply to public colleges and universities that elect to follow the American Institute of Certified Public Accountants (AICPA) College Guide model (as permitted by GASB Statement 15 [GASBS 15], *Governmental College and University Accounting and Financial Reporting Models*). These entities should follow the provisions of the AICPA College Guide model for assigning income, including changes in the fair value of investments to funds. Similarly, state and local governmental entities that apply the provisions of GASB Statement 29 (GASBS 29), *The Use of Not-for-Profit Accounting and Financial Reporting Principles by Governmental Entities*, and elect to follow the AICPA Not-for-Profit model should follow the provisions of that pronouncement.

Accounting and Financial Reporting Standards for External Investment Pools and Individual Investment Accounts

In addition to providing accounting and financial reporting for investments held by governments, GASBS 31 also provides accounting and financial reporting guidelines for external investment pools and individual investment accounts.

Generally, the accounting and financial reporting guidelines presented in the preceding pages related to governments are applicable to all investments held by external investment pools, except that money market investments and participating insurance contracts must be reported by external investment pools at fair value and that 2a7-like pools may report their investments at amortized cost. One other clarification is that external investment pools may report short-term debt investments with remaining maturities of up to ninety days at the date of the financial statements at amortized cost, provided that the fair value of those investments is not significantly affected by the impairment of the credit standing of the issuer or by other factors. For an investment that was originally purchased with a longer maturity, the investment's fair value on the day it becomes a short-term investment should be the basis for purposes of applying amortized cost.

External investment pool financial reporting. Separate stand-alone annual financial reports for governmental external investment pools should include a statement of net assets and a statement of changes in net assets prepared on the economic resources measurement focus and the accrual basis of accounting. GASBS 31 does not require that a statement of cash flows be presented. All applicable GASB pronouncements should be used to prepare these stand-alone reports.

Financial reporting by sponsoring governments. GASBS 31 provides additional financial statement requirements for *sponsoring governments*, defined as governmental entities that provide investment services, whether an investment pool or individual investment accounts, to other entities, and therefore have a fiduciary responsibility for those investments.

A sponsoring government of an external investment pool should report the external portion of each pool as a separate investment trust fund (that is, a fiduciary fund) that reports transactions and balances using the economic resources measurement focus and the accrual basis of accounting.

- The external portion of an external investment pool is the portion of the pool that belongs to legally separate entities that are not part of the sponsoring government's financial reporting entity.
- The internal portion of each external investment pool is the portion of the pool that belongs to the primary government and its component units. The internal portion should be reported in the same manner as the equity in internal investment funds, described earlier in this chapter.

The sponsoring government should present in its financial statements for each investment trust fund a statement of net assets and a statement of changes in net assets. The difference between the external pool assets and liabilities should be captioned "net assets held in trust for pool participants. The accounting for investment trust funds is described in Chapter 11.

Individual Investment Accounts

An individual investment account is an investment service provided by a governmental entity for other legally separate entities that are not part of the same reporting entity. With individual investment accounts, specific investments are required for individual entities, and the income from and changes in the value of those investments affect only the entity for which they were acquired. GASBS 31 requires that governmental entities that provide individual investment accounts to other, legally separate entities that are not part of the same reporting entity report those investments in one or more separate investment trust funds. The disclosure requirements relating to stand-alone reports for external investment pools would not apply to individual investment accounts.

DISCLOSURE REQUIREMENTS— DEPOSITS AND INVESTMENTS

As described in the first part of this chapter, some specific disclosure requirements for investments and external investment pools are a result of the issuance of GASBS 31. However, the main disclosure requirements for investments and deposits were the result of the issuance of GASBS 3. The following section of the chapter describes some of the background material on investments and the various types of risks to which governmental investors are subject, as well as providing the detailed disclosure requirements contained in GASBS 3.

Background

Governmental entities often have cash available for short-, intermediate-, and long-term investment. For example, the general fund may have cash available for a short period until current obligations are paid in the course of normal operations. The capital projects fund may have bond proceeds available for investment for an intermediate term pending their use for a construction project. Fiduciary funds may have funds available that the government is holding in a fiduciary capacity available for long-term investment.

The deposit and investment authority of governmental entities is usually determined by statutes. These statutes may specify

- The types of deposits and investments that may be made
- The financial institutions with which deposits can be made
- The collateral requirements for deposits with financial institutions
- Liquidity requirements

Deposit and investment risk. Depositors and investors face several different types of risks. The two major types of risk are credit risk and market risk.

- *Credit risk* is the risk that another party to a deposit or investment transaction (the counterparty) will not fulfill its obligations.
- *Market risk* is the risk that the market value of an investment, collateral protecting a deposit, or securities underlying a repurchase agreement will decline.

Risks for deposits. The risks for depositors are primarily credit risks. Generally, the risk is that the institution in which the deposits are held will fail, and the deposit balances in excess of the Federal Deposit Insurance Corporation (FDIC) insurance limits will not be recoverable in their entirety. In addition to investigating the creditworthiness of the financial institutions with which it has deposits, a government may also seek to reduce the credit risk associated with its deposits through the use of collateral. There are several measures that depositors may take to ensure that the collateral that they require on uninsured deposits protects those deposits. Governmental depositors may establish (through written contract with the financial institution pledging the collateral) their unconditional right to the collateral. These rights generally include the right to liquidate the collateral in the event of default of the financial institution and the right to additional collateral if the market value of the collateral falls below the required level. Depositors may also reprice the market value of collateral periodically to make sure that it has not fallen below the required level. If a decline occurs, additional collateral is obtained or part of the deposit is recovered.

The degree of credit risk associated with uninsured deposits varies depending on who holds the collateral. If collateral is held by the pledging financial institution, or by its trust department or agent, but not in the name of the depositor, the depositor's access to the collateral and its rights to liquidate the collateral may not be clear in the event of default by the financial institution. There is less risk associated with collateral held by the financial institution's trust department or agent in the depositor's name, and even less risk associated with collateral held by the depositor or by an independent third-party agent of the depositor in the depositor's name.

Risks for investments. Governmental entities employ similar techniques to minimize the credit risk associated with investments as they do for deposits. Ways in which governments safeguard their investments include having the securities held by their custodian or registered in their name, having broker-dealer insurance coverage, and investigating the creditworthiness of issuing and custodial counterparties.

Governmental investors may hold securities themselves or have them held by the broker-dealer, its agent or trust department, or an independent third-party custodian. The degree of credit risk associated with a transaction is affected by who holds the securities and whether the securities are held in the name of the investor.

An investor may safeguard ownership of securities by having the securities registered in the investor's name. If securities are not registered or have been endorsed in blank by the registered owner, they become negotiable by anyone who has them. Having securities in these forms makes transactions easier because they can be bought, sold, or transferred in less time and with less paperwork. However, because they are so easily negotiable, the risks associated with them increase.

Cash and securities held in customer accounts by SEC-registered broker-dealers may be insured by the Securities Investor Protection Corporation (SIPC). In addition, many broker-dealers have insurance in addition to the SIPC coverage.

Required Note Disclosures for Deposits with Financial Institutions and Investments, Including Repurchase Agreements

Disclosures about deposits and investments are designed to help the users of state and local government financial statements assess the risks an entity takes in investing public funds. Governmental entities are required to make disclosures such as

- Legal or contractual provisions for deposits and investments, including repurchase agreements
- Deposits and investments, including repurchase agreements, at the balance sheet date and during the period

The disclosures described below should distinguish between the primary government and its discretely presented component units. The reporting entity's financial statements should present the accounts of the primary government (including its blended component units) and provide an overview of the discretely presented component units. Accordingly, the reporting entity's financial statements should make those discretely presented component unit disclosures that are essential to the fair presentation of the financial reporting entity's basic financial statements.

Investment Disclosures

GASBS 3 requires that the carrying amount and market value of investments including repurchase agreements as of the balance sheet date be disclosed in total and for each type of investment. With the issuance of GASBS 31, the carrying amount and the fair value of many investments will be the same as the carrying amount.

Other Disclosure Requirements—Derivative Financial Instruments

In addition to the disclosure requirements of GASBS 31 and GASBS 3, GASB Technical Bulletin 94-1, *Disclosure About Derivatives and Similar Debt and Investment Transactions*, (GASBTB 94-1) requires specific disclosures for investment transactions involving derivative financial instruments. (GASBTB 94-1 includes within its scope disclosures for derivatives issued along with a government's debt; this section also includes these disclosure requirements.)

Derivatives are generally defined as contracts whose value depends on, or derives from, the value of an underlying asset, reference rate, or index. The Technical Bulletin applies to similar transactions, such as structured financial instruments, such as mortgage backed securities, sometimes referred to as Collateralized Mortgage Obligations, or CMOs.

If derivatives have been used, held, or written during the period being reported upon (regardless of whether the assets or liabilities resulting from these transactions are reported on the balance sheet), the following should be disclosed:

- The nature of the transactions and the reasons for entering into the transactions
- A discussion of the entity's exposure to

  — Credit risk (the exposure to the default of another party to the transactions, such as the counterparty)
  — Market risk (the exposure to changes in the market, such as a change in interest rates or a change in the price or principal value of a security)
  — Legal risk (the exposure to a transaction's being determined to be prohibited by law, regulation, or contract)

The above risk disclosures should be made only to the extent that these risks are above and beyond those risks that are apparent in the financial statements or otherwise disclosed in the notes to the financial statements.

NOTE: For example, if a pension system reported as a pension trust fund invests in CMOs and whose risk is limited to the amount of the CMO, the risks described above may be apparent from the investment that is reported as an investment on the balance sheet and the disclosures ordinarily provided by GASBS 3. In this simplistic case, the risk disclosure requirements of GASBTB 94-1 would be met.

- If an entity is exposed to risk by indirectly using, holding, or writing derivatives, such as through participation in a mutual fund or investment pool that holds derivatives, these risks should be disclosed to the extent that the invormation is available. If the information is not available, that fact should be disclosed.

The government-wide financial statements and entities that use proprietary fund accounting must also consider the disclosure requirements of SFAS 52, *Foreign Currency Translation*, and SFAS 80, *Accounting for Futures Contracts*. In addition, those entities that elect to apply FASB statements and interpretations issued after November 30, 1989, are subject for FASB statements and interpretations that include disclosures about derivatives. These entities will also need to consider the requirements of SFAS 133, *Accounting for Derivative Instruments and Hedging Activities*, which goes beyond disclosures of derivatives and requires that these financial instruments be recorded on the balance sheet. The requirements of SFAS 133 would apply only to derivatives that are currently reported off-balance-sheet and that are not covered by SFAS 52 or SFAS 80. GASBS 31 applies to derivatives reported on-balance sheet and SFAS 52 and SFAS 80 apply to derivatives that are hedges.

SUMMARY

GASBS 31 provides governmental entities with accounting and financial reporting guidance for most of the investments that they hold; these investments generally are carried in the financial statements at fair value. In addition, GASBS 3 provides somewhat extensive disclosure requirements for investments and bank deposits held by governments. Coupled with the requirements of GASBS 28 for securities lending transactions, investments involve intricate accounting and financial reporting requirements that must be adhered to by governmental entities.

16 ACCOUNTING FOR SECURITIES LENDING TRANSACTIONS

INTRODUCTION

Governmental entities, particularly large ones, sometimes enter into transactions in which they loan securities in their investment portfolios to broker-dealers and other entities in return for collateral that the governmental entity agrees to return to the broker-dealer or other borrower when that entity returns the borrowed security to the governmental entity. The GASB issued Statement 28 (GASBS 28), *Accounting and Financial Reporting for Securities Lending Transactions*, in May 1995 to provide accounting and financial reporting requirements for these types of transactions.

This chapter discusses the requirements of GASBS 28 and describes some of the implementation issues encountered by governments that have implemented the statement.

NATURE OF SECURITIES LENDING TRANSACTIONS

Securities lending transactions are defined by GASBS 28 as transactions in which governmental entities transfer their securities to broker-dealers and other entities for collateral—which may be cash, securities, or letters of credit—and simultaneously agree to return the collateral for the same securities in the future. The securities transferred to the broker-dealer or other borrower are referred to as the *underlying securities*.

The governmental lender in a securities lending transaction that accepts cash as collateral to the transactions has the risk of having the transaction bear a cost to it, or it may make a profit on the transaction. For example, assume that the governmental lender of the securities invests the cash received as collateral. If the returns on those investments exceed the agreed-upon rebate paid to the borrower, the securities lending transaction generates income for the government. However, if the investment of the cash collateral does not provide a return exceeding the rebate or if the investment incurs a loss in principal, part of the payment to the borrower would come from the government's resources.

Of course, the situation is different if the collateral for the transaction is not in the form of cash, but instead consists of securities or a letter of credit. In this case, the borrower of the security pays the lender a loan premium or fee in compensation for the securities loan. In some cases, the government may have the ability to pledge or sell the collateral securities before being required to return them to the borrower at the end of the loan.

Governmental entities that lend securities are usually long-term investors with large investment portfolios. Governmental entities that typically use these transactions include pension funds, state investment boards and treasurers, and college and university endowment funds. Governments that enter into securities lending transactions are usually long-term investors; a high rate of portfolio turnover would preclude the loaning of securities because the loan might extend for a period beyond the intended holding period. At the same time, securities lending transactions are generally used by governmental entities that are holders of large investment portfolios. There are several reasons for this, such as the degree of investment sophistication needed to authorize and monitor these types of transactions, as well as the existence of enough "critical mass" of investments available to lend to allow the governmental entity lender to earn enough profit on these transactions to have an acceptable increase in the overall performance on the investment portfolio. In addition, many lending agents are not interested in being involved with securities lending transactions for smaller portfolios.

GASBS 28 applies to all state and local governmental entities that have had securities lending transactions during the period reported. Because securities lending transaction programs are often found in governmental entities with large investment portfolios, they are commonly found in the balance sheets (or statements of plan net assets) for pension plans.

GASBS 28'S EFFECT ON THE BALANCE SHEET

GASBS 28 requires the following basic accounting treatment for securities lending transactions:

- The securities that have been lent (the underlying securities) should continue to be reported in the balance sheet.
- Collateral received by a government as a result of securities lending transactions should be reported as an asset in the balance sheet of the governmental entity if the following collateral is received:
  — Cash is received as collateral.
  — Securities are received as collateral, if the governmental entity has the ability to pledge or sell them without a borrower default.
- Liabilities resulting from these securities lending transactions should also be reported in the balance

sheet of the governmental entity. The governmental entity has a liability to return cash or securities that it received from the securities borrower when the borrower returns the underlying security to the government.

For purposes of determining whether a security received as collateral should be recorded as an asset, governmental lenders are considered to have the ability to pledge or sell collateral securities without a borrower default if the securities lending contract specifically allows it. If the contract does not address whether the lender can pledge or sell the collateral securities without a borrower default, it should be deemed not to have the ability to do so unless it has previously demonstrated that ability or there is some other indication of the ability to pledge or sell the collateral securities.

Securities lending transactions that are collateralized by letters of credit or by securities that the governmental entity does not have the ability to pledge or sell unless the borrower defaults should not be reported as assets and liabilities in the balance sheet. Thus, in these two cases only the underlying security remains recorded in the balance sheet of the lending governmental entity.

NOTE: The obvious result of applying the requirements of GASBS 28 is the "grossing-up" of the governmental entity's balance sheet with an asset for the collateral received and a corresponding liability, which are both in addition to the underlying security, which remains recorded as an asset.

In determining the amount of collateral received by the governmental entity lender, generally the market value of securities received as collateral is slightly higher than the market value of the securities loaned, the difference being referred to as the margin. The margin required by the lending government may be different for different types of securities. For example, the governmental entity might require collateral of 102% of the market value of securities loaned for lending transactions involving domestic securities, and it might require collateral of 105% of the market value of securities loaned for lending transactions involving foreign securities.

GASBS 28'S EFFECT ON THE OPERATING STATEMENT

The above discussion focuses on the accounting and financial reporting requirements of GASBS 28 relative to grossing-up a governmental entity's balance sheet. GASBS 28 has a similar effect on a governmental entity's operating statement—amounts will be grossed-up, but there is no net effect of applying the requirements of the statement.

GASBS 28 requires that the costs of securities lending transactions be reported as expenditures or expenses in the governmental entity's operating statement.   These costs should include

- Borrower rebates (These payments from the lender to the borrower as compensation for the use of the cash collateral provided by the borrower should be reported as interest expenditures or interest expense.)
- Agent fees (These are amounts paid by a lender to its securities lending agent as compensation for managing its securities lending transactions and should be reported along with similar investment management fees.)

In either of the above two cases, these costs of securities lending transactions should not be netted with interest revenue or income from the investment of cash collateral, any other related investments, or loan premiums or fees.

When the above requirements are applied, investment income and expenses are effectively "grossed-up" for the interest earned on the collateral securities received by the lending governmental entity (or on the invested cash received as collateral), and expenditures or expenses are increased for a similar amount representing the amounts that would be paid to the securities borrower in compensation for holding the collateral asset, as well as the investment management expenses relating to securities lending transactions.   Prior to the issuance of GASBS 28, these amounts would typically be netted, with the net income from securities lending transactions reported as part of the investment income of the portfolio.

POOLED SECURITIES

If a government pools money from several funds for investment purposes and the pool, rather than the individual funds, has securities lending transactions, the governmental entity should report the assets and liabilities arising from the securities lending transactions in the balance sheets of the funds that have the risk of loss on the collateral assets.   In many cases, this will involve a *pro rata* allocation to the various funds based on their equity in the pools.

In addition, the income and costs arising from pooled securities lending transactions should be reported in the operating statements of the funds.   If the income from lending pool securities that represent equity owned by one fund becomes the asset of another fund because of legal or contractual provisions, the reporting treatment should be based on the specific language of those provisions. In other words, if the legal or contractual provision requires a transfer of the amounts to another fund, the income and costs should be reported in the fund that owns the equity, with an operating transfer to the recipient fund. However, if the legal or contractual provisions require that the securities lending income be that of another fund, no transfer of resources should be reported. Instead, the amounts should be reported as income and costs in the recipient fund.

If the amounts become the assets of another fund for reasons other than legal or contractual provisions (such as because of a management decision), the income and costs should be recognized in the fund that reports the equity. The transfer of those amounts to the recipient fund should be reported as an operating transfer.

The provisions of GASBS 28 for reporting assets, liabilities, income, and costs from securities lending transactions apply to the financial statements of a governmental reporting entity that sponsors an investment pool in which there are participating entities that are legally separate from the sponsoring government. The reporting requirements of GASBS 28 for assets, liabilities, income and cost do not extend to the legally separate entities that participate in the pool. Thus, these legally separate entities do not need to obtain information form the sponsoring government about securities lending transactions to report in their own financial statements.

DISCLOSURE REQUIREMENTS

GASBS 28 contains a number of disclosure requirements relative to securities lending transactions.

- The governmental entity should disclose in the notes to the financial statements the source of the legal or contractual authorization for the use of securities lending transactions and any significant violations of those provisions that occurred during the period. This is consistent with the requirements under GASBS 3 to disclose the types of investments in which an entity is legally or contractually permitted to invest. Securities lending transactions can be viewed as a significant part of investing activities, and the governmental entity would typically be legally or contractually permitted to enter into these types of transactions.

- Governmental entities should also disclose in the notes to the financial statements a general description of the securities lending transactions that occurred during the period. This disclosure should include the types of securities lent, the types of collateral received, whether the government has the ability to pledge or sell collateral securities without a borrower default, the amount by which the value of the collateral provided is required to exceed the value of the underlying securities, any restrictions on the amount of the loans that can be made, and any loss indemnification provided to the governmental entity by its securities lending agents. The entity also should disclose the carrying amount and market or fair values of the underlying securities at the balance sheet date. (An indemnification is a securities lending agent's guarantee that it will protect the lender from certain losses. A securities lending agent is an entity that arranges the terms and conditions of loans, monitors the market values of the securities lent and the collateral received, and often directs the investment of cash collateral.)

- Governmental entities should also disclose whether the maturities of the investments made with cash collateral generally match the maturities of their securities loans, as well as the extent of such matching at the balance sheet date. This disclosure is intended to give the financial statement reader some information as to whether the governmental entity has subjected itself to risk from changes in interest rates by not matching the maturities of the securities held as collateral with the maturities of the securities lending transactions.

- GASBS 28 also requires disclosures relative to credit risk, if any, related to securities lending transactions. *Credit risk* is defined by GASBS 28 as the aggregate of the lender's exposure to the borrowers of its securities. In other words, if the borrower of the security does not return the security, what exposure does the lending government have? The effective use of collateral is clearly a good mechanism to reduce or eliminate credit risk. A lender has exposure from credit risk if the amount a borrower owes the lender exceeds the amount the lender owes the borrower. The amount the borrower owes the lender includes the fair value of the underlying securities (including accrued interest), unpaid income distributions on the underlying securities, and accrued loan premiums or fees. The amount the lender owes the borrower includes the cash collateral received, the fair value of collateral securities (including accrued interest), the face value of letters of credit, unpaid income distributions on collateral securities, and accrued borrower rebates.

If the governmental entity lender has no credit risk, that fact should be stated in the notes to the financial statements. If there is some amount of credit risk, the net amount due to the borrower should be disclosed in the notes to the financial statements.

Credit risk must be evaluated on a borrower-by-borrower basis and may need to be evaluated by contract with individual borrowers. For example, amounts due to one borrower cannot be offset by amounts due from other borrowers, so in determining the amount of credit risk, the financial statement preparer must ensure that none of these amounts are offset. In addition, the governmental entity lender may not have the right to offset amounts due from one individual borrower from one loan with amounts due to the same borrower on another loan. In determining the amount of credit risk to disclose, the financial statement preparer must also make sure that these due-to and due-from amounts are not offset.

- GASBS 28 requires that governmental entities also disclose the amount of any losses on their securities lending transactions during the period resulting from the default of a borrower or lending agent. Amounts recovered from prior-period losses should also be disclosed if not separately displayed in the operating statement.
- As was more fully described in Chapter 14, GASBS 3 requires that investments included on the balance sheet of a governmental entity as of the end of a reporting period be categorized in terms of custodial credit risk. Because the collateral for securities lending transactions is reported on the balance sheet of the lending governmental entity (when it meets the criteria described earlier in this chapter), the disclosures required by GASBS 3 for collateral included on the balance sheet are required to be made. Accordingly, the carrying amounts and market or fair values of these investments should be disclosed by type of investment as required by GASBS 3, and as more fully described in Chapter 14. GASBS 28 provides the following specific guidance relative to securities lending transactions:

- Collateral that is reported in the balance sheet should be classified by category of custodial credit risk as defined in GASBS 3, unless it has been invested in a securities lending collateral investment pool or another type of investment that is not classified in accordance with GASBS 3. A securities lending collateral investment pool is an agent-managed pool that for investment purposes commingles the cash collateral provided on the securities lending transactions of more than one lender.

- Underlying securities should not be classified by category of custodial credit risk if the collateral for those loans is reported in the balance sheet. The reason for not classifying the underlying securities is that the custodial credit risk related to these securities is effectively reflected in the classification of the custodial credit risk of the collateral. The underlying securities are really not in the custody of the lending government, so custodial risk is transferred effectively to the securities held as collateral.

As described earlier in this chapter, securities received as collateral for securities lending transactions are not always reported as assets on the balance sheet of the lending government. For purposes of complying with the GASBS 3 disclosure requirements, underlying securities should be classified by category of custodial risk if the collateral for those loans is not reported as an asset in the balance sheet of the lending government. The categories in which the underlying securities are classified should be based on the types of collateral and the custodial arrangements for the collateral securities.

SUMMARY

The requirements of GASBS 28 do not apply to the majority of governmental entities because most governmental entities do not have securities lending programs. For those governmental entities that do have these programs, the effect of applying this Statement may have a significant effect on the balance sheet and operating statement by increasing assets, liabilities, revenues, and expenditures/expenses. However, the effect is really a grossing-up of these amounts with no effect on net assets or net results of operations. In addition, the required disclosures of GASBS 28 assist readers of governmental financial statements in understanding and evaluating the use of these transactions by governmental entities in enhancing their investment portfolio performance.

17 COMPENSATED ABSENCES

INTRODUCTION

Governmental entities almost always provide benefits to their employees in the form of *compensated absences*—which is a catch-all phrase for instances where an employee is not at work, but is still paid. Vacation pay and sick leave represent the most common and frequently used forms of compensated absences.

SCOPE OF GASBS 16

GASB Statement 16, *Accounting for Compensated Absences* (GASBS 16) establishes accounting and financial reporting requirements for compensated absences for state and local governmental entities. Compensated absences are absences from work for which employees are still paid, such as vacation, sick leave, and sabbatical leave. GASBS 16's requirements apply regardless of which reporting model or fund type is used by the governmental entity to report its transactions and prepare its financial statements. Therefore, GASBS 16 applies to all state and local governmental entities, including public benefit corporations and authorities, public employee retirement systems, governmental utilities, governmental hospitals and other health care providers, and governmental colleges and universities.

Simply because GASBS 16's requirements generally apply to all governmental entities does not mean that the presentation of the amounts in the various different types of entities' financial statements calculated using its guidance will be the same. The amounts calculated as a liability under GASBS 16 will be the same regardless of the basis of accounting or measurement focus used by the entity or fund to which the liability applies. However, the recording of the liability and recognition of compensation expense or expenditure in preparing fund financial statements will be different based on whether the liability relates to a governmental fund (which uses the modified accrual basis of accounting and the current financial resources measurement focus) or a fund or entity that uses proprietary fund accounting (which uses the full accrual basis of accounting and the economic resources measurement focus). Under the new financial reporting model, the government-wide financial statements will report the liability and compensation expense using the accrual basis of accounting and the economic resources measurement focus.

Additional discussions of these differences will be described later in this chapter.

BASIC PRINCIPLE

The underlying principle for accounting for compensated absences is that a liability for compensated absences that are attributable to services already rendered and are not contingent on a specific event outside the control of the employer and the employee should be accrued as employees earn the rights to the benefits. On the other hand, compensated absences that relate to future services or are contingent on a specific event outside the control of the employer and employee should be accounted for in the period those services are rendered or those events take place.

While this conceptual principle sounds good, to put it into practice the three main types of compensated absences—vacation, sick leave, and sabbatical leave—need to be examined individually to determine when to actually calculate the liability. Guidance is provided later in this chapter as to how to compute the liability, once it is determined that a liability should be recorded.

Vacation Leave (and Other Compensated Absences with Similar Characteristics)

GASBS 16 requires that a liability be accrued for vacation leave and other compensated absences with similar characteristics and should be recorded as the benefits are earned by the employees if both of these conditions are met.

1. The employees' rights to receive compensation are attributable to services already rendered.
2. It is probable that the employer will compensate the employees for the benefits through paid time off or some other means, such as cash payments at termination or retirement.

For purposes of applying these requirements, other compensated absences have characteristics similar to vacation leave if paid time off is not contingent on a specific event outside the control of the employer and the employee. These types of leave include leave whose use is conditional only on length of service, an event that is essentially controllable by the employer or employee, rather than arising from an unforeseen and uncontrollable event such as an illness.

In applying this criterion, three different scenarios will arise.

1. The employee is entitled to the vacation pay, and no other criteria need be met. A liability for this amount should be recorded.

    An employer governmental entity would accrue a liability for vacation leave and other compensated leave with similar characteristics that were earned but not used during the current or prior periods and for which the employees can receive compensation in a future period.

    Some governmental entities provide their employees with military leave. Recording a liability in advance of such leave is not appropriate under GASBS 16 because an employee's right to compensation for military leave is not earned based on past service. Instead, compensation is based on the future military service. In other words, if the employee resigned prior to the start of his or her military leave, he or she would not be entitled to any compensation relating to the future military leave. No military leave was specifically "earned" during the time that the employee was working.

2. The employee has earned time, but the time is not yet available for use or payment because the employee has not yet met certain conditions.

    Benefits that have been earned but that are not yet available for use as paid time off or as some other form of compensation because employees have not met certain conditions (such as a minimum service period for new employees) should be recorded as a liability to the extent that it is probable that the employees will meet the conditions for compensation in the future.

3. The employee has earned vacation benefits, but the benefits are expected to lapse and not result in compensation to the employee.

    Benefits that have been earned but that are expected to lapse and thus not result in compensation to employees should not be accrued as a liability.

Sick Leave (and Other Compensated Absences with Similar Characteristics)

GASBS 16 requires that a liability for sick leave and other compensated absences with similar characteristics should be accrued using one of the following termination approaches:

- The termination payment method
- The vesting method

(For purpose of determining which compensated absences would have similar characteristics to sick leave, financial statement preparers should consider whether the paid time off is contingent on a specific event outside the control of both the employer and the employee. An example of this situation would be jury duty.)

The following are descriptions of the two methods of recording a liability for sick leave.

Termination payment method. A liability should be accrued for sick leave as the benefits are earned by the employees if it is probable that the employer will compensate the employees for the benefits through cash payments conditioned on the employees' termination or retirement (referred to as the *termination payments*).

An additional explanation of termination payments may be necessary to implement this requirement. Termination payments usually are made directly to employees. In some cases, however, a government's sick leave policy may provide for the value of sick leave at termination to be satisfied by payments to a third party on behalf of the employee. For example, some governments allow the value of a sick leave termination payment be used to pay a retiring employee's share of postemployment health care insurance premiums. These amounts, just as cash payments made directly to employees, are termination payments for purposes of applying GASBS 16. However, termination payments do not include sick leave balances for which employees only receive additional service time credited for pension benefit calculation purposes.

In applying the termination payment method, a liability is recorded only to the extent that it is probable that the benefits will result in termination payments, rather than be taken as absences due to illness or other contingencies, such as medical appointments or funerals. The liability that is recorded would be based on an estimate using the governmental entity's historical experience of making termination payments for sick leave, adjusted for the effect of any changes that have taken place in the governmental entity's termination payment policy and other current factors that might be relevant to the calculation.

NOTE: Some governments compensate employees for sick leave at termination based on some reduced payment scheme. For example, the government may have a policy that an employee must have a minimum of ten years of service to be entitled to any ter-

mination payment for sick leave, and the termination payment may be calculated based on some fraction of the total unused sick days that the terminating employee has at the date of termination. For example, a government might have a policy that only employees with a minimum of ten years of service will be compensated for sick leave and that compensation will be equal to the compensation for one-third of the total of the unused sick days that the employee has left on termination.

Vesting method. As an alternative to the termination payment method described above, an employer governmental entity may use the method described as the "vesting" method under GASBS 16. Under the vesting method, a governmental entity should estimate its accrued sick leave liability based on the sick leave accumulated at the balance sheet date by those employees who currently are eligible to receive termination payments, as well as other employees who are expected to become eligible in the future to receive such payments. To calculate the liability, these accumulations should be reduced to the maximum amount allowed as a termination payment. Accruals for those employees who are expected to become eligible in the future should be based on assumptions concerning the probability that individual employees or classes or groups of employees will become eligible to receive termination payments.

Both of these methods should usually produce a similar amount for the liability that a government should record for sick leave and other compensated absences with similar characteristics.

Sabbatical Leave

Determining how or if a liability for sabbatical leave should be calculated and reported based on the nature and terms of the sabbatical leave available to employees. The accounting for sabbatical leave depends on whether the compensation during the sabbatical is for service during the period of the leave itself, or instead for past service.

Some governmental entities permit sabbatical leave from normal duties so that employees can perform research or public service or can obtain additional training to enhance the reputation of or otherwise benefit the employer. In this case, the sabbatical constitutes a change in assigned duties and the salary paid during the leave is considered compensation for service during the period of the leave. The nature of the sabbatical leave is considered to be restricted. In this situation, the sabbatical leave should be accounted for in the period the service is rendered. A liability should not be reported in advance of the sabbatical.

On the other hand, sometimes sabbatical leave is permitted to provide compensated unrestricted time off. In this situation, the salary paid during the leave is compensation for past service. Accordingly, in this situation, a liability should be recorded during the periods the employees earn the right to the leave if it is probable that the employer will compensate the employees for the benefits through paid time off or some other means.

NOTE: In the two extreme cases of sabbatical leave described above, restricted and unrestricted, the determination of whether a liability is recorded seems clear. However, in actual practice, the nature of sabbatical leave may not be as clear as in these two examples. For example, an employee may be given compensated time off to pursue research or other learning experience that is completely at the discretion of the employee. Determination of whether this compensation is related to past service may require the use of considerable judgment on the part of the financial statement preparer. Governmental employers should develop a reasonable policy for whether a liability is recorded and apply this policy consistently among similarly situated employees who are provided with compensated sabbatical leave.

Other Factors Affecting the Liability Calculation

Two other factors need to be considered by the governmental financial statement preparer in calculating liability amounts for compensated absences—the rate of pay that is used to calculate the liability and the additional salary-related costs that should be considered for accrual. These two factors are discussed in the following paragraphs.

GASBS 16 specifies that the liability for compensated absences should be based on the salary rates in effect at the balance sheet date. There is no need to project future salary increases into a calculation that considers that when the vacation or sick leave is actually paid, it is likely to be at a higher rate of pay than that in place at the balance sheet date. On the other hand, if a governmental employer pays employees for compensated absences at other than their pay rates or salary rates (sometimes at a lower amount that is established by contract, regulation, or policy), then the other rate that is in effect at the balance sheet date should be used to calculate the liability.

As for salary-related payments, GASBS 16 specifies that an additional amount should be accrued as a liability for those payments associated with compensated absences. These amounts should be recorded at the rates in effect at the balance sheet date. Salary-related payments subject to accrual are those items for which an employer is liable to make a payment directly and incrementally associated with payments made for compensated absences on termination. These salary-related payments would include the employer's share of social security and Medicare taxes and might also include an employer's contribution to a pension plan. For example, an accrual for the required contribution to a defined contribution or a cost-sharing multiple-employer defined benefit pension plan should be made if the employer is liable for a contribution to the plan based on termination payments made to employees for vacation leave, sick leave, or other compensated absences. An additional accrual should not be made relating to single-employer or agent multiemployer defined benefit plans.

In applying the requirements of the preceding paragraph, the accrual should be made based on the entire liability for each type of compensated absence to which the salary-related payments apply. In other words, payments directly and incrementally associated with the payment of sick leave termination payments should be accrued for the entire sick leave liability. Salary-related payments associated with termination payments of vacation leave should be accrued for the entire vacation leave liability, including leave that might be taken as paid time off, rather than paid as termination payments.

FINANCIAL REPORTING CONSIDERATIONS

The accounting and financial reporting for compensated absences for state and local governments must take into consideration the differences between the governmental fund and the proprietary fund accounting basis and measurement focus with respect to

- Fund long-term liabilities and general long-term liabilities
- Current liabilities and noncurrent liabilities

The accounting and financial reporting differ on whether the liability is recorded in a proprietary fund or a governmental fund. The differences are not in how the amount of the liability is calculated. Both types of funds calculate the liability in the manner described in the preceding sections in this chapter. The difference in the accounting and financial reporting relates to where and how the liability is recorded.

For governmental funds, the long-term portion of the liability for compensated absences is one that is usually only recorded in the government-wide financial statements and not in the governmental fund. Consistent with the modified accrual basis of accounting and the current financial resources measurement focus, the long-term portion of the compensated absence liability will not be liquidated with the expendable available financial resources of the governmental funds to which it relates. The amount of the compensated absences accrued as a liability (with a corresponding expenditure accrual) within a governmental fund at the end of the fiscal year is the amount of the total compensated absence liability that will be paid with expendable available resources. The balance of the liability for compensated absences is recorded in the general long-term debt account group.

NOTE: As a practical matter, many governments report the entire liability for compensated absences that relate to governmental funds only in the government-wide financial statements and report expenditures for compensated absences generally on a pay-as-you-go basis.

For proprietary funds, the accounting and financial reporting for recording the liability for compensated absences more closely resembles that used by commercial enterprises (and the government-wide financial statements). The total applicable compensated absence liability is recorded in the proprietary funds, and the corresponding amount of the liability that must be accrued is recorded as an expense in the proprietary fund.

NOTE: When a government adopts the new financial reporting model, the government-wide financial statements will record compensated absences in a manner similar to that used by proprietary funds. However, the liability that is recorded will need to be reported in two components—the amount estimated to be due in one year and the amount estimated to be due in more than one year. Furthermore, changes in the liability reported on the government-wide statement of net assets (and not the governmental fund) will result in an increase or decrease of expense reported on the government-wide statement of activities. The increase or decrease in expense should be allocated by program/function on the government-wide statement of activities.

SUMMARY

This chapter has presented the basic accounting requirements and guidelines for governments to use in calculating the liability for compensated absences. These general rules should ideally be used to develop a working model for estimating this liability, allowing the governmental entity to meet the requirements of GASBS 16 in a useful and cost-effective manner.

18 EMPLOYER'S ACCOUNTING FOR PENSIONS

INTRODUCTION

This chapter describes the accounting and financial reporting for pensions by state and local governmental entities. Accounting and financial reporting for pensions has been an area for which guidance from the GASB was developed over a very long period. Governmental employers are well known as significant users of pensions as important benefits for their employees. Governments generally pay their employees less than their counterparts in private industry make. However, one factor offsetting these somewhat lower salaries is fairly generous pension benefits that retiring employees enjoy at a relatively young age. Accordingly, the accounting and financial reporting for pension plan costs and financial reporting by governmental pension plans is an important area.

GASBS 27 SCOPE AND APPLICABILITY

GASBS 27 applies to the financial statements of all state and local governmental employers that provide or participate in pension plans, including general-purpose governments, public benefit corporations and authorities, utilities, hospitals and other health care providers, colleges and universities, and public employee retirement systems that are themselves employers.

The requirements of GASBS 27 apply to these entities regardless of whether the employer's financial statements are presented in separately issued, stand-alone statements or are included in the financial reports of another governmental entity. In addition, the requirements of GASBS 27 are applicable regardless of the fund types used to report the employer's pension expenditures or expenses.

The majority of the requirements of GASBS 27 relate to governmental employers that have defined benefit pension plans; however, there is some guidance in the Statement for employers with defined contribution pension plans.

A **defined contribution plan** is defined by GASBS 27 as "a pension plan having terms that specify how contributions to a plan member's account are to be determined, rather than the amount of retirement income the member is to receive." In a defined contribution plan, the amounts that are ultimately received by the plan member as pension benefits depend only on the amount that was contributed to the member's account and the earnings on the investment of those contributions. In addition, in some cases, forfeitures of benefits by other plan members may also be allocated to a member's account. Accordingly, in this type of pension plan there is no guaranteed pension benefit based on an employee's salary, length of service, and so forth.

A **defined benefit pension plan** is defined by GASBS 27 as "A pension having terms that specify the amount of pension benefits to be provided at a future date or after a certain period of time...." In this type of pension plan, it is the amount of the benefit that is specified, rather than the amount of the contributions, which is specified in a defined contribution plan. The defined benefit in this type of plan is usually a function of one or more factors, including age, years of service, and level of compensation.

A defined benefit plan provides retirement income, but it may also provide other types of postemployment benefits. In determining whether these types of benefits are included in the scope of GASBS 27, a governmental financial statement preparer must be careful about two issues: (1) Are the postemployment benefits paid by the pension plan, or are they paid by plans set up by the employer that do not pay pension benefits? (2) Are the postemployment benefits considered postemployment health care benefits? The following paragraphs will help to sort out these questions.

Postemployment benefits are those provided during the period between the termination of employment by the employee and retirement, and the period after retirement (therefore, it is more inclusive than the term *postretirement*, because it may include benefits before a terminated employee's retirement date). Postemployment benefits may typically include disability benefits, death benefits, life insurance, and health care.

If postemployment benefits are paid from an employee benefit plan that does pay pension benefits in addition to the postemployment benefits, then the postemployment benefits are considered to be part of the pension benefits and are included in the scope of GASBS 27, unless the postemployment benefits are postemployment health care benefits. If the postemployment benefits are postemployment health care benefits, they should never be considered pension benefits for purposes of determining whether they fall within the scope of the accounting guidance of GASBS 27.

GASBS 27 REQUIREMENTS FOR DEFINED BENEFIT PENSION PLANS

The GASBS 27 requirements for defined benefit plans can be divided into two basic areas.

1. Measurement of annual pension cost and its recognition by the employer
2. Calculation of the amounts disclosed for the unfunded actuarial liability

The following material addresses these two basic requirements in considerable detail. It is important to keep these two basic objectives in mind, however, not to lose sight of these very basic objectives of GASBS 27 when considering the very technical and detailed nature of its specific requirements.

Measurement of Annual Pension Cost and Its Recognition by the Employer

The first step in measuring and recognizing annual pension cost for a defined benefit pension plan is to determine what type of plan the defined benefit pension plan is. These types are carryovers from the definitions provided under GASBS 5, but are reviewed in the following paragraphs. The two main types of defined benefit pensions are

1. Single-employer or agent multiemployer plans
2. Cost-sharing multiemployer plans

The following paragraphs explain how to determine into which of these two categories an employer's defined benefit pension plan should be classified.

Single-employer or agent multiemployer plans. A single-employer plan is fairly simple to identify. It is a plan that covers the current and former employees, including beneficiaries, of only one employer. An agent multiemployer plan is one in which more than one employer aggregates the individual defined benefit pension plans and pools administrative and investment functions. Each plan for each employer maintains its own identity within the aggregated agent plan.

Cost-sharing multiemployer plans. A cost-sharing multiemployer plan is one pension plan that includes members from more than one employer where there is a pooling or cost-sharing for all of the participating employers. All risks, rewards, and costs, including benefit costs, are shared and are not attributed individually to the employers. A single actuarial valuation covers all plan members regardless of which employer they work for. The same contribution rates apply for each employer, usually a rate proportional to the number of employees or retired members that the employer has in the plan.

Measuring Annual Pension Cost—Single-Employer and Agent Plans

For employers with single-employer or agent multiemployer plans, the annual pension cost should be equal to the annual required contribution (ARC) to the plan for the year, calculated in accordance with the requirements of GASBS 27. The calculation of the ARC is described in the following sections.

CALCULATION OF THE ARC

The basic step in calculating the ARC is to have an actuarial valuation performed for the plan for financial reporting purposes. The valuation is performed by an actuary at a specific point in time and determines pension costs and the actuarial value of various assets and liabilities of the plan.

The actuarial valuation is generally performed as of the beginning of the fiscal year reported. Two other limitations are described in GASBS 27 for the timing of the actuarial valuation.

1.   The ARC reported by an employer for the current year should be based on the results of an actuarial valuation performed as of a date not more than twenty-four months before the beginning of the employer's fiscal year.

2.   A new actuarial valuation should be performed if significant changes have occurred since the previous valuation was performed. These significant changes might be alterations in benefit provisions, the size and/or composition of the population of members covered by the plan, or any other factors that would significantly affect the valuation.

PARAMETERS FOR ACTUARIAL CALCULATIONS, INCLUDING THE ARC

GASBS 27 does not specify a method for performing actuarial calculations, including the calculation of the ARC. In fact, its provisions are quite broad and flexible as to how the ARC is calculated (so flexible that the then-chairman of the GASB dissented from its issuance, citing this flexibility as one of the reasons for his dissension). The flexibility of

GASBS 27 is achieved by the introduction of a concept referred to as the *parameters*. The parameters are a set of requirements for calculating actuarially determined pension information included in financial reports. (This information includes the ARC.)

The ARC and all other actuarially determined pension information included in an employer's financial report should be calculated in accordance with the parameters.

Before looking at the specific parameters, there are two broad concepts that should be covered.

1. The actuarial methods and assumptions applied for financial reporting purposes should be the same methods and assumptions applied by the actuary in determining the plan's funding requirements (unless one of the specific parameters requires the use of a different method or assumption).

2. A defined benefit pension plan and its participating employer should apply the same actuarial methods and assumptions in determining similar or related information included in their respective reports. This same provision (and the same parameters) is included in GASBS 25 for the plan's financial statements.

The specific parameters with which the actuarial calculations must comply are as follows:

- Benefits to be included
- Actuarial assumptions
- Economic assumptions
- Actuarial cost method
- Actuarial value of assets
- Employer's annual required contribution—ARC
- Contribution deficiencies and excess contributions

The following paragraphs describe each of these parameters. Again, while these are fairly technical requirements that may be made more understandable by actuaries, the financial statement preparer should be familiar enough with these requirements to determine whether the actuary has performed his or her calculations in accordance with them.

Benefits to Be Included

The actuarial present value of total projected benefits is the present value (as of the actuarial valuation date) of the cost to finance benefits payable in the future, discounted to reflect the expected effects of the time value of money and the probability of payment. Total projected benefits include all benefits estimated to be payable to plan members (including retirees and beneficiaries, terminated employees entitled to benefits who have not yet received them, and current active members) as a result of their service through the valuation date and their expected future service.

Actuarial Assumptions

Actuarial assumptions are those assumptions that relate to the occurrence of future events affecting pension costs. These include assumptions about mortality, withdrawal, disablement and retirement, changes in compensation and government-provided pension benefits, rates of investment earnings and asset appreciation or depreciation, procedures used to determine the actuarial value of assets, characteristics of future members entering the plan, and any other relevant items considered by the plan's actuary. GASBS 27 requires that actuaries select all actuarial assumptions in accordance with Actuarial Standard of Practice 4, *Measuring Pension Obligations*, which is issued and periodically revised by the Actuarial Standards Board.

Economic Assumptions

Economic assumptions used by the actuary are included with the requirements described above for the actuarial assumption parameter. However, GASBS 27 provides additional guidance in a specific parameter relating to economic assumptions. The two main economic assumptions frequently used in actuarial valuations are the investment return assumption and the projected salary increase assumption.

- The *investment return assumption* (or *discount rate*) is the rate used to adjust a series of future payments to reflect the time value of money. This rate should be based on an estimated long-term investment yield for the plan, with consideration given to the nature and mix of current and expected plan investments and to the basis used to determine the actuarial value of plan assets (discussed further below).
- The projected salary increase assumption is the assumption made by the actuary with respect to future increases in the individual salaries and wages of active plan members; that is, those members who are still active employees. The expected salary increases commonly include amounts for inflation, enhanced productivity, employee merit, and seniority. In other

words, this assumption recognizes that a current employee who will retire in ten years will likely be earning a higher salary at the time of retirement, and this higher salary has an impact on the amount of pension benefits that will be paid to the employee. (Some of these benefits have already been earned by the employee.)

The discount rate and the salary assumption (and any other economic assumptions) should include the same assumption with regard to inflation. For example, consider a plan that invests its assets only in long-term fixed-income securities. In considering an appropriate discount rate, the actuary will consider the various components of the investment return on long-term fixed-income securities, consisting of "real, risk-free" rate of return, which the actuary adjusts for credit and other risks, including market risk tied to inflation. The inflation assumptions that the actuary uses in this calculation should be consistent with the inflation assumption used for determining the projected salary increases.

Actuarial Cost Method

An actuarial cost method is a process that actuaries use to determine the actuarial value of pension plan benefits and to develop an actuarially equivalent allocation of the value to time periods. This is how the actuary determines normal cost (a component of the ARC that is described later) and the actuarial accrued liability (the principal liability for benefits that is disclosed, also described later in this chapter).

GASBS 27 requires use of one of the following actuarial cost methods:

- Entry age
- Frozen entry age
- Attained age
- Frozen attained age
- Projected unit credit
- Aggregate method

GASBS 27 provides a brief description of each of these actuarial methods.

Actuarial Value of Assets

The actuarial value of assets will not necessarily be the same as the value of the assets reported in the plan's financial statements. Governmental pension plans report assets at fair value (which will be more fully covered in Chapter 18's analysis of GASBS 25), which is similar to, but not the same as, the market-related actuarial value for assets prescribed by GASBS 27. As used in conjunction with the actuarial value of assets, a market-related value can be either an actual market value (or estimated market value) or a calculated value that recognizes changes in market value over a period of time, typically three to five years. Actuaries value plan assets using methods and techniques consistent with both the class and the anticipated holding period of assets, the investment return assumption, and other assumptions used in determining the actuarial present value of total projected benefits and current actuarial standards for asset valuation.

The reason that other factors are considered by the actuary in valuing assets for purposes of the actuarial valuations is to smooth out year-to-year changes in the market value of assets. Significant year-to-year changes in the stock and bond markets might otherwise cause significant changes in contribution requirements, pension cost recognition, and liability disclosures. When consideration of the factors described in the preceding paragraph leads the actuary to conclude that such smoothing techniques are appropriate, there is a more consistent calculation of contributions, costs, and liabilities from year to year.

Employer's Annual Required Contribution—ARC

As previously mentioned, the ARC is calculated actuarially in accordance with the parameters. The ARC has two components.

1. Normal cost
2. Amortization of the total unfunded actuarial accrued liability

The following paragraphs describe how actuaries arrive at these two amounts.

Normal cost. The normal cost component of the ARC represents the portion of the actuarial present value of pension plan benefits and expenses allocated to a particular year by the actuarial cost method. The descriptions of the actuarial cost methods provided in the preceding sections each include a determination of how the normal cost component is determined under each method.

Amortization of the total unfunded actuarial accrued liability. The total unfunded actuarial accrued liability is the amount by which the actuarial accrued liability exceeds the actuarial value of the assets of the plan. This value may also be negative, in which case it may be expressed as a negative amount, representing the excess of the actuarial value of assets of the plan over the actuarial accrued liability. This negative amount is also referred to as the "funding excess." The actuarial accrued liability is an amount determined by the actuary as part of the actuarial valuation. It represents the amount of the actuarial present value of pension benefits and expenses that will not be provided for by future normal cost.

GASBS 27 has some very specific requirements as to how the unfunded actuarial accrued liability should be amortized. These requirements are beyond the scope of this Field Guide. However, the amortization period should be between ten and thirty years.

NET PENSION OBLIGATION

The net pension obligation of a governmental employer is a strictly defined term under GASBS 27. To avoid getting lost in the details of its calculation, however, a very general way to view the net pension obligation is the cumulative amount by which an employer has not actually contributed the ARC to the pension plan. Thus, its purpose is to highlight where an employer is not making sufficient contributions into the plan for the plan to pay its pension benefit and expenses. (Conversely, the net pension obligation may be negative because of excessive contributions.) While a net pension obligation does not indicate that the plan will run out of funds in the near future, it does highlight that it is likely that the employer will need to increase its contributions to the plan in the future for the plan to pay its pension benefits and expenses over the long term.

The employer's net pension obligation consists of

- A liability (or asset) at the transition to GASBS 27
- The cumulative difference from the effective date of GASBS 27 between annual pension cost and the employer's contributions, excluding short-term differences and unpaid contributions that have been converted to pension debt

The following paragraphs describe each of these two basic components.

Liability (or Asset) at the Transition to GASBS 27

GASBS 27 adopted an arbitrary look-back period for determining whether a transition liability or asset exists. During this look-back period, the employer should determine whether it made the actuarially determined contributions to each of its pension plans for each of the years in the transition period. In addition, interest on the net pension obligation amounts should be added to the unpaid amounts (in a similar manner as described below for any current-period net pension obligations).

GASBS 27 specifies that when an employer has a net pension obligation, annual interest cost should be equal to the sum of the following:

- The ARC
- One year's interest on the net pension obligation
- An adjustment to the ARC

In computing each of these three amounts, the following should be considered:

- The calculation of the ARC was discussed at length earlier in this chapter.
- The interest on the net pension obligation should be calculated on the balance of net pension obligation at the beginning of the year reported, and should be calculated using the investment return rate used in calculating the ARC.
- An adjustment of the ARC is needed because the calculation of interest is independent of the actuarial calculation, so the ARC should be adjusted to offset the amount of interest, and principal if applicable, already included in the ARC for amortization of past contribution deficiencies or excess contributions by the employer. The amount of the ARC attributable to contribution deficiencies or excesses will not be precisely determinable. The adjustment of the ARC should be equal to the discounted present value of the balance of the net pension obligation at the beginning of the year, calculated using the same amortization method used in determining the ARC for that year. A new calculation should be made each year. The adjustment should be calculated using the same

  — Amortization method (level dollar or level percentage of projected payroll)
  — Actuarial assumptions used in applying the amortization method
  — Amortization period used in determining the ARC for the year

The adjustment should be deducted from the ARC, if the beginning balance of the net pension obligation is positive (that is, if cumulative annual pension cost is greater than cumulative employer contributions) or added to the ARC if the net pension obligation is negative.

NOTE: It is important not to lose sight of the intuitive need for this adjustment by concentrating on the details of the calculation. For example, assume that an employer does not make any contribution to a pension plan for a year, when the actuarial contribution would have been $1 million. Since the plan does not have that $1 million, the unfunded actuarial accrued liability subject to the amortization described above is larger. The actuarial accrued liability is the same, but the plan net assets would be $1 million lower. However, when interest on the net pension obligation is added to the ARC in determining annual pension cost, there is a double counting of the interest cost to the pension plan of not having the assets from the contribution.

Employers with Multiple Plans and Multiple Funds

When an employer has more than one pension plan, all recognition requirements discussed above should be applied separately for each plan.

When an employer makes ARC-related contributions to the same plan from more than one fund, the employer should determine what portion of the ARC applies to each fund. Similarly, when an employer has a net pension obligation and the related liability (asset) is allocated to more than one fund, or a fund and the liability recorded on the government-wide statement of net assets, the employer should allocate the interest and the ARC adjustment components of annual pension cost to each liability (asset), based on its proportionate share of the beginning balance of the net pension obligation.

Cost-Sharing Multiemployer Plans

The preceding part of this chapter describes the accounting and financial reporting requirements for governmental employers that participate in single-employer or agent multiemployer plans. The requirements of GASBS 27 for governmental employers that participate in cost-sharing multiemployer plans are much simpler. These employers should recognize annual pension expenditures or expenses equal to their contractually required contributions to the plan. Recognition should be on the modified accrual or accrual basis, whichever is applicable for the type of employer or for the fund types used to report the employers' contributions. For these types of plans, pension liabilities and assets result from the difference between the contributions required and contributions made. Pension liabilities and assets to different plans should be offset in the financial statements.

NOTE: A useful way to view the relationship of a cost-sharing multiemployer plan and its participating employers is that the plan bills the employers for their annual contributions. The employers' handling of these pension bills is similar to how they handle other types of bills that they pay, which, of course, depends on whether they follow governmental or proprietary fund accounting.

SUMMARY

The overall requirements of GASBS 27 for accounting for pensions by governmental entities provide a good deal of flexibility as to accounting and financial reporting decisions. However, even with this flexibility, there are a number of very specific and detailed requirements that the financial statement preparer must be familiar with to ensure compliance. Obtaining the assistance of an actuary who is well-versed in the requirements of GASBS 27 will make the transition to and continuing compliance with this statement slightly easier.

19 ACCOUNTING FOR POSTRETIREMENT BENEFITS OTHER THAN PENSIONS

INTRODUCTION

Employers, including governmental employers, often offer benefits to their employees that do not start or take effect until after the employee leaves employment. The Financial Accounting Standards Board (FASB) addressed the issue of accounting for the costs of these plans (and the recognition of the extent of the future potential liability for these plans) in Statement of Financial Accounting Standards 106 (SFAS 106), *Employer's Accounting for Postretirement Benefits other than Pensions*. This FASB Statement had a tremendous impact not only on the financial statements of commercial enterprises, but also sometimes on the postretirement benefits actually being offered by these organizations. For example, the recognition of the current costs of these benefits and the recognition the their related liabilities caused some employers to reduce or eliminate the benefits provided under these plans.

Governmental employers have not yet had to deal with accounting and financial reporting requirements as stringent as those of SFAS 106. Governmental employers are generally on the "pay-as-you-go" method, whereby costs are recognized when paid, and no recognition is given to the earned liability for these benefits. However, the GASB currently has a project to develop accounting and reporting standards for postemployment benefits. The final standard that results from this GASB project may well result in governments being required to account for and report the current costs and liabilities of these plans. As an interim measure, the GASB issued Statement 12 (GASBS 12) *Disclosure of Information on Postemployment Benefits other than Pension Benefits by State and Local Government Employers*. This Statement generally includes only disclosure requirements, with no change in accounting for postemployment benefit plans by governments. Accounting issues will be addressed when and if a Statement is issued by the GASB as a result of their current project on postemployment benefit plans.

NOTE: As the GASB has completed its work on the financial reporting model project, readers should be aware that this area was one of the first significant areas to receive the GASB's attention. An Exposure Draft is expected to be issued during the first quarter of 2002.

APPLICABILITY OF GASBS 12 REQUIREMENTS

The requirements of GASBS 12 apply to state and local governmental employers that provide postemployment benefits other than pensions (OPEBs) where the cost of the OPEBs is borne by the employer in whole or part. Included in this group of employers would be public benefit corporations and authorities, public employee retirement systems (PERS), governmental utilities, hospitals and other health care providers, and colleges and universities.

In determining what benefits are "other" than pension benefits, the financial statement preparer needs to understand what the GASB considers to be pension benefits. The term *pension benefits* refers principally to retirement income, but also includes other pension-related benefits (except postemployment health care) when they are provided to plan participants or their beneficiaries through a PERS. Thus, OPEBs would include all postemployment benefits other than pensions not provided by a public employee retirement system, pension plan, or other arrangement, and would also include postemployment health care benefits, even if they are provided by a PERS.

For example, disability income provided by a pension plan would not be considered an OPEB under GASBS 12. If the disability income is provided not through a pension plan but through a separate disability income plan paid for by the employer, then the disability income plan would be considered an OPEB and would be included in the scope of GASBS 12. On the other hand, postemployment health care benefits under a pension plan would be considered an OPEB, regardless of the fact that the pension plan itself provides the benefit, not a separate plan of the employer.

Thus, the disclosure requirements of GASBS 12 apply to the following types of OPEBs:

- All postemployment health care benefits (whether or not provided by a PERS), such as medical, dental, vision, or hearing benefits
- Other postemployment benefits not provided by a PERS
  - Disability income
  - Tuition assistance
  - Legal services
  - Other assistance programs

The above is not an all-inclusive list, but it does cover the major types of postemployment benefits typically found in state and local governmental employers.

The employer's promise to provide OPEBs may take a variety of forms, and an employer may not set aside assets on an actuarially determined basis to pay future benefits as they become due (referred to as *advance funding*). The disclosure requirements of GASBS 12 apply to postemployment benefits regardless of the legal form of the promise, or whether the employer advance-funds the benefits or uses a pay-as-you-go approach.

DISCLOSURE REQUIREMENTS

GASBS 12 requires that employers that provide OPEBs should, at a minimum, disclose the following information. The disclosures may be made separately for one or more types of benefits or as an aggregate for all OPEBs provided.

- A description of the OPEB provided, the employee groups covered, the eligibility requirements to receive the benefits, and the employer and participant obligations to contribute that are quantified in some manner. For example, the approximate percentage of the total obligation to contribute that is borne by the employer and the participants for the benefits might be disclosed. Alternatively, the dollar or percentage contribution rates might be disclosed.
- A description of the statutory, contractual, or other authority under which OPEB provisions and obligations to contribute are established.
- A description of the accounting and financing or funding policies followed by the employer. For example, a statement should be included as to whether the employer's contributions are on a pay-as-you-go basis or are advance-funded on an actuarially determined basis.
- If OPEBs are advance-funded on an actuarially determined basis, the employer should also disclose the following:
  — The actuarial cost method used
  — Significant actuarial assumptions, including the interest rate used and, if applicable, the projected salary increase assumption and the health inflation assumption used to determine the funding requirements
  — The method used to value plan assets

- Depending on whether OPEBs are financed on a pay-as-you-go basis or are advance-funded on an actuarially determined basis, the following additional disclosures are required.

Pay-As-You-Go Basis

- The amount of OPEB expenditures or expenses recognized in the financial statements during the reported period. (The amount disclosed should be net of participant contributions.)
- The number of participants currently eligible to receive benefits. Participants currently eligible to receive benefits are retirees, terminated employees, and beneficiaries for whom the employer is currently responsible for paying all or part of the premiums, contributions, or claims for OPEBs. Covered dependents of participants should be counted as one unit with the participant.
- If the amount of expenditures or expenses for the OPEB cannot readily be separated from expenditures or expenses for similar types of benefits provided to active employees and their dependents, the employer should use reasonable methods to approximate OPEB expenditures or expenses. If a reasonable approximation cannot be made, the employer should state that the OPEB expenditures or expenses cannot be reasonably estimated.
- The pay-as-you-go requirements listed above apply when employers set aside assets for future OPEB payments but do not advance-fund OPEBs on an actuarially determined basis. Employers in this category should disclose the amount of net assets available for future benefit payments.

Advance-Funded on an Actuarially Determined Basis

- The number of active plan participants
- The employer's actuarially required and actual contributions for the reported period. These amounts should be reported net of participant contributions.
- The amount of the net assets available for OPEBs
- The actuarial accrued liability and unfunded actuarial accrued liability for OPEB, according to the actuarial cost method used

NOTE: Ironically, those employers that take a more conservative approach to OPEBs by advance-funding these benefits on an actuarially determined basis are required to disclose the unfunded accrued actuarial liability for OPEBs. On the other hand, those employers that use the less conservative pay-as-you-go funding approach have no obligation to disclose any similarly determined liability amount, although the extent of the liability for pay-as-you-go funding would logically be much higher, since in most cases assets are not being set aside for the benefits.

OTHER DISCLOSURES

In addition to the disclosures listed above, the employer should disclose the following:

- A description (and the dollar effect, if it is measurable) of any significant matters that affect the comparability of the disclosures required by GASBS 12 with those of the previous period. An example of this type of change would be a change in benefit provisions.
- Any additional information that the employer believes will help users assess the nature and magnitude of the cost of the employer's commitment to provide OPEBs.

SUMMARY

GASBS 12 provides some limited disclosure requirements for the OPEBs that are included within its scope. Except for the required disclosures, GASBS 12 specifically states that until the GASB project on OPEBs is completed, state and local governmental employers are not required to change their accounting and financial reporting for OPEBs.

20 RISK FINANCING AND INSURANCE-RELATED ACTIVITIES/PUBLIC ENTITY RISK POOLS

INTRODUCTION

Governmental organizations are subject to many of the same risks of "doing business" as commercial enterprises, including risks related to various torts, property damage awards, personal injury cases, and so forth.

Governments are most often self-insured for these types of risks. Sometimes the government establishes or participates in a *public entity risk pool* that acts somewhat like an insurer against various types of risks.

This chapter is divided into two main sections. The first addresses the accounting and financial reporting guidance for the risk financing and insurance-related activities of state and local governments (other than public entity risk pools). The second section of this chapter addresses the accounting and financial reporting requirements for public entity risk pools.

The primary accounting and financial reporting guidance for both of the sections listed above is found in GASB Statement 10 (GASBS 10), *Accounting and Financial Reporting for Risk Financing and Related Insurance Issues*. This guidance was enhanced by the GASB's *Guide to Implementation of GASB Statement 10*, which provides GASB staff guidance on the application of GASBS 10. Recently, the GASB issued Statement 30 (GASBS 30), *Risk Financing Omnibus*, which was a way of fine-tuning the previously issued guidance to address some of the problems that state and local governmental entities were having in operating under the provisions of GASBS 10. The guidance from all three of these sources is included in this chapter.

RISK FINANCING AND INSURANCE ACTIVITIES OF STATE AND LOCAL GOVERNMENTS (OTHER THAN PUBLIC ENTITY RISK POOLS)

As will be seen in the following discussion, the accounting and financial reporting for risk financing contained in GASBS 10 are quite similar to the accounting requirements of the FASB's Statement of Financial Accounting Standards 5 (SFAS 5), *Accounting for Contingencies*. GASBS 10 includes in its scope the risks of loss from the following kinds of events:

- Torts (wrongful acts, injuries, or damages not involving a breach of contract for which a civil action can be brought)
- Theft or destruction of, or damage to, assets
- Business interruption
- Errors or omissions
- Job-related illnesses or injuries to employees
- Acts of God (events beyond human origin or control, such as natural disasters, lightning, windstorms, and earthquakes)

The accounting and financial reporting requirements discussed in this section also apply to losses resulting when a governmental entity agrees to provide accident and health, dental, and other medical benefits to its employees and retirees and their dependents and beneficiaries, based on covered events that have already occurred. For example, a retiree incurs a doctor bill that will be reimbursed by the government for a doctor's visit occurring prior to the end of the government's fiscal year. However, these requirements do not apply to postemployment benefits that governmental employers expect to provide to current and future retirees, their beneficiaries, and their dependents in accordance with the employer's agreement to provide those future benefits. Also excluded from these requirements are medicaid insurance plans provided to low-income state residents under Title XIX of the Federal Social Security Act.

GASBS 10 provides that when a risk of loss or a portion of the risk of loss from the types of events listed above has not been transferred to an unrelated third party, state and local governmental entities should report an estimated loss from a claim as an expenditure/expense and a liability if both of the following conditions are met:

1. Information available before the financial statements are issued indicates that it is probable that an asset had been impaired or a liability had been incurred at the date of the financial statements. (The date of the financial statements means the end of the most recent accounting period for which financial statements are being presented.) It is implicit in this condition that it must be probable that one or more future events will also occur confirming the fact of the loss.
2. The amount of the loss can be reasonably estimated.

In determining whether the amount of a loss can be reasonably estimated, it is quite possible that the amount of the loss can reasonably be estimated as a range of amounts, rather than as one specific amount. If this is the case, the amount of the loss is still considered to be reasonably estimable. First, determine if some amount within the range appears to be a better estimate than any other amount within the range, and use this amount for the estimate. Second, if no amount within the range is a better estimate than any other amount, the minimum amount of the range should be used as an estimate to be accrued.

When a loss contingency exists, the likelihood that the future event or events will confirm the loss or impairment of an asset or the incurrence of a liability can range from probable to remote. GASBS 10 (like SFAS 5) uses the terms *probable*, *reasonably possible*, and *remote* to identify three areas within that range. The terms are defined as follows:

- *Probable*—the future event or events are likely to occur
- *Reasonably possible*—the chance of the future event or events is more than remote, but less than likely
- *Remote*—the chance of the future event or events occurring is slight

Disclosure of Loss Contingencies

If no accrual is made for a loss contingency because it has not met the conditions of being probable or reasonably estimable, disclosure of the loss contingency should be met if it is at least reasonably possible that a loss may have been incurred. The disclosure should indicate the nature of the contingency and should give either an estimate of the possible loss or range of loss or state that such an estimate cannot be made. Disclosure is not required of a loss contingency involving an unreported claim or assessment if there has been no manifestation of a potential claimant or an awareness of a possible claim or assessment, unless it is considered probable that a claim will be asserted and there is a reasonable possibility that the outcome will be unfavorable.

A disclosure of loss contingency should also be made when an exposure to loss exists in excess of the amount accrued in the financial statements and it is reasonably possible that a loss or additional loss may have been incurred. For example, if a loss is probable and is estimated with a range of amounts and the lower amount of the range is accrued in the financial statements, the reasonably possible amount of the loss in excess of the amount accrued should be disclosed.

A remote loss contingency is not required to be accrued or disclosed in the financial statements.

The following summarizes the expenditure/expense and liability recognition and disclosure requirements under GASBS 10:

Likelihood of Loss Contingency	*Accounting/Disclosure*
Probable and can be reasonably estimated	Recognize expenditure/expense and liability
Probable and cannot be reasonably estimated	Disclosure required/no expenditure/expense and liability recognition
Reasonably possible	Disclosure required/no expenditure/expense and liability recognition
Remote	No disclosure required no expenditure/expense and liability recognition

Incurred-but-not-reported claims. GASBS 10 requires that incurred-but-not-reported claims (IBNR) be evaluated. When a loss can be reasonably estimated and it is possible that a claim will be asserted, the expenditure/expense and liability should be recognized.

IBNR claims are claims for uninsured events that have occurred but have not yet been reported to the governmental entity. IBNR claims include (1) known losses expected to be presented later as claims, (2) unknown loss events expected to become claims, and (3) expected future developments on claims already reported.

Amount of loss accrual. Estimates for claims liabilities, including IBNR, should be based on the estimated ultimate cost of settling the claims, including the effects of inflation and other societal and economic factors, using experience adjusted for current trends and any other factors that would modify experience.

GASBS 10 specifies that claims liabilities should include specific, incremental claim adjustment expenditures/expenses. In other words, incremental costs should include only those costs incurred because of a claim. For example, the cost of outside legal counsel on a particular claim is likely to be treated as an incremental cost. However, assistance from internal legal staff on a claim may be incremental because the salary costs for internal staff normally will be incurred regardless of the claim.

Discounting. The practice of presenting claims liabilities at the discounted present value of estimated future cash payments is neither mandated nor prohibited by GASBS 10. However, claims liabilities associated with structured settlements should be discounted if they represent contractual obligations to pay money on fixed or determinable dates. A structured settlement is a means of satisfying a claim liability and consists of an initial cash payment to meet specific present financial needs combined with a stream of future payments designed to meet future financial needs. For example, a government may enter into a settlement with someone injured by a government vehicle, whereby the government agrees to pay the injured party's hospital claims up front, and then a monthly fixed amount for the remaining life of the injured party. The monthly payment cash flow streams should be discounted when a government recognizes this loss in its financial statements.

Annuity contracts. A governmental entity may purchase an annuity contract in a claimant's name to satisfy a claim liability. If the likelihood that the entity will be required to make future payments on the claim is remote, the governmental entity is considered to have satisfied its primary liability to the claimant. Accordingly, the annuity contract should not be reported as an asset by the governmental entity, and the liability for the claim should be removed from the governmental entity's balance sheet. However, GASBS 10 requires that the aggregate outstanding amount of liabilities that are removed from the governmental entity's balance sheet be disclosed as long as those contingent liabilities are outstanding. On the other hand, if annuity contracts used to settle claims for which the claimant has signed an agreement releasing the governmental entity from further obligation and for which the likelihood that the governmental entity will be required to make future payments on those claims is remote, then the amount of the liability related to these annuity contracts should not be included in this aggregate disclosure. If it is later determined that the primary liability will revert back to the governmental entity, the liability should be reinstated on the balance sheet.

Use of a single fund. GASBS 10 requires that if a single fund is used to account for a governmental entity's risk financing activities, that fund should be either the general fund or an internal service fund. Entities reported as proprietary funds or trust funds and that are component units of a primary government may participate in a risk-financing internal service fund of that primary government. However, other stand-alone entities that are reported as proprietary or trust funds and are not considered to be a part of another financial reporting entity should not use an internal service fund to report their own risk financing activities.

Risk Retention by Entities other than Pools

The following summarizes the accounting and financial reporting considerations that must be made when either the general fund or an internal service fund is used to account for risk retention retained by entities other than pools.

General fund. An entity that uses the general fund to account for its risk financing activities should recognize claims liabilities and expenditures in accordance with the criteria described earlier in this chapter.

Claims liabilities should be reduced by amounts expected to be recovered through excess insurance. Excess insurance is a way to transfer the risk of loss from one party to another when the risk transferred is for amounts that exceed a certain sum. For example, a government may retain the risk of loss for amounts below a relatively high dollar amount, such as $5 million. However, the governmental entity may transfer the risk (that is, buy insurance) for losses in excess of this $5 million amount. Any amounts that are expected to be recovered from this excess amount should be deducted from claim liability recorded in the general fund.

NOTE: Readers should refer to Chapter 13, which discusses recording long-term obligations on the government-wide statement of net assets. There are certain liabilities of governmental funds (which obviously include the general fund) that, when not liquidated with expendable financial resources, are not recorded as liabilities of the fund, but are instead recorded only in the government-wide financial statements. Liabilities for claims and judgments discussed in this chapter are one of these liabilities that, for governmental funds, would only be recorded in the government-wide financial statements and not be recorded as a fund liability when they are not expected to be liquidated with expendable financial resources. Thus, when the general fund is used to account for risk financing activities, the liability recognized in the financial statements may well be reported only in the government-wide financial statements, since most, if not all, of the liability will not be liquidated with expendable financial resources.

One useful way in which governments can determine how much, if any, of the judgments and claims liability should be reported in the general fund itself is to look at those liabilities that have been settled in principle, but not payment, prior to the end of the fiscal year, and accrue these settlements as expenditures and liabilities in the general fund as of the end of the fiscal year, with the remainder of the judgments and claims liability recorded only in the government-wide financial statements.

While the "single" fund for accounting for risk financing activities may be met by accounting for these activities in the general fund, that does not mean that the general fund cannot allocate the costs of claims that are recognized to other funds. GASBS 10 provides that the governmental entity may use any method it chooses to allocate loss expenditures/expenses to other funds of the entity. The allocated amounts should be treated as expenditures in the funds to which they are allocated and as a reduction of the expenditures of the general fund, from which the costs are allocated. (However, if the total amount so allocated exceeds the total expenditures and liabilities, the excess should be treated as operating transfers.)

NOTE: Keep in mind that proprietary funds use the accrual basis of accounting and the economic resources measurement focus. Accordingly, the recording of liabilities related to these funds should follow that for proprietary funds; that is, the expense and the liability should be recorded in the proprietary fund itself, and not in the general long-term debt account group.

Internal service fund. A governmental entity may elect to use an internal service fund to account for its risk financing activities. Claims expenses and liabilities should be recognized using the criteria described in the earlier part of this chapter. As is the case when the general fund is used to account for risk financing activities, claims expenses should be reduced by amounts expected to be recovered through excess insurance. In additions, claims amounts that are probable but not reasonably estimable should be disclosed, in addition to the disclosures of loss that are reasonably possible.

The internal service fund may use any basis considered appropriate to charge other funds of the governmental entity. However, GASBS 10 includes three conditions that must be met in charging these amounts to other funds.

1. The total charge by the internal service fund to the other funds for the period reported is calculated in accordance with the earlier section of this chapter, *or*

2. The total charge by the internal service fund to the other funds is based on an actuarial method or historical cost information adjusted over a reasonable period of time so that internal service fund revenues and expenses are approximately equal. (The actuarial method can be any one of several techniques that actuaries use to determine the amounts and timing of contributions needed to finance claims liabilities so that the total contributions plus compounded earnings on them will equal the amounts needed to satisfy claims liabilities. It may or may not include a provision for anticipated catastrophic losses.)

3. In addition to item 2. above, the total charge by the internal service fund may include a reasonable provision for expected future catastrophic losses.

Charges made by internal service funds in accordance with these provisions should be recognized as revenue by the internal service fund and as expenditures/expenses by the other funds of the governmental entity. Deficits, if any, in the internal service fund resulting from application of items 2. and 3. above do not need to be charged back to the other funds in any one year, as long as adjustments are made over a reasonable period of time. A deficit fund balance in an internal service fund, however, should be disclosed in the notes to the financial statements. Retained earnings in an internal service fund resulting from application of item 3. above should be reported as equity designated for future catastrophic losses in the notes to the financial statements.

On the other hand, if the charge by an internal service fund to the other funds of the governmental entity is greater than the amount resulting from application of the preceding three conditions, the excess should be reported in both the internal service fund and the other funds as an operating transfer. However, if the charge by the internal service fund to the other funds fails to recover the full cost of claims over a reasonable period of time, any deficit fund balance in the internal service fund should be charged back to the other funds and reported as an expenditure/expense of those funds.

NOTE: These principles for the charging of costs by the internal service fund for risk financing are similar to those normally used by internal service funds for charging of other costs. Refer to Chapter 10 for additional information.

Governmental Entities That Participate in Risk Pools

As will be more fully described in the second part of this chapter, a governmental entity may participate in a public entity risk pool when there is a transfer or a pooling of risk. On the other hand, a governmental entity may participate in a public entity risk pool when there is no transfer of risk to the public entity risk pool, but rather the governmental entity contracts with the pool to service the governmental entity's uninsured claims. The following two sections describe the governmental entity's accounting and financial reporting considerations in each of these two instances.

Entities Participating in Public Entity Risk Pools with Transfer or Pooling of Risk

If a governmental entity participates in a pool in which there is a transfer or pooling (or sharing) of risks among the participants, the governmental entity should report its premium or required contribution as an insurance expenditure or expense. If the pooling agreement permits the pool to make additional assessments to its members, the governmental entity should consider the likelihood of additional assessments and report an additional expenditure or expense and liability if an assessment is probable and can be reasonably estimated. Assessment amounts that are probable but not reasonably estimable should be disclosed, along with disclosure of assessments that are reasonably possible.

NOTE: In other words, instead of the governmental entity evaluating the likelihood of losses due to claims that it directly pays, the governmental entity is making the same considerations as to the likelihood that it will need to pay more money to the public entity risk pool because of the claims experience of the pool requiring additional resources.

If the pool agreement does not provide for additional member assessments and the pool reports a deficit for its operations, the pool member should consider the financial capacity or stability of the pool to meet its obligations when they become due. If it is probable that the governmental entity will be required to pay its own obligations if the pool fails, the amount of those obligations should be reported as an expenditure/expense and as a liability if they can be reasonably estimated. Additionally, the same disclosure requirements for losses that are probable but not estimable and for losses that are reasonably possible apply.

Capitalization contributions. When state or local governmental entities join to form a public entity risk pool or when a governmental entity joins an established pool, the pooling agreement may require that a capitalization contribution be made to the pool to meet the initial or ongoing capital minimums established by the pooling agreement itself or by statute or regulation.

A capitalization contribution to a public entity risk pool with a transfer or pooling of risk should be reported as a deposit if it is probable that the contribution will be returned to the governmental entity either upon the dissolution of or the approved withdrawal from the pool. This determination should be based on the governmental entity's review of the provisions of the pooling agreement and an evaluation of the pool's financial capacity to return the contribution. (Governmental funds that record the capitalization contribution as a deposit should reserve a fund balance to indicate that the deposit is not appropriable for expenditure.)

If it is not probable that the contribution will be returned to the governmental entity, the following guidance should be used, depending on the fund type or type of entity involved:

- Proprietary funds. The contribution should be reported initially as an asset (prepaid insurance), and an expense should be recognized over the period for which the pool is expected to provide coverage. The periods expected to be covered should be consistent with the periods for which the contribution is factored into the pool's determination of premiums, but should not exceed ten years if this period is not readily determinable.
- Governmental funds. The entire amount of the capitalization contribution may be recognized as an expenditure in the period of the contribution. Reporting the capitalization contribution as prepaid insurance is not required. However, if the governmental entity elects, the governmental fund can initially report the capitalization contribution as an asset (prepaid insurance), and expenditures should be allocated and recognized over the periods for which the pool is expected to provide coverage. Similar to the method used by proprietary funds, the periods expected to be covered should be consistent with the periods for which the contribution is factored into the pool's determination of premiums paid, but should not exceed ten years if the period is not determinable.

- Colleges and universities. In the unrestricted current funds of colleges and universities that apply the AICPA College Guide model, the capitalization contribution should be treated in the same manner as described above for proprietary funds.

NOTE: Government-wide financial statements prepared under the new financial reporting model would account for capitalization contributions in a manner similar to proprietary funds. Judgement will be required to determine whether the asset recorded is a current or noncurrent asset based upon the facts of the particular situation.

Entities Participating in Public Entity Risk Pools without Transfer or Pooling of Risk

Governmental entities sometimes contract with other entities to service their uninsured claims. In this situation, there is no transfer of risk to the pool or pooling of risk with other pool participants. The governmental entity should recognize and measure its claims liabilities and related expenditures/expenses in accordance with the requirements described earlier in this chapter (essentially as if the governmental entity were servicing its own claims). Payments to the pool, including capitalization contributions, should be reported either as deposits or as reductions of the claim liability, as appropriate. A deposit should be recorded when the payment is not expected to be used to pay claims. A reduction of the claims liability should be made when payments to the pool are used to pay claims as they are incurred.

Other Matters for Entities other than Public Entity Risk Pools

In addition to some disclosure requirements (which follow the next section), GASBS 10 provides some other specific guidance for accounting and financial reporting for risk financing activities for governmental entities that are not public entity risk pools. These additional topics are as follows, and are discussed in the following paragraphs:

1. Insurance-related transactions

   a. Claims-made policies
   b. Retrospectively rated policies
   c. Policyholder or pool dividends

2. Entities providing claims servicing or insurance coverage to others

Insurance-Related Transactions

Claims-made policies. A *claims-made* policy or contract is a type of policy that covers losses from claims asserted against the policyholder during the policy period, regardless of whether the liability-imposing events occurred during the current period or any previous period in which the policyholder was insured under the claims-made contract or other specified period before the policy period (the policy retroactive date). For example, a governmental entity may purchase a claims-made policy to cover claims made during its fiscal year, July 1, 1999 through June 30, 2000. A claim resulting from an accident which occurred on May 1, 1999, that was filed on July 31, 1999, would be covered by this claims-made policy. However, an accident that occurred on August 1, 1999, for which a claim was not filed until August 31, 2000, would not be covered by the policy, unless of course the policy was renewed for the next fiscal year.

While this type of policy represents a transfer of risk within the policy limits to the insurer or public entity risk pool for claims and incidents reported to the insurer or the pool, there is no transfer of risk for claims and incidents not reported to the insurer or pool. As a result, a governmental entity that is insured under a claims-made policy should account for the estimated cost of those claims and incidents not reported to the insurer as it would for other IBNR claims as described in the earlier part of this chapter.

If, on the other hand, the governmental entity purchases "tail coverage," the premium or contribution for this additional insurance would be accounted for as an expenditure or expense in the financial statements of the period presented. *Tail coverage* is a type of insurance policy that is designed to cover claims incurred before but reported after the cancellation or expiration of a claims-made policy. It is also referred to as *extended discovery coverage*. In this case, the risk for the IBNR claims up to the limit of the policy is transferred to the insurance company or pool that is providing the tail insurance coverage.

Retrospectively rated policies. A *retrospectively rated* policy is one that uses a method of determining the final amount of an insurance premium by which the initial premium is adjusted based on actual experience during the period of coverage, sometimes subject to minimum and maximum adjustment limits. It is designed to encourage safety by the insured (since increased claims will result in higher premiums) and to compensate the insurer if larger than expected losses are incurred.

A governmental entity with a retrospectively rated policy or contract where the minimum or required contribution is based primarily on the entity's loss experience should account for the minimum premium as an expenditure or expense over the period of the coverage under the policy and should also accrue estimated losses from reported and unreported claims in excess of the minimum premium. This accrual should be determined as would other claims accrual as was described earlier in this chapter. However, any estimated losses should not be accrued in excess of a stipulated maximum premium or contribution requirement.

If the governmental entity is insured under a retrospective policy that is based on the experience of a group of entities, it would account for the claims costs as in the preceding paragraph, although it would use the group's experience in determining any additional amounts that would need to be accrued to reflect anticipated premium adjustments. In addition, GASBS 10 specifies that the governmental entity should disclose

- That it is insured under a retrospectively rated policy
- That premiums are accrued based on the ultimate cost of the experience to date of a group of entities

In addition, if the governmental entity cannot estimate losses on its retrospective policies, it should disclose the existing contingency in the notes to the financial statements, provided that the additional liability for premiums is probable or reasonably possible.

Policyholder or pool dividends. If a governmental entity receives or is entitled to receive a policyholder dividend or return of contribution related to its insurance or pool participation contract, that dividend should be recognized as a reduction of original insurance expenditures or expenses at the time that the dividend is declared. This treatment is appropriate since policyholder dividends are payments made or credits extended to the insured by the insurer, usually at the end of the policy year, that result in a reduction in the net insurance cost to the policyholder. The accounting treatment in the preceding paragraph is appropriate regardless of whether the dividends are paid in cash to the policyholder or are applied to the insured to reduce premiums due for the next policy year.

Entities providing claims servicing or insurance coverage to others. Sometimes a governmental entity may provide insurance-like services to other entities. The circumstances of the nature and extent of the services provided need to be considered to determine the most appropriate accounting treatment. The following general principles apply:

- If a governmental entity provides insurance or risk management coverage to other entities outside the government's reporting entity that is separate from its own risk management activities and involves a material transfer or pooling of risk among the participants, then these activities should be accounted for as a public entity risk pool. (See the second part of this chapter for further details.)

- If a governmental entity provides risk transfer or pooling coverage combined with its own risk management activities to individuals or organizations outside of its reporting entity, those activities should continue to be reported in the general fund or internal service fund only as long as the governmental entity is the predominant participant in the fund. If the governmental entity is not the predominant participant in the fund, then the combined activities should be accounted for as a public entity risk pool, using an enterprise fund and the accounting and financial reporting requirements described in the second part of this chapter.

- If a governmental entity provides claims servicing functions which are not insurance functions for individuals and organizations that are not a part of its financial reporting entity, amounts collected or due from those individuals or organizations and paid (or to be paid) to settle claims should be reported as a net asset or liability on an accrual basis, as appropriate. In other words, as a claims service, the governmental entity may collect more from the other entity than it has paid out to settle claims on behalf of the other entity, in which case it owes the excess amount back to the other entity. On the other hand, the governmental entity may have paid out more to settle claims for the other entity than it has received from the other entity, in which case it has a receivable for the difference from the other entity. In addition, the operating statement of the governmental entity should report claims servicing revenue and administrative costs as described in the second section of this chapter.

In addition to the accounting requirements relating to risk financing activities described in the preceding section of this chapter, GASBS 10 also contains a number of disclosure requirements relating to these activities.

ACCOUNTING AND FINANCIAL REPORTING FOR PUBLIC ENTITY RISK POOLS

This section of the chapter briefly describes the accounting and financial reporting requirements for risk financing and insurance-related activities of public entity risk pools. A complete discussion of public entity risk pool accounting and financial reporting is beyond the scope of this Field Guide. These standards are primarily derived from those of GASBS 10, as subsequently amended by GASBS 30.

What Is a Public Entity Risk Pool?

A *public entity risk pool* is a cooperative group of governmental entities joining together to finance an exposure, liability, or risk. The risks may include property and liability risks, workers, or employee health care. The pool may be a stand-alone entity or be included as part of a larger governmental entity that acts as the pool's sponsor.

There are four basic types of public entity risk pools. They are

1. **Risk-sharing pool**—An arrangement by which governments pool risks and funds and share in the cost of losses

2. **Insurance-purchasing pool**—An arrangement by which governments pool funds or resources to purchase commercial insurance products (This arrangement is also referred to as a *risk-purchasing group*.)

3. **Banking pool**—An arrangement by which monies are made available on a loan basis for pool members in the event of loss

4. **Claims-servicing or account pool**—An arrangement in which a pool manages separate accounts for each pool member from which the losses of that member are paid

NOTE: Only the risk-sharing and insurance-purchasing pools are considered to represent a transfer of risk.

Risks of loss from the following kinds of events are included within the scope of this discussion of public entity risk pools that represent a transfer of risk:

- Torts (wrongful acts, injuries, or damages not involving a breach of contract for which a civil action can be brought)
- Theft or destruction of, or damage to, assets
- Business interruption
- Errors or omissions
- Job-related illnesses or injuries to employees
- Acts of God (events beyond human origin or control, such as natural disasters, lightning, windstorms, and earthquakes)
- Other risks of loss of participating entities assumed under a policy or a participation contract issued by a public entity risk pool.

The rules discussed in this section also apply to losses assumed under contract by a public entity risk pool when a participating employer agrees to provide accident and health, dental, and other medical benefits to its employees and retirees and their dependents and beneficiaries based on covered events that have already occurred. The scope of this section excludes all postemployment benefits that governmental employers expect to provide to current and future retirees. In addition, the scope of GASBS 10's guidance for public entity risk pools excludes medicaid insurance plans provided to low-income state residents under Title XIX of the Federal Social Security Act, although it is unlikely that a state would use a public entity risk pool for medicaid insurance plans anyway.

Specific Accounting and Financial Reporting Requirements

In addition to the background information described above, GASBS 10 provides specific guidance as to the accounting and financial reporting requirements of a public entity risk pool. These requirements are beyond the scope of this Field Guide.

Claim cost recognition. The basic principle for claim cost recognition by public entity risk pools is that a liability for unpaid claims (including IBNR) should be accrued when insured events occur.

For claims-made policies, a liability should be accrued in the period in which the event that triggers coverage under the policy or participation contract occurs.

The recorded liability should be based on the estimated ultimate cost of settling the claims (including the effects of inflation and other societal and economic factors), using experience adjusted for current trends and any other factors that would modify experience.

Claims accruals for IBNR claims should be made if it is probable that a loss has been incurred and the amount can be reasonably estimated. Changes in estimates of claims costs resulting from the continuous review process and differences between estimates and payments for claims should be recognized in results of operations of the period in which the estimates are changed or payments are made.

Estimated recoveries on unsettled claims should be evaluated in terms of their estimated and realizable value and deducted from the liability for unpaid claims. Estimated recoveries on settled claims also should be deducted from the liability for unpaid claims.

Claims adjustment expenses.   Liabilities for claims adjustment expenses should be accrued when the related liability for unpaid claims is accrued. Claims adjustment expenses include all costs that are expected to be incurred in connection with the settlement of unpaid claims. These costs can be either allocated or unallocated.

SUMMARY

Risk financing activities are typically very significant for state and local governmental entities, regardless of whether risks are transferred to public entity risk pools. This chapter addressed the accounting and financial reporting requirements for both the state and local governmental entities, and for public entity risk pools.

21 ACCOUNTING FOR LEASES

INTRODUCTION

Accounting for leases is one of the more technically challenging areas in accounting, including governmental accounting. This chapter describes the accounting and financial reporting requirements for both lessees and lessors. Essentially, these accounting requirements depend on whether the lease is classified as an operating lease or a capital lease. This classification is made in the same manner by governmental entities as by commercial enterprises. Two important differences must be considered, however. The first is whether the lease is accounted for by a governmental fund or a proprietary fund. The accounting and financial reporting requirements differ significantly. The second is whether an operating lease has scheduled rent increases inherent in its terms and conditions. The accounting for such scheduled rent increases differs for governmental entities from the accounting used by commercial enterprises for scheduled rent increases.

This chapter provides guidance for all of these situations, first from the point of view of the lessee and second from the point of view of the lessor.

ACCOUNTING BASIS

The accounting and financial reporting requirements discussed in this chapter originate with NCGA Statement 5 (NCGAS 5), *Accounting and Financial Reporting Principles for Lease Agreements of State and Local Governments.* NCGAS 5 directs state and local governments to use the accounting and financial reporting standards of FASB Statement 13 (SFAS 13), *Accounting for Leases,* including subsequent amendments. NCGAS 5 provides guidance to state and local governments on applying the requirements of SFAS 13 in a manner consistent with that of governmental accounting. In other words, governmental funds need to account for the capital assets and long-term liabilities resulting from accounting for a lease as a capital lease consistent with how capital assets and long-term liabilities are otherwise accounted for by governmental funds. The requirements of SFAS 13, as amended, can be applied by proprietary funds directly, since these funds use the same basis of accounting and measurement focus as commercial funds, resulting in identical accounting treatment for these leases. The effect of recording capital leases on the government-wide financial statements must also be considered. The government-wide statements record leases in a manner similar to propriety funds.

NOTE: One important consideration in lease accounting for capital leases for governments concerns leases between a primary government and its component units. The accounting differs for blended component units and discretely presented component units.

- ***Blended component units.*** *Capital leases between the primary government and a blended component unit (or between two component units) should not be reported as capital leases in the financial reporting entity's financial statements. The component unit's debt and assets under the lease are reported as a form of the primary government's debts and assets.*

- ***Discretely presented component units.*** *Capital leases between the primary government and a discretely presented component unit should be accounted for as usual capital leases under SFAS 13 as described in this chapter. However, related receivables and payables should not be combined with other amounts due to or from component units or with capital lease receivables and payables with organizations outside of the reporting entity. In these cases, governments may want to consider elimination entries for the lease assets and liabilities, since a double counting of these assets and liabilities results from this accounting treatment.*

The accounting for leases is derived from the view that a lease that transfers substantially all of the benefits and risks of ownership should be accounted for as the acquisition of an asset and the incurrence of a liability by the lessee (that is, a capital lease), and as a sale or financing by the lessor (that is, a sales-type, direct-financing, or leveraged lease). Other leases should be accounted for as operating leases; in other words, the rental of property.

Lessee Accounting

A lessee accounts for a lease as one of the following:

- Capital lease
- Operating lease

If a lease meets any one of the following four classification criteria, it is a capital lease:

1. The lease transfers ownership of the property to the lessee by the end of the lease term. (To be a capital lease, a land lease must meet this criterion.)
2. The lease contains a bargain purchase option. A *bargain purchase option* is a provision allowing the lessee, at its option, to purchase the lease property for a price sufficiently lower than the expected fair

value of the property at the date the option becomes exercisable, and that exercise of the option appears, at the inception of the lease, to be reasonably assured.

3. The lease term is equal to 75% or more of the estimated economic life of the leased property. However, if the beginning of the lease term falls within the last 25% of the total estimated economic life of the lease property, including earlier years of use, this criterion should not be used for purposes of classifying the lease. The *estimated economic life* of leased property is defined by SFAS 13 as the estimated remaining period during which the property is expected to be economically usable by one or more users, with normal repairs and maintenance, for the purpose for which it was intended at the inception of the lease without limitation of the lease term.

   NOTE: A good example of the "economic" life of an asset that is being leased would be the life of a personal computer, or PC. While the actual hardware may be expected to function perfectly well for ten years, it would be hard to justify an economic life of more than three to five years, given the rapid changes in PC technology coupled with increasing demands on PC hardware by software packages.

4. The present value at the beginning of the lease term of the minimum lease payments, excluding executory costs, equals or exceeds 90% of the excess of the fair value of the leased property. If the beginning of the lease term falls within the last 25% of the total estimated economic life of the lease property, including earlier years of use, this criterion should not be used for purposes of classifying the lease.

Minimum lease payments include only those payments that the lessee is obligated to make or can be required to make in connection with the leased property. Contingent rentals should not be considered part of the minimum lease payments.

In determining the present value of lease payments, the lessee should use its incremental borrowing rate unless the following two conditions are met:

1. It is practical for the lessee to determine the implicit interest rate that the lessor used to compute the lease payments.

2.   The implicit rate computed by the lessor is less than the lessee's incremental borrowing rate.

If both of these conditions are met, then the lessee should use the interest rate that is implicit in the lease instead of its incremental borrowing rate in computing the present value of the minimum lease payments. The lessee's incremental borrowing rate is the estimated interest rate that the lessee would have had to pay if the leased property had been purchased and financed over the period covered by the lease.

Recording operating and capital leases by the lessee. The following pages provide an illustration of how a lessee would record both an operating lease and a capital lease. The recording is also affected by whether the fund that is recording the lease is a governmental or a proprietary fund. These differences are also illustrated.

Operating lease. The recording of an operating lease is basically the same for both governmental funds and proprietary funds. The lease is accounted for as any other recurring payment. Remember that an operating lease is treated simply as a rental of property with no assets or liabilities recorded, assuming that the governmental entity makes the lease payments on time and there is no overlapping prepaid periods.

Capital lease. In recording a capital lease, the governmental entity records an amount equal to the present value of the minimum lease payments. (However, the amount recorded should not exceed the fair value of the property being leased.) Both an asset and a liability are recorded because a capital lease is accounted for as if the lessee had actually purchased the leased property. In other words, it records the leased property on its books as an asset and records the same amount as a liability, reflecting that the substance of the lease transaction is that the lessee is purchasing the asset from and financing the purchase with the lessor.

Governmental fund. In governmental funds, the primary emphasis is on the flow of financial resources, and expenditures are recognized on the modified accrual basis of accounting. Accordingly, if a lease agreement is to be financed from general governmental resources, it must be accounted for and reported on a basis consistent with governmental fund accounting principles.

Capital assets used in governmental activities acquired through lease agreements should be capitalized in the government-wide statement of net assets at the inception of the agreement in an amount determined by the criteria of SFAS 13, as amended. A liability in the same amount should be recorded simultaneously in the government-wide statement of net assets. When a capital lease represents the acquisition or construction of a general fixed asset, it should be reflected as an expenditure and an other financing source, consistent with the accounting and financial reporting for general obligation bonded debt. (See Chapter 8 for further information on accounting for general fixed asset acquisition by a capital projects fund.) Subsequent governmental fund lease payments are accounted for consistently with the principles for recording debt service on general obligation debt. (See Chapter 9 for accounting for debt service payments by a debt service fund.)

Proprietary funds. Capital lease accounting for proprietary funds should follow SFAS 13, as amended and interpreted, without modification. All assets and liabilities of proprietary funds are accounted for and reported in the respective proprietary fund. Therefore, transactions for proprietary fund capital leases are accounted for and reported entirely within the individual proprietary fund.

Disclosure requirements. Both governmental funds and proprietary funds are required to follow the disclosure requirements of SFAS 13, as amended and interpreted. The details of these disclosure requirements are beyond the scope of this Field Guide.

Lessor Accounting

Lessors also classify leases according to whether they are in substance sales of property or equipment or true rentals of property or equipment. A lessor classifies leases into one of the following categories:

- Operating leases
- Direct financing leases
- Sales-type leases
- Leveraged leases

For governmental entities, the two predominate leases are operating leases and direct financing leases. Sales-type leases arise when there is a manufacturer's profit built into the lease payment. Leveraged leases involve the financing of the lease through a third-party creditor. Both of these types of leases are outside the discussion of the leasing activities of governmental entities, but are included in SFAS 13 because of their relevance to commercial enterprises.

The direct financing lease for a lessor is the equivalent of the capital lease for a lessee. A direct financing lease transfers substantially all of the risk and rewards of ownership from the lessor to the lessee. In a direct financing lease, the owner of the property is in substance financing the purchase of the property by the lessee, which is evident from the title of this type of lease. In the government-wide financial statements, the accounting for a direct financing lease would be the same as that described in later sections on proprietary funds.

SFAS 13 requires that a lease be classified as a direct financing lease when any of the four capitalization criteria (described earlier in the chapter) are met and when both of the following additional criteria are satisfied:

- Collectibility of the minimum future lease payments is reasonably predictable. However, a lessor is not precluded from classifying a lease as a direct financing lease simply because the receivable is subject to an estimate of uncollectibility based on the experience with groups of similar receivables.
- No important uncertainties surround the amount of nonreimbursable costs yet to be incurred by the lessor under the lease. Important uncertainties might include commitments by the lessor to guarantee performance of the leased property in a manner more extensive than the typical product warranty or to effectively protect the lessee from obsolescence of the leased property. However, the necessity of estimated executory costs to be paid by the lessor does not by itself constitute an important uncertainty for purposes of this criterion.

The lessor's investment in the lease consists of the present value of the minimum lease payments, including any residual values that accrue to the benefit of the lessor and any rental payments guaranteed by a third party not related to the lessor or lessee (similar to a leveraged lease). In determining the present value of the minimum lease payments, the interest rate implicit in the lease is used. This rate is the discount rate that, when applied to the minimum lease payments and the residual value accruing to the benefit of the lessor, causes the aggregate present value at the beginning of the lease term to be equal to the fair value of the leased property to the lessor at the inception of the lease.

NOTE: This sounds more complicated than it is. Simply, it means that a lessor that enters into a direct financing lease agreement does so at the fair value of the property being leased. Included in the monthly lease payments is an interest factor that reflects the fact that the lessor is receiving the money over time, rather than at once. The interest rate needed to discount the monthly lease payments to arrive at the fair value of the property at the beginning of the lease is the implicit interest rate.

Once the present value of the minimum lease payments is determined, this amount is compared with the carrying amount of the asset that is recorded on the books of the lessor at the time the lease is signed. The difference between the present value of the minimum lease payments and the carrying amount is recorded as deferred income at the time the lease is signed. The amount of deferred income is amortized into income over the lease term, using the effective interest method.

As was seen with accounting for capital leases by lessees, whether the fund recording the lease is a governmental fund or a proprietary fund has a significant effect on how leases, particularly capital leases, are accounted for and reported.

Direct financing lease—Governmental funds. In governmental funds, lease receivables and deferred revenues should be used to account for leases receivable when a state or local government is the lessor in a lease situation. Only the portion of lease receivables that represents revenue/other financing sources that are measurable and available should be recognized as revenue/other financing sources in governmental funds. The remainder of the receivable remains deferred.

There are two factors that need to be considered by governmental funds in recording direct financing leases: initial direct costs and allowance for uncollectible accounts.

Initial direct costs. The governmental entity may incur costs related to the negotiation and execution of the lease, such as legal and accounting costs, credit investigations, and so on. The governmental fund would recognize these costs as expenditures when incurred, with an equal amount of unearned revenue recognized in the same period.

Proprietary funds. Proprietary funds record direct financing leases in the same way that commercial enterprises would record these leases. These leases are recorded in the government-wide financial statements in the same manner. One significant difference is that since the asset being leased is already on the balance sheet of the proprietary fund, the amount of deferred revenue to be amortized is much smaller, consisting of the deferred interest income on the lease and the difference between the fair value of the asset leased and the carrying amount of the asset.

Disclosure requirements. There are a number of disclosure requirements contained in SFAS 13 that must be made, where applicable, by governmental entities that are lessors. The details of this requirement is beyond the scope of this Field Guide.

OTHER LEASING ISSUES FOR GOVERNMENTAL ENTITIES

In addition to the specific considerations for accounting and financial reporting for leases that pertain to governmental entities that are lessees and lessors, there are two additional crosscutting matters related to leasing activities that need to be considered.

- Operating leases with scheduled rent increases
- Fiscal funding and cancellation clauses

These topics are addressed in the remaining sections of this chapter.

Operating Leases with Scheduled Rent Increases

GASB Statement 13 (GASBS 13), *Accounting for Operating Leases with Scheduled Rent Increases,* establishes accounting requirements for those types of leases that differ from the accounting and financial reporting for those by commercial organizations. GASBS 13's requirements for operating leases with scheduled rent increases apply regardless of whether a governmental or proprietary fund is used to account for the lease. The requirements apply to all state and local governmental entities, including public benefit corporations and authorities, public employee retirement systems, and governmental utilities, hospitals, other health care providers, colleges, and universities.

Scheduled rent increases are fixed by contract. The increases take place with the passage of time and are not contingent on future events. The increases in rent may be based, for example, on such factors as anticipated increases in costs or anticipated appreciation of property values, although the amount of the increase is specified in the lease agreement. Scheduled rent increases are not contingent rentals, in which the changes in rent payments are based on changes in future specific economic factors, such as future sales volume or future inflation.

Measurement criteria. Transactions that arise from operating leases with scheduled rent increases should be measured based on the terms and conditions of the lease contract when the pattern of payment requirements, including the increases, is systematic and rational.

NOTE: For example, a governmental entity leases office space for a three-year period in which the rents are as follows: Year 1, $1,000; Year 2, $1,100; Year 3, $1,200. The governmental entity would recognize an expenditure/expense of $1,000 in Year 1, $1,100 in Year 2, and $1,200 in Year 3. This is different from the requirements of commercial accounting, where the total payments under the lease ($3,300) would be recognized on a straight-line basis over the life of the lease, or in this case $1,100 in each year.

In applying this requirement, GASBS 13 provides the following examples of payment schedules that are considered systematic and rational:

- Lease agreements specify scheduled rent increases over the lease term that are intended to cover (and are reasonably associated with) economic factors relating to the property, such as the anticipated effects of property value appreciation or increases in costs due to factors such as inflation. Rent increases because of property value appreciation may result from the maturation of individual properties as well as from general appreciation of the market. Lower lease property values (and rents) may exist, for example, when a new office building has only a few tenants, but more are expected in the future.
- Lease payments are required to be made on a basis that represents the time pattern in which the lease property is available for use by the lessee.

In some cases, an operating lease with scheduled rent increases contains payment requirements in a particular year or years that are artificially low when viewed in the context of earlier or later payment requirements. This situation may take place, for example, when a lessor provides a rent reduction or rent holiday that is in substance a financing arrangement between the lessor and the lessee. Another example provided by GASBS 13 is where a lessor provides a lessee with reduced rents as an inducement to enter into the lease. In this case, GASBS 13 stipulates that the operating lease transactions be measured using either of the following methods:

1. **The straight-line method.** This is the method described above that is normally used by commercial enterprises in accounting for all operating leases with scheduled rent increases. The periodic rental expenditure/expense and rental revenue are equal to the total amount of the lease payments divided by the total number of periodic payments to be made under the lease.

2. **The fair value method.** The operating lease transactions may be measured based on the estimated fair value of the rental. The difference between the actual lease payments and the fair value of the lease property should be accounted for using the interest method, whereby an interest amount (whether expenditure/expense or revenue) is recorded at a constant rate based on the amount of the outstanding accrued lease receivable or payable. However, if the fair value of the rental is not reasonably estimable, the straight-line method should be used.

In applying these requirements for using the straight-line and estimated fair value methods, there is a distinction in the accounting between governmental funds and proprietary funds.

- Entities that report operating leases with scheduled rent increases in proprietary and similar trust funds should recognize rental revenue or expense each period as it accrues over the lease term, as described above for the straight-line and estimated fair value methods. This would apply to the government-wide financial statements as well.
- Entities that report operating leases with scheduled rent increases in governmental funds should recognize rental revenue or expenditures each period using the modified accrual basis of accounting. That is, the amount recognized as rental revenue (either on a straight-line basis or an estimated fair value basis) should be recognized as revenue to the extent that it is available to finance expenditures of the fiscal period. Accrued receivables should be reported in the fund and offset by deferred revenue for the portion not yet recognized as revenue. The lessee should recognize expenditures and fund liabilities to the extent that the amounts are payable with expendable, available financial resources. Any remaining accrued liabilities calculated in accordance with either the straight-line basis or the estimated fair value basis should be reported as an additional liability in the government-wide statement of net assets.

Fiscal Funding and Cancellation Clauses

In applying the criteria of SFAS 13 to lease agreements of state and local governments, legal restrictions of governments must be considered. One type of legal restriction relates to debt limitation and debt incurrence that prohibits governments from entering into obligations extending beyond the current budget year. Because of this type of restriction, a governmental lease agreement usually contains a clause (called either a *fiscal funding clause* or a *cancellation clause*) that permits the governmental lessee to terminate the agreement on an annual basis if funds are not appropriated to make required payments.

This issue was addressed by FASB Technical Bulletin 79-10 (TB 79-10), *Fiscal Funding Clauses in Lease Agreements,* which states

> ...*Statement 13 requires that a cancelable lease, such as lease contain a fiscal funding clause [a clause that generally provides that the lease is cancelable if the legislature or other funding authority does not appropriate the funds necessary for the governmental unit to fulfill its obligations under the lease agreement] be evaluated to determine whether the uncertainty of possible lease cancellation is a remote contingency...a lease which is cancelable (1) only upon occurrence of some remote contingency...shall be considered noncancelable for purposes of this definition.*

The economic substance of most lease agreements with fiscal funding clauses is that they are essentially long-term contracts, with only a remote possibility that the lease will be canceled because of the fiscal funding clause. Accordingly, fiscal funding clauses should not prohibit lease agreements from being capitalized. If a lease agreement meets all other capitalization criteria except for the noncancelable criterion, the likelihood of the lease being canceled must be evaluated, and if the possibility of cancellation is remote, the lease should be capitalized.

SUMMARY

The accounting and financial reporting for lease agreements is an area that usually presents an interesting challenge to financial statement preparers. This challenge is due to the diversity in the types and nature of lease agreements that must be accounted for, as well as the complexity of the accounting rules that must be applied. The financial statement preparer for a governmental entity must be familiar with the requirements of commercial accounting for leases in order to effectively and correctly apply this guidance to lease agreements that are entered into by a governmental entity.

22 LANDFILL CLOSURE AND POSTCLOSURE CARE COSTS

INTRODUCTION

The GASB issued Statement 18 (GASBS 18), *Accounting for Municipal Solid Waste Landfill Closure and Postclosure Care Costs,* to address a very narrow issue, the accounting and financial reporting for landfill closure and postclosure care costs. However, since many governmental entities operate these types of facilities, GASBS 18 affected many governmental entities.

GASBS 18 was issued in response to requirements promulgated by the United States Environmental Protection Agency (EPA). Landfill operators became obligated to meet certain requirements of the EPA as to closure and postclosure requirements. The postclosure requirements extend for a period of thirty years. Landfill operators are also subject to closure and postclosure care costs resulting from state and local laws and regulations. The GASB issued GASBS 18 to require governments to recognize the liability for these closure and postclosure conditions as the landfill is being used, so that by the time the landfill becomes full and no longer accepts waste, the liability is recorded in the financial statements of the governmental entity that operates the landfill and is responsible for these requirements.

This chapter describes the applicability and requirements of GASBS 18. It also provides examples of detailed calculations of the liabilities for these types of costs that must be recorded in the governmental entity's financial statements.

APPLICABILITY

The provisions of GASBS 18 apply to all state and local governmental entities, including public benefit corporations and authorities, governmental utilities, governmental hospitals and other health care facilities, and governmental colleges and universities. GASBS 18 establishes accounting and financial reporting standards for municipal solid waste landfill (hereafter MSWLF, or simply landfill) closure and postclosure care costs that are required by federal, state, and local laws and regulations. In order to meet these requirements, financial statement preparers need to understand (1) what a MSWLF is and how it operates and (2) closure and postclosure care costs that will be incurred and are covered by this Statement. These two items are addressed in the following paragraphs.

MUNICIPAL SOLID WASTE LANDFILLS

A municipal solid waste landfill is an area of land or an excavation that receives household waste. What makes a landfill "municipal" is not the ownership of the landfill, but the type of waste that is received by the landfill—municipal waste means household waste. Thus, a private, nongovernmental enterprise could own and operate a MSWLF (although it wouldn't be subject to the requirements of GASBS 18).

Landfills (which, for purposes of this chapter, is used interchangeably with MSWLF) operate in many different ways. Their operating methods, along with their closure and postclosure care plans, are filed with regulatory bodies. Many landfills operate on a "cell" basis, where the total landfill is divided into sections that are used one at time. Each cell can then be closed when it reaches capacity and the waste is then received by the next cell that will be used.

Certain of the closure materials and equipment used to contain wastes and to monitor the environmental impact of landfill operations (such as liners and leachate collection systems) must be installed before the cells are ready to receive waste. These prereception activities are sometimes needed in order to comply with federal, state, or local regulations or requirements. After each cell (or the entire landfill, if it is operated as one large cell) is filled to capacity and no longer accepts waste, a final cover is applied to the cell. Sometimes even when the landfill is operated as a number of cells, the final cover is not applied until the entire landfill is filled to capacity and no longer accepts solid waste.

Estimated Total Current Cost of Closure and Postclosure Care

There are a variety of costs that the operator of a landfill will incur for protection of the environment. These costs will be incurred during the period that the landfill is in operation and after the landfill is closed and no longer accepting waste. GASBS 18 addresses the recording of costs relating both to the closure of the landfill and to costs incurred after the landfill is closed (postclosure costs). These costs include the cost of equipment and facilities (such as leachate collection facilities and final cover) as well as the cost of services (such as postclosure maintenance and monitoring costs). Certain of these costs, which result in the disbursement of funds near or after the date that the landfill stops accepting solid waste and during the postclosure period, are included in the "estimated total current cost" of landfill closure and postclosure care, regardless of whether they are capital or operating in nature. (Current cost is the amount that would be paid if all equipment, facilities, and services included in the estimate were acquired during the current period.)

GASBS 18 requires that the estimated total current cost of landfill closure and postclosure care, based on the applicable federal, state, and local laws and regulations, include the following:

- The cost of equipment expected to be installed and facilities expected to be constructed (based upon the landfill's operating plan) near or after the date that the landfill stops accepting solid waste and during the postclosure period. Equipment and facilities that are considered as part of these costs should only be those that will be used exclusively for the landfill. This may include gas monitoring and collection systems, storm water management systems, groundwater monitoring wells, and leachate treatment facilities. The costs for equipment and facilities that are shared by more than one landfill should be allocated to each user landfill based on the percentage of use by each landfill.
- The cost of final cover (sometimes called capping) expected to be applied near or after the date that the landfill stops accepting waste.
- The cost of monitoring and maintaining the expected usable landfill area during the postclosure period. Postclosure care may include maintaining the final cover; monitoring groundwater; monitoring and collecting methane and other gases; collecting, treating, and transporting leachate; repairing or replacing equipment; and remedying or containing environmental hazards.

In determining the estimated total current costs, the governmental financial statement preparer should consider whether all of the requirements of the EPA, as well as state or local requirements, apply as to what facilities need to be installed and what activities need to take place for the closure and postclosure periods. In other words, what is the governmental operating the landfill required to do and what does it plan to do to close and thereafter care for the landfill? The current cost of these facilities and activities need to be considered as part of the total estimated current cost.

NOTE: The calculation of the estimated current cost of closure and postclosure care for a landfill realistically requires the assistance of either in-house or consulting engineers. Some con-

*sulting engineers have teamed with accounting or financial con-
sulting firms to prepare these estimates and calculations for governmental entities, including the preparation of the required disclosures in a draft footnote. While using these services may be
effective or convenient, the financial statement preparer ultimately takes responsibility for the amounts recorded and disclosed, and should therefore seek to understand and concur with
the calculations, even if outside specialists are used.*

After the governmental entity makes an initial calculation of the estimated current cost of landfill closure and postclosure costs, the estimate should be adjusted each year to reflect any changes that should be made to the estimate. For
example, the current cost or the estimated costs may increase
or decrease simply due to inflation or deflation. On the other
hand, there may be changes in the operating conditions of the
landfill that may affect the closure and postclosure costs.
These changes might include the type of equipment that will
need to be acquired, as well as facilities or services that will
be used to perform closure and postclosure care. In addition,
there may be changes in cost estimates due to changes in the
technologies that will be used for closure and postclosure care
activities, changes in the expected usable landfill area, and
changes in closure and postclosure legal and regulatory requirements that must be considered.

Recording Closure and Postclosure Care Costs—
Proprietary Funds and Government-Wide Financial
Statements

The true impact of applying GASBS 18's requirements
of recognizing a liability is seen in the government-wide financial statements and in proprietary funds. This is because
as a liability is recorded proportionally each year for total estimated current costs, a corresponding expense is recorded in
the operating statements. This results in a matching of the period in which the cost of the closure and postclosure care activities occur with the period that is benefited by the landfill
activities—that is, when the solid wastes are actually put into
the landfill.

Recording Closure and Postclosure Care Costs—
Governmental Funds

For landfills reported using governmental funds, the
measurement and recognition of the accrued liability for landfill closure and postclosure care should be consistent with the
calculations described above for proprietary funds. However,

the governmental funds should recognize expenditures and fund liabilities using the modified accrual basis of accounting. The additional liability that is not recorded in the fund should be included in the government-wide financial statements.

SUMMARY

The accounting and financial reporting for landfills is an important consideration for the financial statement preparer of a governmental entity that operates or owns a landfill. While the accounting itself for landfill closure and postclosure costs is not complicated, the determination and estimation of these future costs often requires the work of a specialist to assist the financial statement preparer in complying with the accounting and disclosure requirements of GASBS 18.